The Last Imperialist

The Last Imperialist

Sir Alan Burns' Epic Defense of the British Empire

Bruce Gilley

REGNERY
HISTORY
Washington, D.C.

Regnery History™ is a trademark of Salem Communications Holding Corporation
Regnery® is a registered trademark and its colophon is a trademark of Salem Communications Holding Corporation

First paperback edition published 2024

ISBN: 978-1-68451-520-2
eISBN: 978-1-68451-222-5
LCCN: 2022507014

Cataloging-in-Publication data on file with the Library of Congress

Published in the United States by
Regnery History
An Imprint of Regnery Publishing
A Division of Salem Media Group
Washington, D.C.
www.Regnery.com

Manufactured in the United States of America

10 9 8 7 6 5 4 3 2 1

Books are available in quantity for promotional or premium use.
 For information on discounts and terms, please visit our website:
www.Regnery.com.

Dedicated to the family of Sir Alan Burns

For more information on The Last Imperialist, *including photos, author interviews, and original documents, please visit the book's website: www.web.pdx.edu/~gilleyb/TheLastImperialist.html*

Contents

List of Figures

Abbreviations Used in Notes

ACB   Sir Alan Cuthbert Maxwell Burns

Allen   Charles Allen, "Oral History Interview: Sir Alan Burns,"
        BBC Productions (1978), Imperial War Museum, Catalogue #
        4708/03. Cassette numbers 1, 2, and 3.

CBAA   Sir Alan Burns, *Colonialism Before and After* (unpublished, ca.
        1973).

CCC   Sir Alan Burns, *Colonial Civil Servant* (London: George Allen &
        Unwin, 1949).

CCT-G   Sir Alan Burns, "Constitutional Changes in the Tropics," Talk at
        Centre for Industrial Studies, Geneva, October 20, 1953.

C.O.   Colonial Office.

CO/   Colonial Office archives, Public Records Office, London.

CP   Sir Alan Burns, *Colour Prejudice, With Particular Reference to
        the Relationship Between Whites and Negroes* (London: George
        Allen & Unwin, 1948).

CPCW-G Sir Alan Burns, "Colour Prejudice in a Changing World," Talk at
        Centre for Industrial Studies, Geneva, October 21, 1953.

CRP-G   Sir Alan Burns, "Colour and Racial Prejudice," Talk at Centre
        for Industrial Studies, Geneva, October 29, 1951.

DWPA   Richard Rathbone, "Death and Politics: West Africa in the
        1940s," *History Today* (1993).

FCO/   Foreign and Commonwealth Office archives, Public Records
        Office, London.

FO/   Foreign Office archives, Public Records Office, London.

FBCE-G Sir Alan Burns, "The Future of the British Colonial Empire,"
        Talk at Centre for Industrial Studies, Geneva, February 1, 1950.

HBWI	Sir Alan Burns, *History of the British West Indies* (London: George Allen & Unwin, 1954).
HON	Sir Alan Burns, *History of Nigeria*, 8th edition (London: George Allen & Unwin, 1972).
HS/	Special Operations Executive archives, Public Records Office, London.
IDOC	Sir Alan Burns, *In Defence of Colonies: British Colonial Territories in International Affairs* (London: George Allen & Unwin, 1957).
KV/	Security Service archives, Public Records Office, London.
MCGC	Richard Rathbone, "A Murder in the Colonial Gold Coast: Law and Politics in the 1940s," *Journal of African History* (1989).
MPCG	Richard Rathbone, *Murder and Politics in Colonial Ghana* (1993).
OPT	Sir Alan Burns, "The Movement Towards Self-Government in British Colonial Territories," *Optima*, June 1954.
RCD-G	Sir Alan Burns, "Recent Constitutional Developments in British Colonial Territories," Talk at Centre for Industrial Studies, Geneva, October 29, 1951.
TCCC-G	Sir Alan Burns, "The Colonial Civil Service," Talk at Center for Industrial Studies, Geneva, October 11, 1951.
UN-G	Sir Alan Burns, "The United Nations," Talk at Centre for Industrial Studies, Geneva, October 21, 1953.
UN/	Official records of the United Nations. Available at: https://digitallibrary.un.org.

Part I

FOUNDATIONS

Chapter 1

The Fate of Lesser Persons

The man straightened up in the airport waiting room and lowered his newspaper. His face was contorted with a mixture of emotions—anger, fear, sadness—at what he had just read. His rumpled suit and outdated waistcoat strained under the pressure. They'd killed Danquah.

Danquah had been Sir Alan Burns' nemesis. Danquah stood for opportunism and politics, while Burns stood for justice and administration. Danquah claimed to have ended Burns' career. A promised post as governor of exotic Malaya was withdrawn and replaced by a taxing, high-profile decade at the United Nations—all because of Danquah. The last time they met, at the ceremony for Ghana's independence in 1957, the animosity was palpable. There were no handshakes, despite encouragement from bystanders. Danquah, a leading Ghanaian nationalist, boasted of how much pain he had inflicted on Burns, a former colonial governor. Full of confidence, Danquah was a man of the future, while Burns was a man of the past. Danquah was surrounded by reporters. Burns was ignored and flew home to shudders about the whole colonial enterprise. Now, eight years later, Danquah was dead, devoured by the revolution he started. Ghana was in steep decline, and the lives of close friends were at risk.

Accra, Ghana, February 4, 1965, New York Times Service—Dr. Joseph B. Danquah, a leader in the struggle for Ghanaian independence who later broke bitterly with President Kwame Nkrumah, died in detention today, the Government announced. The official statement said that Dr. Danquah, who was 69 years old, had died of a heart attack. He had been imprisoned since Jan. 8, 1964, under Ghana's Preventive Detention Act. In the decades before the Gold Coast became independent from Britain and changed its name to Ghana, Dr. Danquah was the colony's unquestioned political leader. After independence, he led the

opposition against Kwame Nkrumah under a government that tolerated opposition less and less.[1]

It was the twilight days of European empire. As colonial judges, station masters, revenue collectors, regimental commanders, and district officers came
home, a long shadow of global indifference had spread over the affairs of
newly independent countries like Ghana. Under that shadow, stories like the
death of Danquah were now common. No one really cared anymore. Unless,
like Sir Alan Burns, they remembered.

In retrospect, it was surprising how long Danquah had survived.[2] A witty
and self-effacing lawyer, Joseph Danquah was the sort of person that colonial
officials like Sir Alan Burns hoped would assume power in newly independent states. He was pushed aside in 1947 by the radical Nkrumah, who had
been trained in London by Britain's Communist Party and in the United
States by black racialists. Nkrumah abandoned the lawyerly constitutionalism
of his mentor in favor of violent street protest. In the election prior to independence, Nkrumah's party trounced the moderates represented by Danquah
with promises of untold riches and freedom once the British left.

The moment the Union Jack was lowered, Nkrumah introduced a series of
repressive measures and steered West Africa's most prosperous economy into
a wall. Eleven of the twelve opposition members in Parliament were soon in
prison. By 1965, wages had fallen to levels not seen since the 1930s, while
Ghana's foreign reserves, carefully built up under the British, had evaporated.
Cocoa farmers, the backbone of the economy, were paid half the market price
by Nkrumah. The British had paid them 50 percent above the market price.[3]
Backbenchers in the ruling party began to grumble that things were worse
than in colonial days. Danquah wrote to Nkrumah about an "anti-climax of
repression after liberation."

In the first presidential election after independence, a sham really, Danquah
won only 2 percent of the vote against Nkrumah's 98 percent. Danquah
warned that his erstwhile colleague was becoming a "despot, autocrat, or
dictator . . . or God." Amid the unbridled enthusiasm for an end to colonialism, such sentiments now seemed churlish. President Kennedy toasted the
diminutive Nkrumah in Washington in early 1961 despite warnings from
the State Department of an "alarming trend toward authoritarian socialism."[4]
Kennedy's ill-chosen words at the departure ceremony — "We ourselves are a
revolutionary people[,] and we want to see for other people what we have been
able to gain for ourselves" — seemed only to encourage Nkrumah's fanaticism.

As living standards plummeted in 1961, a strike erupted among railway
and dock workers over a government budget that would reduce wages
and raise taxes. The strike rapidly spread to other sectors of the economy.
Workers accustomed to the beginnings of prosperity under colonialism felt

jilted by Nkrumah's promise of "paradise in ten years" after the British left. The ruling party newspaper insisted that parliamentary criticisms of the budget were evidence of "the utter fraudulence and ineffectiveness of the bogus British colonialist system" and that the striking workers were "agents of neo-colonialism."[5] Nkrumah, on vacation in Russia, instructed his cabinet to declare martial law. The British and Canadian officers on staff in the Ghanaian army probably prevented the military from overthrowing Nkrumah in absentia. When Nkrumah returned from his Soviet-sponsored rest on the Black Sea, he jailed fifty of the strike leaders.

Danquah was arrested for demanding a "sensible" budget and spent eight months in prison. He and his fellow detainees smuggled out copies of protest letters to the United Nations, just as they had during colonial days, expecting it would cause a sensation. But for some reason, the defenders of justice at the United Nations did not seem to care about black lives now that the British were gone.

Believing that Nkrumah would eventually be thrown out of office, the CIA station in Accra began paying Danquah's wife a small monthly stipend during his incarceration, hoping that this comparatively prudent nationalist would halt Nkrumah's destructive march.[6] President Kennedy was furious when he learned of the payments, knowing that Nkrumah, and generations of his admirers, would cite them as proof that any opposition to his baleful policies was merely a Western plot.

When he was released in 1962, Danquah wrote of a sense among Ghanaians that they had been "misled" by expectations of freedom and prosperity after independence. Under constant police supervision, he was forced to watch Nkrumah receive the Soviet Union's Lenin Peace Prize in Accra. At the ceremony, Nkrumah observed sullenly that Danquah had grown fat on "bacon and egg." He ordered the country's expanding ranks of political prisoners—586 people detained in 1963 alone and 1,200 by 1965—to be fed only a dried bread made from cassava flour known as *garri*.

In 1964, the latest of several attempts to assassinate Nkrumah was foiled by security guards. When interrogated, the assassin commented that Danquah would benefit from Nkrumah's death. The police commissioner concluded that Danquah had nothing to do with it.[7] But in the dystopian politics of post-colonial countries, police reports were now irrelevant. Danquah was locked up again, this time in a bare concrete cell in the condemned prisoners' section. He was not allowed to stand for the first three months and not allowed outside for the first six. On the *garri* diet, he lost forty pounds. No Ghanaian doctors attended him. Instead, imported doctors from communist Yugoslavia issued upbeat reports on his health. Small acts of kindness from the Ghanaian guards—peeling oranges for the weakened man or bathing him in his cell—persisted.

Four letters to Nkrumah, a combination of flattery and hectoring, went unanswered. In one, Danquah contrasted his cruel conditions with how the British had treated them both when they were detained briefly following a riot in 1948: "They treated us as gentlemen, and not as galley slaves, and provided each of us with a furnished bungalow (two or three rooms) with a garden, together with opportunity for reading and writing. In fact, I took with me my typewriter and papers for the purpose . . . and there was ample opportunity for correspondence." The Irish district commissioner had provided three square meals a day from his own table. A colonial judge had released them both against the wishes of the colonial administration, because there was no evidence to justify continued detention. "The reason why detention in 'free' and civilized and humane Ghana is" so much worse than under British colonialism, Danquah wrote to Nkrumah, "has never been understood by me."[8]

By early 1965, Danquah's letters took on a measure of desperation: "It was our people's love for justice that compelled them to ask the British in 1843 to come back to Ghana [after evacuating in 1828] . . . Our people's love of British justice . . . compelled our ancestors to welcome the return of the British. Now the British people have gone away from us only some seven years ago . . . and already some people are asking in regard to certain incidents: 'Is this justice?'"[9] Shaming Nkrumah with unfavorable comparisons to colonialism was unlikely to persuade. By now, Danquah realized that his rival—Black Star of Africa, Messianic Majesty of Ghana, Man of Destiny, Redeemer and Victor, Party Chairman For Life, President of the Ghana Academy of Sciences, and Senior Captain of a new 7,500-ton luxury yacht— had no intention of relenting. Nkrumah declared Ghana a one-party state and the 1965 election unnecessary.

The constant interrogations of Danquah intensified as his health sputtered. He began to make preparations to die, asking Nkrumah to tell his wife that he had sought to make peace with him. "When I am rendered incapable of acting for myself by any fatality, such as death or insanity, there will be a legitimate provision to stabilize her in life and enable her to sustain me in her memory."

Twelve days later, after more than a year in prison, Danquah was let out for a five-minute bath. On returning, he found his cell ransacked, his Bible lying shredded on the floor. A storm of anger arose. "Cows and fools!" he berated the warders. They claimed he overreacted and suffered a heart attack. No one really knew. A later inquiry led by a British judge concluded that the horrific treatment of "a man of his standing and intellect . . . beggars description."[10] The Ghanaian opposition leader living in Britain offered to return from exile and stand trial in a neutral African state if Nkrumah would stand trial for Danquah's murder.[11] Nkrumah declined. But he made a show of retreating to his ancestral village, where the state-run press was instructed to photograph him in brooding postures.[12]

News of Danquah's death brought recriminations from across Africa. "If independence means the substitution of indigenous tyranny for alien rule," declared Nigerian president Nnamdi Azikiwe a few days after the death, "then those who struggled for the independence of former colonial territories have not only desecrated the cause of freedom, they have betrayed their peoples."[13] As a young nationalist, Azikiwe had spent three years working alongside Danquah in Ghana (then known as the Gold Coast), between 1934 and 1937, where he launched a nationalist newspaper, the *African Morning Post*, published a book on African independence, and consorted with anti-colonial leaders from across the region. Azikiwe now understood that those newspapers, organizations, orderly societies, and civic freedoms under colonialism did not just "happen." "It is an irony of history," Azikiwe would say about Danquah's death, "that a great pioneer of Ghanaian scholarship should die in a detention camp barely eight years after his country had become free from foreign domination."[14] Ghana's official radio station called Azikiwe a "witless parrot" and the rest of his cabinet "mad dogs" for their cautious approach to decolonization.[15]

An official funeral was out of the question. Danquah's family insisted on a ceremony in his hometown. Nkrumah, the Afro-centrist, banned the use of traditional Akan drums intended to give Danquah's spirit influence over the living. Instead, the brass band of the local Presbyterian church was allowed to play. There was something fitting in this. Danquah's life and career had been critically shaped by his father's embrace of Presbyterianism and by his own love of British colonial administration and constitutionalism. The brass band sounded a universal loss in a way that the Akan drums could not. "His death was seen as parricidal by many who considered Danquah the father of the nation, and Nkrumah his wayward son," wrote a British historian who was a graduate student in Ghana at the time.[16] A few days after the death, a Pentagon analyst for Africa raised the obvious question in a letter to the *New York Times*: "If a man who named the state ends in this manner, what may be the fate of lesser persons?"[17]

As Sir Alan Burns sat with his wife Katie at New York's newly renamed John F. Kennedy International airport on the morning of February 5th, 1965, the news of Danquah's death was disquieting. Knowing that this man who vilified him as governor had died brought little joy. Any sense of vindication was overshadowed by anxiety for the "lesser persons" left behind. Somewhere in rural Ghana was his niece Marca, daughter of his brother Emile. It was Emile who led the training of Nkrumah in London by the British Communist Party. The Burns brothers never lost their mutual love despite being ideologically divided on colonialism and pretty much everything else. Marca, a veterinarian and animal geneticist, picked up the communist bug from her father. After independence, she volunteered to run a state-owned goat farm for Nkrumah. The state-run farms produced only 20 percent as much per worker as private farms, and they embezzled most of what they produced.[18] Marca remained a dogged Nkrumahist even as her father retired, agog and confused by the failures of communism. Sir Alan, the undiminished man of affairs, continued to take an active "colonial" interest in the fate of individual lives in the newly independent states. Marca needed his help.

In Accra, meanwhile, was Lady Dinah Quist, a close friend and confidante of Sir Alan. She was the wife of the first African speaker of the legislature, whom Burns promoted in the last days of empire. A noble West African woman, he kept her photo and letters tucked away in his belongings. She supported him at the very worst time of his life, when the British press and Parliament—especially the self-important Winston Churchill—were calling for his resignation over the death sentences of local men convicted of a "ritual murder." Danquah had led the defense, pettifogging the colonial legal system until Burns commuted most of the sentences. "You have not done anything wrong[,] and why should you go away in this manner?" Lady Quist had written to him at the height of the drama. She stood by Burns in the worst of times. Now it was his turn to stand by her.

With these thoughts, Burns folded his newspaper. He and wife Katie were returning to the fly-blown colonies of the British Caribbean, where they were born and raised. It was their fiftieth anniversary—time to make up for the hardships and lost moments of life in the colonial civil service. Burns worried about Katie's fragile health. But the death of Danquah would loom over the five weeks they spent in Antigua and St. Kitts.

The 1960s were a decade of self-doubt for the West. The Soviet Union and Mao's China were heralded as the future. The deaths of millions in the newly independent countries were politely ignored by Western progressives as the "price of freedom." Burns remained the most prominent and eloquent defender of Western colonialism, as determined as he was charming. He had expected a quiet retirement after the Gold Coast. But London sent him to the United Nations to make a last stand for the British Empire. In a dramatic four months at the United Nations in 1955, he had tried to slow the global rush to decolonization. His failure signified the last hope for the preservation of the millions of human lives that would be lost in the subsequent collapse of colonial rule. Ten years later, Danquah was dead, and Burns had become a lone voice, seen as a dinosaur and reactionary by the left and an embarrassment by the right. Yet with each new crisis like Ghana, the warnings he made seemed more prescient.

The small sailboats twisted and turned in the light breeze off the jetty at Basseterre, capital of St. Kitts. As a young man, Burns had literally sailed from one assignment to the next in these islands, sometimes with prisoners under his charge manning the jib. From the verandah of the St. Kitts Club in 1965 with drink in hand, it could seem like nothing had changed in the sixty-odd years since he began his colonial career. His father's photograph still hung over the reading room inside.

But those "tender and new-dedicate foundations" created by colonial rule, as Kipling called them, were everywhere under threat from tyrants like Nkrumah. At age seventy-seven, Burns remained politely contrarian, refusing to accept the anti-colonial viewpoints that had swept the West's intellectual canvas. Human lives were being lost at an alarming rate in the former colonial areas, and no one seemed to care now that the colonizers were gone. His first task was to find Marca and Lady Quist. Perhaps in other ways, this lone figure who stood against a global catastrophe could still make a difference. "You have not done anything wrong[,] and why should you go away in this manner?"

Sir Alan Burns was one of the most experienced and articulate British colonial officials of the twentieth century. He served in top posts in the Bahamas, British Honduras (Belize), the Gold Coast (Ghana), and Nigeria, as well as in the Colonial Office in London, and for ten critical years after World War II, he was the most passionate voice for European colonialism at the United Nations. Pugnacious, likeable, spare of words, humorous, and impatient with humbug, Burns was widely published and even more widely traveled. He wrote books about the United Nations, colonialism, the history of Nigeria, travel decorum, the British West Indies, and the game of bridge, among other topics. After leaving the UN, he continued his "colonial" life, working to avert ethnic conflict in Fiji and trying to hold the British Commonwealth together. He loved birds, philately, rum punch, and Woodpecker-brand cider. He lived just long enough to witness the catastrophic consequences of sudden decolonization across the Third World, writing a final unpublished manuscript that presciently predicted the rise of humanitarian intervention in failed states.

Burns may seem an unlikely topic for a biography. The views he defended are out of fashion today. He was an obdurate defender of colonialism as a legitimate form of alien rule that brought more justice, opportunity, and prospects for human flourishing than would have otherwise arisen in the places it was found. Those are big claims, but his life was lived at a commensurate scale—he was an ostrich-feathered governor of West Africa's richest country, a member of the British delegation to the United Nations for a decade, and a revered scholar on Nigeria whose history of that country defined the field for half a century. His personal story covers the full arc of the story of Western colonialism—its rise, flourishing, embattlement, and collapse. He not only lived through colonialism but debated it with its fiercest critics.

These included his brother Emile, a leading member of Britain's Communist Party who trained Third World tyrants like Nkrumah and consorted with Soviet Union agents under the watchful eye of Britain's MI5.

Anti-colonial perspectives are so dominant today that an admiring biography of Sir Alan Burns would seem to lack a modern sensibility. But new voices and research are starting to reclaim some degree of objectivity about the causes and consequences of colonialism. The life of Sir Alan Burns shows us in intimate detail why and how colonialism spread so rapidly and easily; how its universalizing ethos so quickly won out over the parochial worldviews it displaced; how this inevitably created its own demise by asserting the centrality of human dignity, rights, and national identity that must lead to self-government; how this productive tension between colonial rule and rising nationalism, which could have set many countries onto a stable path, was broken by the West's sudden loss of confidence (and resources) after World War II; how the precipitous end of European colonial rule brought catastrophic consequences for most of the newly independent countries; and how, despite the entrenchment of anti-colonial ideology globally, new voices and leaders in the Third World began to reclaim those lessons in the 1980s and 1990s, to good effect. Burns not only lived this reality, dying in 1980 just as the first shoots of a renewed positive interest in colonialism were appearing; he also wrote it.

A leading scholar of colonial officialdom considered Burns to be of "comparable eminence" to Lord Lugard, the storied explorer and governor who amalgamated what became Nigeria.[19] As governor of the Gold Coast, he was praised in Parliament as "one of the very best men the Colonial Service has ever known." Burns was part of the last cohort of colonial officials who were Britain's Greatest Generation. They have been forgotten by a preemptive imperial cringe in that country. Compared to the "great men" like Nkrumah and Gandhi whose intemperate and ill-considered efforts to force colonizers out led to setbacks for their people, these late colonial officials have much to be proud of. Yet they are oddly neglected.

The career of Sir Alan Burns is no less fascinating than are his political views. Burns lived a dramatic life of escape from riots and poverty in St. Kitts into the din of war in the swamps of the Cameroons in World War I. He put down prison riots in the Bahamas as colonial secretary and had his London office shattered by German bombs in World War II. As governor of the Gold Coast, he was variously denounced and praised for his handling of a celebrated "ritual murder" case that filled the London papers for months. His brother's flirtation with Soviet spies meant he was watched closely by Britain's spy chasers even as he was made privy to the most secret information on Soviet behavior. During a decade at the United Nations, he crisscrossed the Atlantic by ship in the company of Thai princes and American tycoons, everywhere making a public defense of the British Empire. Sadly, Burns lived just long enough to see his worst predictions vindicated in the "lost decade" of the 1970s.

An unpretentious Catholic, Burns left behind a loyal family following. He was devoted to his graceful wife Katie. Before dying of cancer in 1970, she bet the farm on a racehorse and lost. Burns did not complain. He had overcome worse setbacks. His relationship with his two daughters was more distant—in part, because he saw so little of them when they were young. But he was fair and generous as a father. His brother Robert was a close confidante, his best friend really, who toiled in the tropics for the colonial civil service like himself but was forced out by deafness. Robert died the same year as Katie, leaving Alan as the unexpected graybeard of his family.

In his final years in the 1970s, living alone in a decaying Britain, Burns would set out from his flat each morning to cross London's grand Pall Mall avenue to his cherished Athenaeum Club. Seeing him step out, the club porter would walk into the road to hold up traffic. In 1978, I was a young Canadian boy visiting Britain for the first time with my parents and siblings. Perhaps on one of those mornings, travelling by London cab to see Buckingham Palace, my family was delayed by Sir Alan's morning ritual. As the cab passed, I imagine pressing my nose to the window to get a glimpse of the tottering old man, amazed at yet another example of the eccentric British. It's as close as I could ever have been to Sir Alan Burns. Fortunately, his memories were carefully preserved by his family. This book exhumes that noble and important life.

NOTES

1. "Joseph Danquah, foe of Nkrumah, leader of independence in Ghana, dies a prisoner," *New York Times*, February 5, 1965.

2. Quotations from Danquah are taken from Lawrence Henry Yaw Ofosu-Appiah, *The Life and Times of Dr. J. B. Danquah* (1974), pp. 241–63; and Joe Appiah, *The Man, J. B. Danquah* (1974).

3. Ales Bulir, "The Price Incentive to Smuggle and the Cocoa Supply in Ghana, 1950–96," *International Monetary Fund Working Papers* (1998).

4. JFKPOF-117b-011 (Presidential Papers of John F. Kennedy), "Ghana: Nkrumah Visit," March 1961.

5. Trevor Jones, *Ghana's First Republic 1960–1966: The Pursuit of the Political Kingdom* (1976), p. 123.

6. Richard Mahoney, *JFK: Ordeal in Africa* (1983), pp. 184–85.

7. Republic of Ghana Commission of Enquiry into Ghana Prisons, *Dr. J. B. Danquah: Detention and Death in Nsawam Prison* (1967), p. 53.

8. Ibid., p. 173.

9. Joe Appiah, op. cit., p. 30.

10. Ibid., p. iii.

11. "Exile's reply to Dr. Nkrumah," *The Times*, April 7, 1965.

12. Jones, op. cit., p. 254.

13. "Nigerians angered by a death," *New York Times*, February 9, 1965.

14. "Africa tyranny condemned," *The Times*, February 8, 1965.

15. Olajide Aluko, *Ghana and Nigeria, 1957–70: A Study in Inter-African Discord* (1976), p. 84.

16. David Birmingham, *Kwame Nkrumah: The Father of African Nationalism* (1998), p. 98.

17. James Hooker, "Danquah's death," *New York Times*, February 21, 1965.

18. Marvin Miracle and Ann Willcox Seidman, *State Farms in Ghana* (1968).

19. Anthony Kirk-Greene, "Scholastic Attainment and Scholarly Achievement in Britain's Imperial Civil Services: The Case of the African Governors," *Oxford Review of Education* (1981), p. 19.

Chapter 2

A Judge of Rum

Late one afternoon in 1897, a group of children stood on a wooden jetty in Basseterre, capital of St. Kitts, in the remotest part of the British Caribbean. They held flowers and Union Jacks. Among them was a nine-year-old boy, Alan Burns, wearing a blue-and-white sailor suit with Jack Tar hat. As dusk fell, a British warship appeared on the horizon. It disgorged a boatload of men who were rowed to the jetty for an appreciative welcome.

The arrivals offered hope in what seemed a hopeless situation. A year earlier, a riot had erupted when a Portuguese plantation owner in St. Kitts had refused demands from his workers for higher wages.[1] Workers on the island, mostly descended from slaves, had been striking and setting fire to cane fields for six months. Alan's father, the treasurer of St. Kitts and a member of its legislature, urged a firm response. The local administrator was hesitant. When the new riot erupted, it coincided with a protest by harbor workers demanding better conditions who were blocking services to visiting ships. The estate and harbor workers made common cause, blowing shells to signify their defiance as they marched into the center of Basseterre. They were joined by the swelling ranks of unemployed. The plantation owners sought refuge in anchored boats while the voluntary police force fled into the bush. The mob smashed windows and street lights, looted stores, and left the town in ruins.

The Burns home, a modest two-story residence on the main street, quickly became a target. "They broke into the rum shops and got gloriously drunk. They then paraded the streets, stoning the houses of the white residents and breaking most of their glass windows, and assaulting any they could find," Alan would recall. Along with his younger brother Emile and their parents, the family huddled behind wooden shutters as the mob besieged their home. "I can remember my mother pushing my younger brother under the bed as stones flew into the room where we were gathered."[2] Alan's father, who had been caught in a similar riot in Antigua as a boy, wielded a revolver. "The local authorities are handicapped and entirely unable to cope with the rioters," one newspaper reported.[3]

By luck, one of the British warships that regularly wintered in the Caribbean, the HMS *Cordelia*, had recently arrived off Basseterre. The local administrator called for assistance. A naval brigade of 66 sailors and marines came ashore. Weathering a rain of stones and broken bottles, they shot 3 rioters dead, wounded another 5, and arrested 150. Fires were extinguished and martial law imposed. It was an unprecedented suspension of liberties on the island, which had been in British hands for nearly 200 years. If the *Cordelia* had not been in harbor that day, the American commercial agent on the island reported, "few of the white people would have escaped with their lives."[4]

"[The attack was] one of the earliest incidents that I can clearly remember," Alan would recall. He and Emile were confined to home during six months of martial law. Top officials, including Alan's father, worked to calm the population of thirty-two thousand, choosing to exile many of the rioters to outlying islands. "A very uneasy feeling existed in the island for some months subsequently," noted the official report on the riot.[5] The Burns family fortunes were collapsing as fast as those of the island. Alan's two older brothers and older sister were at boarding school in England. The cost of schooling three children in England was heavy, and, as economic conditions in St. Kitts worsened following the riots, government salaries were cut and pension promises became a fiction. Just as the British Empire reached its "pinnacle of wealth and power" globally, Alan would recall, the Caribbean colonies were in a state of "economic crisis, financial disaster, and the abandonment of ancient constitutions."[6] Three days after Christmas in 1896, Alan's overworked father, aged forty-four, died.

To be born and raised on the tiny islands of the British Caribbean in the late nineteenth century was to be on the periphery in every sense. Each group—European, African, East Indian, Chinese, Amer-Indian—came from somewhere else and saw itself as a part of an inchoate new people. Alan grew up as a "wild boy" of the islands, hunting blue pigeons in the densely forested mountainous uplands of St. Kitts and sailing for hours in a gaff-rigged dinghy. His best friend was his black nanny, "who was very dear to" him, as he "was dear to her."[7] The Caribbean social milieu was like mud splattered by a spinning wheel: freed blacks working the plantations; Indian and Chinese migrants competing with them; poor white farmers disparaged as "white cockroaches" by the freed blacks; a mixed-race, "whitey-pokey," colored population serving in menial service roles; and a small number of white colonial officials bitterly divided between locals and expatriates. The British Empire in the Caribbean stewed away in the tropical heat—"the Empire's darkest slum," as Britain's top colonial official called it[8]—and every few years a great oily bubble like the St. Kitts riots exploded to the surface.

For the Burns family, the social distance from European civilization was great. The family was originally part of the McGregor clan in Scotland that for centuries had been in and out of trouble with the law. Feuds with rival clans and conflict with British soldiers in his hometown of St. Andrews forced Alan's grandfather to flee. He arrived in Montserrat in 1832 at the age of nineteen and married a well-to-do American woman whose family had settled Hunts Point (later a part of New York City). A reinvented man, he joined the civil service and rose to be assistant colonial secretary of the Leeward Islands colony, dying in 1887, the year that Alan was born.

Alan's father took the family even further from its British roots. He fell in love with a Catholic girl whose family had fled the French Revolution and settled at St. Kitts (which had been divided under a pact between English and French settlers in 1627). In order to marry her, he converted to Catholicism. If there was any Christian group more scorned by the British Empire than the evangelical Protestants, it was the Catholics, whose patriotism was always doubted. Catholic French planters had held British Grenada for a year in 1796, executing the governor and forty-eight of his officials. An attempt by Leeward Island legislators to allow Catholic refugees from the French Revolution to hold government positions was disallowed by the British authorities in 1798. It was not until 1829, with the lifting of such restrictions in Britain itself, that the Catholics were allowed to hold government jobs. Alan was the fourth of five children of this suspicious Catholic union. He attended the Basseterre Roman Catholic grammar school, where the students were an unruly collection of races compared to the orderly English stock at the Anglican school.

The waves of migrants who made up the Caribbean islands were lost. "They had the vaguest idea of their history. . . . Some people spoke of a shipwreck," wrote the Nobel laureate Vidiadhar (V. S.) Naipaul, a Trinidadian of Indian descent.[9] Naipaul powerfully described his need to "make that journey from the periphery to the center" toward what he called the "universal civilization"[10] to be found in Europe and the United States. For Naipaul, in 1950, the journey was as simple as boarding a ship with a scholarship to Oxford. But for Alan Burns in 1897, a nine-year-old boy without a father and with only the shreds of a basic education, the escape from the periphery would be more difficult.

The arrival of Her Majesty's West Indies Royal Commission on the wooden jetty at Basseterre in 1897 suggested a way out. The chief representative of "universal civilization" who walked past the impressionable young Alan that evening was the awe-inspiring Sir Henry Norman; raised in Calcutta, he had been a war hero and commander in India and then a modernizing governor of Jamaica and Queensland in Australia, among other posts. Offered the position of Viceroy of India, Norman declined, fearing the strain. The West Indies commission would be his coda. Many Leeward Islanders were starting to look toward the United States for help—"like Mohammedans to Mecca" as one contemporary American journalist put it.[11] But for the young Alan, Mecca was in the direction of Britain, and it was personified by the regal Sir Henry Norman who clambered onto the jetty that evening.

The commission began its inquiry in British Guiana (later independent Guyana) in January 1897, working its way north.[12] In Antigua, it reported, "Poverty is increasing and houses falling into disrepair and . . . generally a state of depression exists which cannot but cause suffering and discontent."[13] In St. Kitts, it stated, "We regret to have to say that the prospects are no better," and, "The prospect of distress leading perhaps to disturbance . . . is very serious."

Alan pored over the commission's report when it was released in 1898. In all the Caribbean colonies, the report said, "A very serious condition of things is rapidly approaching . . . and the crisis will be reached in a very few years." The colonies were promised ten years of financial support to improve infrastructure, invest in new crops, reform land ownership, and expand education. London would lobby European and American governments to stop subsidizing their sugar production. Alan later recalled every point of its diagnosis and recommendations.[14] Rising above the sordid squabbles of cruel Portuguese planters, angry black cane cutters, cretinous mulatto policemen, and punch-drunk British officials, the report described Alan's world in a new language: the language of governance, universalism, and dispassion. From this colonial perspective came empathy and understanding. "Notwithstanding these riots," Alan would later write, "the general conduct of the inhabitants was good."[15]

Colonialism in the Caribbean, as elsewhere, was not yet in question. A sense of nationalism, of being separate from Britain, did not yet exist. Subject peoples saw themselves as natural parts of European empires. Riots like those in Basseterre were evidence of rising expectations, and the Royal Commission was evidence of a rising response. Alan was present, so to speak, at the prelude to nationalism.

The death of Alan's father prompted one older brother, Robert (known in the family as Bertie), and his elder sister, Agnes Ethel (known as Essie), to return to St. Kitts from boarding school in England. The eldest brother, Cecil, who was at Cambridge as a promising Catholic theologian, would never return to the islands. The dire conditions led the family to desperate measures. While Alan looked to the universal civilization in Britain, his mother, like others on the island, looked to the proximal version in the United States. In the summer of 1897, she led the four children—Bertie, Essie, Alan, and Emile—to New York City, hoping to extract some financial compensation from the family's ancient claims at Hunts Point. Like the comically protracted Jarndyce and Jarndyce proceedings in Dickens's *Bleak House*, the Hunts Point case had dragged on for decades without resolution. It was Alan's first time in a developed Western country, and it does not seem to have been a happy time, not least because the claims came to naught. As in Jarndyce and Jarndyce, lawyers' fees had eaten most of the money.

The failure of the Hunts Point assay forced the family to make some hard choices on returning to St. Kitts. Bertie was now the responsible sibling since Cecil remained in England. Faced with two younger brothers needing an education and family finances on the skids, Bertie abandoned his education, where he had shown promise as a classicist, and took a civil service job in St. Kitts, aged seventeen. Essie also remained in St. Kitts, abandoning her interest in writing. Their sacrifices freed up money to send Alan to England. He would follow his brothers to St. Edmund's College, a Catholic boys' school north of London. Alan arrived in England in August 1900, aged twelve. Having welcomed universal civilization to Basseterre three years earlier, Alan of Basseterre now came ashore in universal civilization.

If New York was miserable, England seems to have been simply a bore to this "wild boy." He was "intelligent but lazy" and spent "too much time playing cricket and tennis," according to his school records. In private, he made unflattering doodles of female staff he wanted to marry. There was no easy road ahead, and he knew it. A letter to his mother reflected his tender determination:

Dear Mater,
This is meant to be a serious letter though I know it will seem funny.
Firstly, in I Ruds. you can learn either Greek or Latin. I am learning
Greek until I hear from you so please send instructions soon.
II. What am I to do when I leave college. Am I to get work in the West Indies
or in England. I finally intend to get in the Indian Civil Service for I am certain
that if I studied hard I could pass any exam of that sort. My health is fairly
good so I am going to have a shot at it. I can study for it when I am working.
III. How long am I to stay at the college.
IV. Please tell me if you see anything on my bill that you think I spend too
much on & especially suits of clothes. I try to make them last as long as I can
but at a college you can't hold up your skirts like a girl & you can't help being
knocked in the dirt sometimes so I fear I spend a lot on clothes (outer).
Please write full answers to these inquiries by next mail.
Your affectionate son,
Alan Burns

During the holidays, Alan remained in Britain, where the debate on colonial-ism had begun. It was prompted by the brutal three-year war from 1899 to 1902 against the Dutch-descended Boer republics in southern Africa, fought in an effort to unify the region under British control. The war was popular among black South Africans, who hoped for an extension of the freedoms of the British Cape Colony to other parts of the region: one hundred thousand of them fought and served on the British side of the war. The local Indian com-munity, meanwhile, which had been streaming into southern Africa because of British rule, expressed its support for the war "unreservedly and uncon-ditionally." In the words of one immigrant, a local lawyer named Mohandas Gandhi, the Indian community's contributions to the war would "bind closer still the different parts of the mighty empire of which" the Indian community was "so proud."[16]

At home, the war was unpopular. Over twenty-two thousand British soldiers died, and vast sums were spent on the campaign. What had once appeared a progressive empire of free trade and civilization seemed to be unraveling into jingoism and over-reach—captured in the title of one criti-cal book that appeared in 1899, *Patriotism and Empire*.[17] A young econo-mist, John Hobson, spent that summer in southern Africa as war loomed, then returning home to join the newly formed League of Liberals Against Aggression and Militarism. His 1902 book *Imperialism: A Study* became the first major critique of colonialism.[18] Hobson's proposal for colonies to be turned into international trusteeships would shape Alan's entire career.

Alan's question to his mother about his future was abruptly resolved in his third year, when brother Emile joined him at St. Edmund's. The cost of supporting two boys was untenable and so, like his brother before him, Alan abandoned his formal education. "As family fortunes had been at a very low ebb ever since my father's death," Alan would write, "it was necessary for me to begin work very young."[19] Cecil remained in England, while Bertie escaped to a customs job in the Gold Coast of West Africa. Sister Essie and Alan's mother migrated to England and settled at a Catholic convent. Alan was the last of the Burns dynasty in the Caribbean.

When he returned to St. Kitts in 1903, aged sixteen, there were no jobs. Alan volunteered at the treasurer's office, an unpaid internship that would last for two years. Not until 1905 did the name Alan Cuthbert Maxwell Burns finally appear in the annals of Western colonialism, when he was formally hired as a junior revenue officer (RO) in the Presidency of St. Christopher–Nevis, aged seventeen. It was the lowliest job in the most insignificant part of the British Empire.

Alan insisted that he "was practically born into the colonial civil service."[20] A fellow colonial official joked that he "imbibed the traditions of a colonial civil servant with his mother's milk."[21] It would be better to say that he developed an affinity for a vocation that was in the family. Brother Cecil, after all, never thought of joining the service, and Bertie was at best a reluctant colonial official. Sister Essie showed little interest in things colonial, while Emile avoided it altogether. For Alan, the colonial service was a dream job: "I cannot remember ever having thought seriously of any other possible career," he wrote, "and if I had the chance to begin again I do not think I should choose any other."[22]

Two-thirds of the men who rose to become governors in Britain's African colonies in the twentieth century had university degrees. Alan considered his lack of formal education an advantage. As his career progressed, he would repeatedly argue against attempts to require a university degree for senior colonial jobs. "A strong character and sound common sense are far more valuable assets to a colonial official than the most brilliant academic distinctions," he would write.[23] The ineffectual governor of the Leeward Islands at the time was a Balliol graduate and former professor of classics. Much later, when summer university courses became mandatory for new recruits, Alan warned that they would produce young officers "full of zeal and theory" lacking what he considered the two essentials: "unlimited patience and a real sympathy for the people among whom the young officer will work."[24]

Burns, RO, was an ideal candidate in this sense: colonial-born, diligent, of practical bent, and with a natural empathy for local needs. The first available photo of him at a desk shows him in a crisp uniform with his equally well-dressed staff—black, colored, and Indian—ready for a day's work (figure 2.1): "A lack of punctuality, untidy offices, and slovenliness in dress may be indications of eccentric genius," he would write, "but they are more likely to be signs of inefficiency."[25]

One advantage of being raised in the British Caribbean was its constitutional traditions. In other colonies, the governor and traditional rulers shared absolute power. In the British Caribbean, as a result of pressures from European settlers and their colored (mixed-race) descendants, legislatures had become more democratic over time. "As the education and development of the inhabitants improved, the system was adapted to meet the growing desire for fuller representation," Alan would later recall.[26] A gradual move to self-government was *normal* in colonial politics for Alan, whose father and grandfather had served in colonial legislatures and cabinets. He would take these assumptions with him, if he could ever escape.

Another advantage was that it was difficult to be parochial in the Caribbean, where everyone was an immigrant and most populations were thoroughly mixed. The color barrier for top colonial posts in the British Empire was broken here first in 1841 when a mixed-race African was appointed president of the island of Nevis, a half hour's sail from St. Kitts.[27] The social diversity

Figure 2.1   Junior Revenue Officer, St. Kitts, 1905. *Source*: Private Collection of Alan Dixon.

gave Alan a cosmopolitan view about race and an enduring interest in race relations. At work, he quickly became an equal opportunity employer: "I was of course prejudiced in those days in favor of the local officials," he would write of his early days, "[because] there were at that time a number of local men, both white and colored, who could more competently have discharged the duties of these posts" filled by expatriates.[28]

Growing up in the Caribbean also meant that Alan *believed* in colonialism. The comparative benefits of being a colony here were obvious. The nonwhite populations were far better off in Barbados, the Bahamas, Bermuda, the Leeward Islands, Jamaica, and Trinidad than in independent countries like Haiti or mainland states like Guatemala or Colombia a hundred years after their anti-colonial revolutions. Black and South Asian workers did not seriously contemplate migration to the noncolonial countries of the region. With worsening sugar conditions, there were appeals for *more* British colonialism, not less. Once you started thinking about the alternatives, colonial rule by a relatively liberal and law-governed state like Britain willing to spend time and resources on your country's economic well-being was preferable to the tragic alternative of premature self-rule as it came to life in places like Haiti and Guatemala. This was why the first nonwhite president of Nevis "identified powerfully with British institutions and values," in the words of one historian.[29] "At its lowest assessment," Alan would write, "British rule was the lesser of two evils."[30]

The same year that Alan joined the colonial service, Kipling wrote his poem "The Pro-Consuls." It was inspired by an editorial in the *Times* that extolled the achievements of the British governor of South Africa, Lord Alfred Milner, in creating a unified state. "The foundations which Lord Milner has laid are firm and strong," the *Times* effused, "But for the decision which he took six years ago, there may now be ruins where a fair and stately building is slowly rising."[31] Alan would learn the poem by heart and, as he rose in the colonial service, would distribute copies to his staff.

The poem captured three central aspects of the colonial project that would suffuse Alan's thinking. First, colonialism filled a governance deficit that would otherwise have been unfilled. "Hid behind the centuries" was a developmental gap that, left ungoverned or poorly governed as in places like Haiti or Liberia, would leave societies ravaged by violence and poverty—"the sea we fear." That was how empire spread: as much by indigenous pull as by European push. The task of colonial government was to build "foundations deep" so that "peace be fitly made." The idea of "foundations" of self-government—articulated by the *Times* and then lyricized by Kipling—would inform Alan's thinking for the next half century: "It takes time to lay foundations," he would write, "and if these foundations are hurriedly laid—and badly laid because of the hurry— the whole building must be insecure."[32]

The later poems of Kipling, of which "The Pro-Consuls" is one, had a new melancholy. Those sleep-deprived colonial officials would receive little thanks for their efforts. Colonial peoples would inevitably turn on their governors as a result of becoming literate, cosmopolitan, healthy, and secure, making full use of the new rights and legal protections that colonialism afforded. "Doubted they are, and defamed / By the tongues their act set free." Successful colonialism created the conditions of its own demise. It was, in one scholar's terms, a "self-defeating enterprise."[33] Western liberalism, and the Christian humanistic thought that produced it, would cause colonial peoples to demand their own rights to be self-governing. That was, in a sense, the plan all along: "Power that must their power displace." Alan would tell new recruits years later what they must accept as colonial officials: ". . . A certain amount of criticism even from those we are trying to help, and we must accept cheerfully the fact that we are training the men who in the end must take our places from us." This was, as Kipling had put it, "foretold of old at our outgoing." As Alan would put it, "You will get little thanks, but does this really matter?"[34]

The deeper sadness in Kipling's later poems related to the home front. Colonial officials could no longer expect praise from "their generation." The

Oxbridge dons were "Scholarly to judge the souls / That go down into the pit." In this last stage of empire, with social esteem fading, a colonial official needed to be motivated "Not by lust of praise or show" but by the knowledge that his absence would make things worse. As Alan would write, intellectuals back home might "believe the worst of colonial administrators and gener-ally of Britons overseas, and . . . credit the inhabitants of colonial territories with the possession of all those virtues which their 'oppressors' so obviously lack."[35] A "defeatist attitude" would creep into the mainstream of British society, insisting that colonialism was "something to be ashamed of."[36] But those who saw foundations rising and lives improved needed to stay the course: "I think there has been far too much sackcloth and ashes[,] and I hope that this unfortunate and entirely unjustified attitude has not depressed the men who are doing such good work in the colonies. There is no reason why it should."[37]

As a junior revenue officer in St. Kitts, one of Alan's daily chores was to row out to newly arrived ships. The heavy surf frequently upset the small boats as they returned to shore. Alan survived one capsize "due more to good luck than anything else as the steersman had little control over the boat once she was caught on the crest of a breaker."[38] This briny career was more than just a problem of safety. How could one catch the notice of the Colonial Office while spending endless days as acting harbor master in St. Kitts? "Stick close to your desks, and never go to sea, and you all may be rulers of the Queen's Navy!" was the witty advice of the Lord of the Admiralty in Gilbert and Sullivan's *H.M.S. Pinafore* of 1878. Alan was quite literally unable to comply; as he summarized his first years: "I spent a great deal of my time on the sea."[39]

To get back on dry land, in 1909 Alan took a job as clerk to the magistrate of Basseterre, where his gift for organization was badly needed. Hundreds of years of Leeward Islands legal code meant that the court clerk was a sort of legal help desk for contending parties. "It was no easy matter to ascertain what laws were actually in force," he recalled.[40] Working with a friend in the court, he compiled a reference book that lawyers and litigants could consult for themselves. The *Index of the Laws of the Federated Colony of the Leeward Islands and of the Several Presidencies Comprising the Same* was not a page turner when it appeared with a London legal house in 1911.[41] Topics included pond drainage, petroleum storage, fire brigades, plant protec-tion, wharfage rates, horse taxes, boards of health, compulsory inoculations, ice-making subsidies, keeping sailors orderly while on shore leave, poor relief, and road maintenance. The authors offered their work with "much diffidence and anxiety." They were each paid twenty pounds. It was the first demonstration of Alan as a "scholar-administrator" that was so important to career advancement in the colonial service.[42] After the *Index*, Alan would write ten more books, all of them considerably more compelling.

These were boisterous days for Alan. The social scene in island society was gay despite the economic woes. Social gatherings took place on Saturday afternoons at the St. Kitts Club, where Alan's father had been an institution— billiards for the gentlemen, bridge for couples, and a social area, favored by unattached men and women, where the club's trademark rum punch was served: "one of sour (lime juice), two of sweet (syrup), three of the strong (rum), and four of the weak (ice)." Alan became an aficionado of bridge and rum punch, the latter "something to remember—and to respect." He would aspire to the highest compliment: "a gentleman and a scholar—and a judge of rum."

Despite the gaiety, the scene was difficult for European women. To escape from the shipwreck of Caribbean society, they turned up for the social events with the crews of visiting British warships, the same crews who had rescued the European population from annihilation in 1896. The major fixture was the annual visit of the British Navy's North American and West Indies Squadron, based in Bermuda. The arrival of even a single cruiser "was an event of some importance," Alan would recall. Cricket, tennis, picnics. Then the main event: a "subscription dance" where the local ladies "could be certain of a sufficiency of partners."

Kathleen (Katie) Hardtman was a local estate girl, the belle of St. Kitts: well-raised in a prominent planter family and three years younger than Alan. She was one of nine children, and even as her family's holdings expanded because of a belief that sugar prices would eventually rebound, actual fortunes were declining. She completed a high school correspondence degree with Cambridge in 1905, aged fifteen, making her better educated than Alan. She was elegant, smart, and most of all ambitious. The visiting sailors did not capture her fancy. These naval officers were too much at sea, never likely to advance beyond a small cottage on the south English coast. Instead, the two Burns boys—Alan and Emile—competed for her affections.

Alan and Emile had been rivals in tennis as well as love. For Alan, tennis was for health and fun—"the best game for the tropics, giving just enough exercise to keep one fit."[43] Emile, by contrast, had begun to hate his upbringing, including tennis. Having spurned the colonial service, he took a place at Cambridge. Katie might have followed. But by now, she was in love with Alan. When Emile heard, he was baffled. Why would she choose a dull colonial clerk over a dashing Cambridge man? "You really are much too nice for Alan," he wrote to Katie.[44]

Like many of his generation at Cambridge, Emile was caught up in the excitement of socialism. Katie preferred a more practical spouse. She was not a Catholic, but that did not matter to Alan, whose faith was ecumenical. Their differences, on the other hand, were complementary. Katie knew that professional advance in British administration required more than a good knowledge of rum punch and a gift for paperwork. She had the instincts for being well-dressed and socially adept, as well as politically savvy, areas where he was weak. She would "bring him up in the way he shouldn't go," as Emile advised, whether tailoring his suits or charming his superiors.

With their nuptials agreed, Katie, aged twenty, decided to leave the islands for New York, where she joined the typing pool of a Wall Street accountancy firm. For the next five years, she and Alan would endure a long-distance relationship as he struggled to advance in the colonial civil service while she added to their meager savings. New York had let down Alan's family, but it might make his marriage.

One advantage of his mother and sister's resettlement in England was that it gave Alan an official anchor in the universal civilization whose colonial cause he supported. When his first leave came up in 1910, he argued that his "home" was Britain. He spent five months in south England, shuttling between the coast and London. It was ten years since he set foot in England, and the intellectual shift against colonialism was now in full motion. While he was in England, the first major conference of colonial critics was organized by economist John Hobson. Among the speakers was the writer and journalist G. K. Chesterton, who was emblematic of a new kind of political animal: the "conservative at home and liberal abroad." "It is undoubtedly better for general human morality that we should leave other people alone," he told the delegates. If there was *any* imperial mission worth defending—"anything that is of our souls and of ourselves"—it was to help each nation achieve "the management of its own affairs."[45]

Modernizing ideas were also taking hold within the Burns family. After a stint in Rome, Cecil had abandoned the priesthood and taken up lecturing on political and social questions in London. He confided his loss of faith to Alan and published a venomous attack on the Vatican in the *Times*, accusing it of persecuting anyone with a "modern spirit."[46] For Cecil, the Vatican had become like a bad colonial power: too worried about its own interests and agenda and not enough about the interests of those it was supposed to serve. Like Hobson, Cecil was not anti-colonial per se. In a 1920 book, he would argue that European colonialism had "on the whole . . . been good" despite its many failures, because the alternatives for ungoverned areas were likely much worse.[47] The task for the colonies, he wrote, was to strengthen consent by creating a voluntary alliance of peoples in self-governing states. Britain might retain a colonial role, but only by invitation: "Imperialism, if it is to develop, must be reconciled with nationalism."[48]

The modern spirit also took hold of Essie, who, despite her devout faith, never quite fit into the regimented life of the convent. With the rich material of the school, she fashioned two of the most popular "strong girl" novels of the day: *The Grand Duchess Benedicta* (1915)—"A real plot and some good illustrations," *The Spectator* magazine affirmed[49]—and *Peggy in Demand* (1924), both stories of devious plots played by convent students against the adults. Neither was adopted in the convent curriculum.

When Alan returned from leave in Britain in 1911, the Colonial Office declared him ready for a "starter colony." The place chosen was the tiny island of Anguilla, population four thousand. The journey to Anguilla took two days by sailboat. When he arrived, there was little to do. "I tried such trifling cases as there were, kept the Treasury books, supervised the repairs of the roads, kept an eye on the customs officers, and directed the energies of the two or three short-term prisoners who remained, almost willingly, in the prison."[50] The friendly locals invited him to share a bottle of rum procured from the nearby French-Dutch island of St. Martin, assuring him earnestly that they kept a special "duty paid" bottle for just such occasions. The medical dispensary had an array of medicines in numbered bottles that Alan was supposed to administer according to a chart left by the previous incumbent. In another colony, the story went, the amateur colonial doctor "found that the symptoms indicated the use of medicine from bottle No. 8, but as this bottle was unfortunately empty he gave the patient a double dose of No. 4; the result is not reported." Alan confined his efforts to bandages and quinine: "None of my patients ever returned a second time," he quipped.

The prisoners were his favorite companions. They turned up at his bungalow each morning for work orders. He sent them to cut grass in the cemetery or to repair roads. At mid-day he would visit. "My coming was the signal for an outburst of energy too good to be true." Sometimes he took them hunting, since they knew every duck pond on the island. "I regret to say that on one occasion I used them to recover birds that I shot[,] and I think they enjoyed that day as much as I did."

The delightful little island of Anguilla would be the site of one of the most comic episodes in post-colonial history—known as the "Bay of Piglets"—when British police and frogmen "invaded" the beaches in 1969 in response to local demands for a restoration of colonial rule. Being stuck here in 1911, however, was no joke. Alan begged for a transfer. When it came, it was momentous. He was sent to the biggest and second most populous island of the Leeward Islands colony, Dominica, to serve as private secretary to the chief administrator.

The commanding heights, even of an island of only twenty-nine thousand people, were exhilarating, even still if his skills in prison management and health care went to waste. The chief administrator of Dominica was a well-connected old sea dog of Canadian birth who had recently served as acting governor of the Leeward Islands and thus had a direct line to London. The advice he gave to Alan was stark: careers were being made in Africa and India, and since the Indian service operated on its own terms, any advance would require a stint in Africa.

The kindly administrator found Alan a post in the greatest African colony of them all: Nigeria, smack in the heart of the "white man's grave" where few officials lasted long and many went mad. Katie promised to join him there as soon as they were married. After just a few months, Alan packed his bags for Lagos. He had escaped, but it was not clear to what: "Most of my friends thought that I was going to almost certain death."[51]

NOTES

1. On the 1896 riots see Vincent Hubbard, *A History of St. Kitts: The Sweet Trade* (2002) and Glen Richards, *Collective Violence in Plantation Societies: The Case of the St. Kitts Labour Protests of 1896 and 1935* (1987).

2. CCC, p. 241.

3. "Devastation of St. Kitts island," *San Francisco Call*, March 10, 1896.

4. Humberto García Muñiz and José Lee Borges, "U.S. Consular Activism in the Caribbean, 1783–1903," *Revista Mexicana del Caribe* (1998).

5. Frank Cundall, *Political and Social Disturbances in the West Indies: A Brief Account and Bibliography* (1906), p. 22.

6. HBWI, p. 651.

7. Allen, cassette 3.

8. Julian Amery, *Life of Joseph Chamberlain* (1951), vol. 4, pp. 241–42.

9. V. S. Naipaul, *The Enigma of Arrival* (1987), p. 162.

10. V. S. Naipaul, *The Writer and the World* (2002), p. 517.

11. Hubbard, op. cit., p. 127.

12. Bonham Richardson, "Depression Riots and the Calling of the 1897 West India Royal Commission," *New West Indian Guide* (1992).

13. Great Britain, *Royal Commission to Inquire into Conditions and Prospects of the Sugar-Growing West India Colonies, 1896* (1897), pp. 55, 57, 17.

14. HBWI, pp. 661–62.

15. Ibid., p. 683.

16. Ashwin Desai and Goolam Vahed, *The South African Gandhi: Stretcher-Bearer of Empire* (2015), p. 53.

17. John Robertson, *Patriotism and Empire* (1899).

18. John Hobson, *Imperialism: A Study* (1902).

19. CCC, p. 10.

20. Ibid., p. 9.

21. Stewart Symes, "Review of 'Colonial Civil Servant,'" *African Affairs* (1950), p. 81.

22. CCC, p. 9.

23. Ibid., pp. 294–95.

24. Ibid., p. 302.

25. Ibid., p. 152.

26. CBAA, p. 33; FBCE-G.

27. Edward Cox, "Ralph Brush Cleghorn of St. Kitts (1804–1842)," *Slavery & Abolition* (2007).

28. CCC, p. 20.

29. Cox, op. cit., p. 55.

30. IDOC, p. 42.

31. "Lord Milner," *The Times*, July 21, 1905.

32. CBAA, p. 157.

33. David Abernethy, *The Dynamics of Global Dominance: European Overseas Empires, 1415–1980* (2000), p. 325.

34. CCC, p. 324.

35. IDOC, p. 299.

36. Ibid., p. 293.

37. CCC, p. 311.

38. Ibid., p. 13.

39. Ibid., p. 13.

40. Ibid., p. 264.

41. Alan Burns and Dudley Henry Semper, *Index of the Laws of the Federated Colony of the Leeward Islands and of the Several Presidencies Comprising the Same* (1911).

42. Anthony Kirk-Greene, "Scholastic Attainment and Scholarly Achievement in Britain's Imperial Civil Services: The Case of the African Governors," *Oxford Review of Education* (1981).

43. CCC, p. 14.

44. Emile Burns, personal letter to Katie Hardtman, November 22, 1909, private collection.

45. Nannie Florence Dryhurst, *Nationalities and Subject Races. Report of Conference Held in Caxton Hall, Westminster, June 28–30, 1910* (1910), pp. 129–30.

46. "Persecution of the Modernists," *The Times*, November 2, 1910.

47. Cecil Delisle Burns, *International Politics* (1920), p. 64.

48. Cecil Delisle Burns, *Political Ideals: Their Nature and Development: An Essay* (1915), pp. 215, 224.

49. "Reviews," *The Spectator*, January 22, 1916.

50. CCC, pp. 16–18.

51. Ibid., p. 27.

Chapter 3

My Old Mahammedan Sergeant

It took Alan three weeks to reach England, where he procured a portable bathtub, mosquito nets, and a thick cotton "spine pad" erroneously believed to protect the wearer from heatstroke. From there, he boarded a steamship for Lagos. Sister Essie saw him off at Southampton, and he had a brief visit with brother Bertie when the ship called at the Gold Coast. Anchored off Lagos, he was unceremoniously lowered in a wooden "mammy-chair," placed in a skiff, reloaded onto a larger tender, and paddled over a hazardous sand bar into port. "Why the hell did you come here? You should go back!" a half-crazed Englishman stumbling around the wharf yelled at him when he disembarked.

Alan sailed on the German steamship *Professor Woermann*, the newest of the "fast service" ships serving the Woermann Line's West Africa route. The German ships set out from Hamburg, called at Southampton and Boulogne, and then knit their way along the west African coast. One German diplomat on board, Alan recalled, "distinguished himself by taking an overdose of quinine . . . with disastrous results."[1]

Carl Woermann was a Hamburg merchant who dominated commerce in the uncolonized area east of British Nigeria. The local Duala people, who populated the coastline, became the chief intermediaries of the trade exporting palm oil, palm kernels, and ivory to Europe in return for cloth, manufactures, guns, salt, and gin. Twice, in 1877 and 1881, the Duala chiefs entreated the British to establish a protectorate over their region. The British declined. The result was a German protectorate, which became the German Cameroons in 1884. The following year, German commercial interests convinced a coastal chief in what became German Togoland to accept a similar arrangement. It was the beginning of Germany's relatively brief thirty-year stint as a colonial power.

The cooperative attitude that emerged from great power conferences on colonialism held in Berlin in 1884 and 1885 meant that there was solidarity among British, French, and German colonial officials. Germany's top colonial official hosted a dinner to honor the retiring British governor of Uganda in 1909 when they found themselves together aboard a homebound German steamer: "We made flowery speeches, vowing eternal friendship between our two nations," the governor recalled.[2] That was changing by 1912, however, as Germany's rebuilding of its navy to support its colonies contributed to an arms race in Europe and as its expansionary colonial diplomacy, known as *Weltpolitik*, posed a challenge to British and French imperial interests. By the time Alan arrived in Africa aboard the *Professor Woermann*, it appeared likely that he would be pressed into service to defend the British Empire against the Woermann legacy.

On joining the colonial service in 1905, Alan enlisted in the St. Kitts militia. The militias formed a basis "on which larger forces can be built up in time of war," he recalled.[3] Besides shooting tournaments with garish trophies, one advantage of militia membership was that in 1911, between assignments in Anguilla and Dominica, Alan was invited to join the ten-member Leeward Islands contingent at the coronation of King George V in London. One thousand soldiers and officers from the British Empire took part in the coronation. It was the largest and most representative gathering of colonial subjects of the British Empire at its peak. The day after the coronation, the colonial contingent was invited to Buckingham Palace to receive medals from the new monarch. "Here they stood in the heart of the great nation that had made this equality of races possible, to receive, as equals in arms and citizenship, the mark of the Royal appreciation of a common patriotism," the *Times* eulogized.[4]

The Mexican writer and Nobel laureate Octavio Paz wrote that "the creation of a universal order . . . was the most extraordinary accomplishment of colonialism."[5] The universalizing transformation of European society that had accompanied Europe's rapid development was exported to other societies. As Alan would write, colonialism "united tribes into nations large enough to take their part in the international community" and in so doing contributed toward a recognition of "the universal brotherhood of man."[6]

Universal rights brought universal responsibilities, however. To make claims on the universal citizenship of colonialism meant making contributions as well. During the coronation, Alan and the rest of the colonial armies were warned that the obligations of empire might shortly be thrust upon them. Any great power of Europe adopting a "Napoleonic policy," the British foreign secretary warned, would threaten British sea power, and thus its ability to protect its colonies and dominions. The empire needed to protect Britain if

Britain were to protect the empire. In a speech to the colonial contingents, the retired commander-in-chief of British forces, Lord Roberts, who was well-known for his warnings about German intentions, admonished the soldiers to be prepared: "It is not enough to have preference for the unity and mainte-nance of the Empire unless we are also animated by the desire to make that unity real and effective against all possible dangers, and to do so before it is too late."[7] His words would be cruelly vindicated when he died of pneumonia visiting Indian troops in France in the first month of World War I.

When the war began in August 1914, Alan was put on active duty as a ser-geant in the Nigeria Land Contingent, a merry band of European volunteers who took shooting practice after dinner. If he had remained in the West Indies Regiment, his chances of survival would have been nil, since it was eventu-ally deployed to the deadly theater of Mesopotamia. In Africa, by contrast, many hoped that hostilities could be avoided. If the Germans stayed put and did not use their colonies to menace sea routes, Africa could in theory remain at peace.

Yet the robust Allied response to German aggression in Europe in August 1914 caused Berlin to rethink its colonial strategy. German colonies could be used to tie down Allied armies and resources that would otherwise be deployed to Europe. A British and French quagmire in Africa would help a German victory in Europe. The Germans invented the term "world war" (*der Welt Krieg*) to describe this globalizing strategy. The British and French, meanwhile, saw that German colonies would be critical resources for sup-porting the war in Europe. A massive 12-tower radio transmitter built in German Togoland in 1914 coordinated all German shipping in the Atlantic. As a result, the defensive colonial strategy of the British and French was abandoned in favor of dismantling the German empire.

If European colonies were being held by force, the outbreak of war would have been a perfect time to throw out the oppressors. Virtually the entire constabulary of Lagos, for example, was packed off to war, while the already thinly policed northern Muslim areas of Nigeria were emptied of a colonial military and police presence. Just two thousand native policemen and about thirty British police officers kept order in a country of twenty million for the next four years. At a time of Arab nationalism against the Ottoman Empire, the peoples of British and French West Africa could easily have styled them-selves as fighting a similar anti-imperial battle.

There was, to be sure, a continuation of everyday protests about every-day issues throughout the war. These revolts invariably involved public authorities, who happened to be colonial ones. Rarely, however, were they "anti-colonial." One of the few that occurred was in the British colony of Nyasaland (today's Malawi) in southeast Africa, where a heavily indebted Baptist pastor radicalized in the United States, John Chilembwe, criticized

the use of Nyasaland natives to fight against German positions in East
Africa—"invited to die for a cause which is not theirs," as he insisted.[8] Yet
Chilembwe's appeals for a mass uprising fell on deaf ears. A remarkable two-
thirds of the adult male population of Nyasaland—215,000 men in total—
fought or served in support roles for British forces during the war. Chiefs and
Muslim leaders spurned the mercurial Chilembwe. When the time came for
his uprising in 1915, it was a flop. Probably fewer than 100 men participated.
After sitting for hours on an old railway bridge, Chilembwe fled and was
caught and killed by native police.

The only recorded attempt in Nigeria to rouse the natives against colonialism during the war occurred in 1915, when a man declared himself "the second Elijah" and led a mob to smash the fetish idols of his neighbors. He was
arrested on extortion and sedition charges. Despite the nationalist mythology
that these failed revolts spawned, their main significance was to demonstrate
the legitimacy and effectiveness of British rule. To the extent that there was
a "national will" in Nigeria or Nyasaland, it was a national will to participate
in the universal civilization of British colonialism. "From all quarters came
manifestations of the loyalty of the African populations," Alan would write.[9]
In the Caribbean, he noted, "the loyalty of the West Indians was impres-
sive" as "large contributions were made to various war funds and the people
accepted cheerfully the inevitable shortages and restrictions imposed on
them."[10] Brother Cecil, in a postwar book based on letters from brother Bertie
in the Gold Coast, noted that "although all British troops were removed from
the colony, there was no native disturbance nor even the suspicion of it."[11] In
all, 1.4 million soldiers from India and 53,000 from British Africa fought for
British forces in the war, in addition to 1 million black Africans and 330,000
Egyptians who served in support roles.

It was appropriate, therefore, that the first British shot in World War I
against the Germans was fired in Africa by an African. On August 7th, 1914,
while patrolling the border with German Togoland, regimental Sergeant-
Major Alhaji Grunshi from the Gold Coast came upon the enemy and discharged his historic shell. The universal civilization of empire was making
its unity "real and effective" as Lord Roberts had insisted. Yet this unity also
existed in German colonies. There too, local tribes that had benefited from
colonialism would put up a spirited defense. The quagmire of the Great War
in Africa loomed. Having fought so hard to escape from the Caribbean, Alan
was now fighting for his life.

Togoland was Germany's model colony. European merchants traded with
native groups and developed commodity production to the advantage of all.
The tiny capital at Lomé exerted minimal control, which remained in the
hands of local chiefs. This meant that the colony was little prepared for war.

The defense force consisted of just eight hundred natives and a dozen German officers. Alan's regiment was put on standby in case the Nigerian forces that had been sent to assist troops from the Gold Coast needed help. Sensing the hopeless situation, the local chiefs of Togoland rebelled. The German garrison in Lomé quickly fell, followed by the garrison protecting the radio transmitter. The colony was split into French and British sectors, and the Allied forces were redeployed.

The rapid conclusion of the Togoland campaign meant that Alan's contingent was reassigned to the bigger challenge: German Cameroons, a mountainous and rain-soaked colony of 3 million people twice the size of Germany. German rule had many allies among the native population here. In the north, the local sultanate of the Islamic Fulanis, which had invaded, plundered, and enslaved rival groups from 1823 until the Germans arrived in 1902, was the willing agent of German control. In the south, German rule operated through the coastal Duala tribes, who became prosperous middlemen. In 1914, the entire colony was policed by only 2,700 native police and soldiers and 200 German officers — or one for every 1,000 residents, between one-fifth and one-tenth the capacity of modern states. "Wherever I went, I heard natives praise the excellent German administration," a Yale historian who conducted his dissertation fieldwork in the inland areas in the 1920s wrote. "The frequently made comment about the Germans was that they were very strict, at times harsh, but always just."[12]

It was only by fluke that this successful colony found itself in fragile health as Alan's contingent readied for battle. In early 1914, a Duala chief and his advisor were imprisoned by the German governor over their opposition to a new port on Duala lands. With the outbreak of war, the Germans hastily convened a trial and hanged both men. An uncle of the dead chief fled to Lagos and placed himself at the service of the British. They put him back ashore in September to gather information and stir rebellion among the Duala, who rose up immediately. The uprising made the British overconfident that they could take the town of Duala (today's Douala) as easily as they had captured Lomé. Three British platoons sent overland were stranded by swollen rivers and cut to pieces by German machine gun fire. The British strategy now shifted: the town would be bombarded from the coast while troops would be put ashore in the thick swamps of the Wuri river delta to capture the town from the sea.

On September 18th, Alan was told that he would be shipping out to take part in the coastal assault. That day, he went to confession, ordered his "chop boxes" for food, and wrote a letter to Katie. He also prepared a personal diary, a leather-bound book with "Burns" written on the cover. The next morning, after attending mass, he boarded the SS *Appam*, a converted passenger ship. The odd-ball flotilla of French and British warships taking part in the assault on Duala included ancient gunboats from the China service, a tug-boat named *Walrus*, a leaking launch named *Alligator*, and the Nigeria governor's yacht. The Germans sunk several ships across the mouth of the Duala harbor and mined the waters. It took the British several days to clear the way. On September 25, with the harbor made safe, an ultimatum was issued. With no surrender received, the Allied forces prepared to land the following day.

The commander of the entire operation was aboard the *Appam*, so Alan and his fellow soldiers (both British and African) were assigned to the commander's regiment. This was "bad luck," Alan recalled, because the regiment was "far inferior, both in discipline and in fighting value" to others taking part.[13] The regiment was divided into five companies of fifty soldiers each, and Alan was assigned to lead a half company of 25 soldiers. In all, 2,400 native soldiers from British regiments and 1,900 natives from French regiments would take part in the attack on Duala. Alan was one of 81 noncommissioned British officers serving alongside 154 British officers. An even bigger role was played by 4,500 native porters, boatmen, river pilots, and scouts.

The events of September 26, 1914, are shrouded in confusion. As Alan wrote to Katie:[14]

> We got up at two o'clock [a.m.] and fell in on deck in a pouring rain at 2:45. After some hot coffee & sandwiches we finally got away about 3:30. I was in charge of the right half of "D" company on the launch Alligator and the various launches went up stream led by an armed picket boat. Then just as day was breaking, we swung out of the main stream and went up a creek. We were landed (if that is the right word) in a mangrove swamp, where we were always up to our knees and often up to our waists in water. It was a most dreadful swamp & the bush was very thick. In these depressing surroundings I received my baptism of fire.[15]

German snipers caught sight of the landing parties flailing in the swamp as dawn broke. At the same time, the HMS *Challenger* and a gunboat, *Remus*, began a steady bombardment of the town. "Topsy-turveydom set in mud and slime" was how one officer described the scene.[16] Alan's party came under heavy fire, as he recalled:

> At about 12 our scouts got in touch with the enemy and the Germans started to fire on our picket boats and the launches. There was a deafening row, the bullets were whistling through the trees and shells were bursting overhead and through it all we could distinctly hear the heavy firing from the "Challenger." I confess that when the bullets started I was frightened but luckily two of my men started

to run and I jumped up and kicked them back into the firing line. That kept me busy and after that I had too much to do to be frightened.

There were 200 German soldiers stationed at one position overlooking the river where they glimpsed the British thrashing in the reeds. The official British report described the blunder: "After groping forward for the enemy, an advancing column found itself suddenly under fire at point blank range in a situation which was bewildering and which afforded little opportunity of judging of the hostile dispositions."[17] Alan was more blunt: "The show was certainly not well thought out. . . . Had the Germans known our position they could have got the lot." As Alan's letter suggests, the confusion operated in both directions. The scattered British forces struggling in the bush apparently made the Germans believe that a great force had surrounded them and might cut off their path of retreat. Shots were firing in every direction even as they retreated. Inevitably, some hit their mark.

> Our casualties were very slight owing to the thickness of the bush. We lost 5 blacks killed and 1 white man & about 15 blacks wounded. Our company lost none. The Germans lost very heavily from the shelling but I doubt if the casualties were much. They certainly left no dead in the ground we advanced over. I think they fell back because they knew we outnumbered them.

By midnight, Alan was back aboard the *Appam* "covered in mud and cuts from thorns & wet through, very hungry & very tired." The next day, the Germans surrendered. In subsequent reports, both British commanding officers were oddly proud of the fiasco. "The only redeeming feature of the episode," the commanding land officer would write, "was that our activity in the river caused the enemy to appreciate the fact that Duala was being threatened from the rear, thus hastening his decision to evacuate and surrender the town."[18] The commanding naval officer was likewise triumphant: "The first attempt seemed to be a complete failure, but, in fact, it was not. The [German] governor and commandant had already left the town, and the threat of the reconnaissance on the main line of retreat was too much for the nerves of those who had been left in charge."[19] Alan, with the passage of time, would employ his characteristic humor in recalling the events: "We were re-embarked . . . having accomplished nothing at all, but as Duala capitulated the following day we took some of the credit to ourselves, while acknowledging that the *Challenger*'s guns may also have had some effect. Perhaps the Germans thought that troops capable of landing at such a place were capable of anything."[20]

A subsequent official history of the operation was more scathing. The hasty disembarkation in uncharted swampland just one day after the ultimatum was partly driven by restlessness aboard the overloaded troop ships, it found.[21] There was only one road from the swamps, and it was never discovered. It was only by coincidence that the Germans were not guarding the river better when Alan's company landed. The whole area was "quite unsuitable as a base for a force of any size," the report noted. If there were any heroes that day, they were the native carriers and pilots who successfully evacuated the troops as night fell—a sort of Dunkirk on the Wuri.

Alan's company was put ashore the following day, and the natives "received us with open arms." The Germans "had made themselves thoroughly hated," and the natives had to be restrained from assaulting the captured Germans. A total of 720 German civilians were deported to camps in West Africa, mainly for their own safety. "The German civilian prisoners seemed bewildered and did exactly what they were told without argument."[22] As they carried their luggage to the quay, the natives jeered and pelted them with garbage. "I don't know what the terms are and whether it means the surrender of all the Cameroons, or only the town of Duala," Alan wrote to Katie that evening. "I will wire you if it is all over so that you will know I am safe." In fact, it was only the coastal Duala who would receive the allied troops with open arms. The Germans retreated inland, where their support was stronger. Alan's real baptism of fire was yet to come.

For a week after the surrender of Duala, Alan's regiment rested. Natives emerged from the forest with fruit and cereals for sale. His diary for October 5th records: "Saved kittens. Acquired typewriter." The respite was short-lived. Following the defeat at Duala, German forces retreated in three directions, one of which was up the Wuri river to the town of Jabassi (today's Yabassi). Britain's strategy of dismantling the German empire meant that the Nigerian forces would pursue the Germans in all three directions. On the evening of October 5th, Alan's company was told that it would take part in an assault on Jabassi.

Jabassi sat on the right (or western) bank of the Wuri River, fifty miles above Duala, behind several hills and ridges. There were only sixty German officers and about three hundred native soldiers guarding the town. The swampy land running down to the river was covered in thick elephant grass. Away from the coastal breezes, the heat was intense, as were the mosquitos. For two days, the British forces moved up the river in tugs and barges. "October 7th: Natives cheering us, cursing Germans," Alan's diary records. The battle of Jabassi on October 8th, 1914, would be the most harrowing day of his life.

The commanding officer, Edmund Gorges, was the same man who had ordered the chaotic landings at Duala. His series of tactical blunders at Jabassi would make it a day of infamy. "I was, in fact, very loath to throw a portion of my small force into such a blind piece of unknown country," Gorges wrote in his memoirs.[23] Two of Alan's letters about this day survive, one to Katie and one to Bertie. They provide a detailed account of the debacle.

The mistakes began when Gorges put his soldiers ashore a full two miles below Jabassi. They were to march overland into battle but did not carry provisions for the day ahead. "We were sent into action without food and pushed on at a terrific pace under a very hot sun. The result was that the white men were exhausted early in the day," wrote Alan. On Gorges' orders, a naval detachment hauled an impractical 12-pound field gun (weighing 1 ton) through the swampland like some ancient idol. Alan's half company of 25 African soldiers passed the sailors "lying on the ground too exhausted to go forward or backward." Then the gunfire began.

> There was no sign of any enemy until we reached an open surface below a small hill when a few scouts opened fire on us. We doubled to the top and they ran but we were unable to catch or shoot any as the men were too nervous to shoot straight. After that I went with my half company to another hill and for the rest of the day was on my own. I occupied three ridges in succession taking them fairly easily and with no casualties, although bullets were buzzing round us all the time. My position was on the extreme left flank of our force and we held off all attacks as I was able to post my men in a very strong position on the last hill.

While Alan's group provided cover from its hilltop position, a disaster was unfolding below. Gorges had ordered the main force split into two, one of which would launch a frontal assault on the town, while the other moved in from the right. The flanking group got lost and emerged from the forest behind the frontal group. The frontal group became confused and scattered as heavy Maxim machine gun fire blared from the town buildings. Alan watched the carnage below:

> All went well til our troops reached the first houses when a most terrific fire broke out and mowed them down. Captain Brand and two white sergeants were killed. Lt. Bennet got a terrible wound in the face. Many natives were killed and I am sorry to say most of the rest ran. Had the men stood, I have no doubt that a bayonet charge would have taken the town as the Germans must have been greatly knocked about by the shell fire from the gunboats. The German Maxims were splendidly served and did terrible damage. Our men refused to advance.

Meanwhile, native scouts for the British had reported earlier in the day that German forces were hiding on the left (or eastern) bank of the river, opposite where the British boats were at anchor. The official report gave a grim account: "These reports of enemy on the left bank do not appear to have been passed on to Colonel Gorges. In any case, their full significance does not seem to have been grasped and no attempts were made to take active countermeasures against enemy action from this direction."[24] This hidden battery opened its cross-fire on the boats and on the back of the troops, adding to the confusion. It took some time for the boats to turn and return fire. Five British sailors were killed. The British boats then fled downstream, leaving the assault forces under fire from the rear with no means of evacuation.

When Gorges arrived on the scene, in his own words, he "found the troops suffering from the effects of the terrific heat, tactical unity completely lost in the dense elephant grass through which officers were trying to lead the men, many of whom showed signs of hanging back under the constant bursts of machine gun fire, of which this was their first experience."[25] The overall British commander of the Cameroons campaign who had ordered Gorges to take Jabassi wrote that "difficult country, novel conditions, and the fact that our native troops encountered machine-gun fire for the first time are contributory causes to failure."[26] Gorges had to relent, as Alan recalled:

> At last the slaughter got so terrible that the General ordered the retreat and I got an order to hold my hill at all costs to cover the retreat. About this time there opened a very heavy Maxim fire on my position and when there were our wounded streaming back through our lines they started to run. I was driven to beating them back to their places with a stick and I had to shoot one fellow in the arm to stop him running. For the next two hours we were under fire from the whole of the German right but they kept at a respectful distance so our losses were not heavy.

In covering the retreat, Alan relied on his command position to steady his nerves.

> If anyone tells you that he likes being in a fight and enjoys being under fire tell him from me that he is a liar. I had to walk up and down our front every now and then to steady the men and when the bullets came close I was horribly frightened. If I had not got to show the men I was not afraid I believe I would have run away myself.

Alan's half company suffered the biggest losses. Eight of his twenty-five men were killed and another eight wounded, of a total of seventeen British forces killed in the failed assault. He attributed his own survival to luck.

Their rifle fire was rotten. One man I saw take four shots at me from about 400 yards. I was standing up and he missed every one. . . . The men did not behave very well but we covered the retreat and I never left my position til every one of the other companies was embarked. It was a terrible day.

The re-embarkation was no better. Falling water caused one boat to go aground. Then, a heavy evening storm blew down the river, making the voyage hazardous. The "ignominious retreat down river was too awful for words," Alan wrote. Gorges called it a "nightmare of nocturnal navigation."[27] Alan was exhausted. "I am sorry to say I fainted when I got on board but the Doctor revived me with a half glass of neat brandy."

As colonial military blunders of World War I go, the ill-fated raid on Jabassi is too trifling to rate a mention in most histories. But for Alan, even small blunders were a disaster in the colonies since the colonial trust demanded an extra duty of care in times of war. The heavy losses and the ignominious retreat bore heavily on him:

> We should never have retreated as we could have held our ground until morning and had another try next day. . . . If we held our ground til next day and I got some rest and food we could easily have gone on and won . . . I felt (as everyone else did) like crying with shame and vexation when I saw our fellows giving up ground they had won at such a cost. The Jabassi show was disgracefully run. . . . Our men behaved disgracefully but the generalship was also a great deal to blame. . . . The General should be shot for having ordered the retirement.

Alan's contingent rested for a week before a larger force was sent to take Jabassi, this time without Alan's company. On the second attempt, the town was easily taken. As with the Duala follies, Gorges later defended the fiasco at Jabassi, writing, "the enemy was fairly shaken, thus paving the way for our success."[28]

For the next two months, Alan's company was on watch up and down the Wuri River. There was sporadic resistance from German forces around Jabassi. A day after its surrender, one of Alan's Nigerian soldiers was shot in the face after his machine gun jammed. He remained at his post to unjam the gun, retreated to have the wound dressed, and then hurried back to rejoin the fight. During a two-week reconnaissance up the river, Alan's company encountered heavy fire. The native canoeists did not flinch, steering the company to safety: "They received little honor and their services were too often overlooked, but without them the troops would have been helpless," Alan recalled.[29]

In the relative calm of these months, Alan's bond with his native soldiers grew. He regularly visited the wounded from the Jabassi battle. He seemed to inspire a devotion usually reserved for senior officers. When his company was briefly stationed at the 35-man Jabassi blockhouse—a concrete box with a machine gun mounted on top—they obeyed him faithfully despite constant enemy harassment. As he wrote:

> The men are improving as they get more accustomed to fire and I always get volunteers to go with me on a sortie. It is rather amusing the way the men try to take care of me. My old Mahammedan sergeant in especial has constituted himself my guardian angel. If I get out of the trench to have a look around he always follows me. And although I order him back under cover he won't go until I do.

The daily activities involved a lot of parading, where Alan took pleasure in being alongside his men: "Those of us who have served with them regard these African soldiers with affection and pride."[30] Being proud, however, also meant being firm. The worst experience was having to give evidence against a native soldier who had fallen asleep while on sentry duty at the blockhouse. As Alan wrote to Katie: "It is a very serious offense as it might have meant the whole lot of us getting scuppered. He has been sentenced to receive 24 lashes. I suppose it is necessary but I hate to witness it in cold blood."

Away from action, Alan's diary recounts a full schedule of diversions: playing skittles in the trenches, walking the lines to inspect barbed wire, removing "jiggers" (fleas that burrow into the feet and cause infections), evening drinks with fellow officers, begging the French bakery for bread, catching snakes, tending to the kittens he had rescued, and oiling his typewriter. Alan was also called upon to sort out the multiple tribes that the British were now supposed to govern. One day he wrote to a senior officer in camp:

> A native has come in and wishes to see you to ask your protection. He was going past Mamba on the Njanga creek when the natives stopped him, took away all the provisions he was taking down to Duala, and beat him and his woman. The local chief tried to protect him and was himself beaten. He also is here. Shall I send them across to see you? A.C. Burns, Lt. W. Afr. Rf.

With his robust health and disposition, the tour seems to have suited Alan. "My beard is long and straggly, my face (nose especially) sunburnt, ditto my arms and knees, but I am very fit. I could use with a good long sleep but otherwise I have never felt better." He expected to be "passing a very unhappy birthday" when he turned 27 that month. But the cooks outdid themselves for his birthday dinner: pea soup, herring, curried bully beef, black rice, ship's biscuit, asparagus ("the best part of the dinner"), gooseberry jam, and coffee. For drinks, they procured a bottle of Medoc from the French and found some rum for the Caribbean boy. Most of all, Alan was tired of his long separation from Katie. "It is far better to think of the time we are going to have together. That is what I do all the time."

Alan would spend two more months on garrison duty. The Cameroons campaign was getting worse as the fighting moved inland. The assumption by Alan and others that a hearty welcome was waiting for the British throughout the colony was false. The Hausa and Jaunde tribes of the interior proved every bit as willing to fight for the Germans as the Nigerian tribes were to fight for the British. In the first attempt to seize the new inland capital at Jaunde (today's capital of Yaoundé), the Allies lost nine hundred soldiers. When the southern areas fell, more than six thousand native soldiers and eight thousand other natives chose to leave with the Germans for the neutral Spanish colony of Rio Muni (today's Equatorial Guinea).

The Germans were succeeding in creating a quagmire for the British and French in Africa. Alan's Nigeria Land Contingent began recruiting more volunteers in Nigeria. Given his administrative experience, Alan was recalled to Lagos to oversee the recruitment and training of this additional cannon fodder. It was a stroke of luck. For the next year, British and French losses in the Cameroons would mount. Not until February 1916 would the last German garrison in the north of the Cameroons surrender. By then, most of Alan's former "D" company would be dead.

After defeating the Germans in West Africa, British forces were sent to East Africa, where native support for German rule ran deep. The quagmire in East Africa had baleful consequences for colonial government in Nigeria. In addition to the manpower strains, the war stretched government services and was "profoundly felt," Alan would write.[31] The newly amalgamated Nigeria needed more government, but the war led to less. The pressures came not just from the loss of police, which created openings for vandals and thieves, but also from the economic costs. Food prices rose, government revenues declined (especially from imports of liquor by German traders), and planned new railways were suspended. Sporadic rebellions broke out, often "at the instigation of German traders," Alan would write. The various disturbances invariably centered on everyday issues: a new tax or a new rule. "In these circumstances, it is remarkable that there was so *little* serious internal trouble," Alan would write, "and in view of the absence on active service of a large proportion of the Nigeria Regiment it was extremely fortunate."

The politeness of the war-time "rioters" particularly impressed him. On one occasion while on his bicycle, he found himself in the middle of a protest over the conviction of a popular native politician. "One of the leaders of the mob came forward and politely enquired whether I wished to pass, and then invited me to follow close behind him 'in case any of the people might be rude.'" On another occasion, a group marched to the governor's house in

Lagos to protest a new water rate. "Please sir, we are a riot," they announced. The governor told them that he was very busy and asked whether they would be so kind as to hold their riot the next day. They obliged, and the governor sent a policeman to fetch them. From the gubernatorial verandah, Alan recalled, "the strange sight was seen of the 'rioters' arriving, led by a police officer on his bicycle."

Alan saw his final war-time action as a result of the pressures caused by the East Africa campaign. About forty miles north of Lagos was a town named Abeokuta that had been populated in the early 1800s by various groups known as the Egba fleeing conquest by other tribes. The morass of refugees in the town played havoc with traditional lines of authority. In 1853, the local British commander estimated that the 140 villages that made up Abeokuta contained no less than 4,000 chiefs—or 29 chiefs per village. "Everyone acts like a chief," the saying went.[32] The lack of authority left them vulnerable to internal strife and external threats. Thus, in 1893, the various groups in Abeokuta signed a treaty with the British under which a single chief, or Alake, was appointed to coordinate the various chiefs.

Shortly after the outbreak of World War I, the Egba tribes signed an updated treaty that called for a full reorganization of Abeokuta into a native administration under the Alake. A head tax was imposed to replace the battery of levies, fines, and tributes that had been prone to corruption and inefficiency. Individuals were to be given title over their land, replacing the refugee tradition that viewed the entire town as communal and temporary. Yet these attempts to manage economic and social change in Abeokuta ran into historical animosities and unresolved power struggles. As agents of the new dispensation, the traditional chiefs became the targets of unrest. "Discontent and misunderstanding had time to grow and to become serious before the Government was aware of what was happening," Alan recalled.[33]

In June 1918, malcontents in Egba began cutting telegraph lines and setting fire to public buildings. Train stations were looted and rail lines sabotaged. The official report estimated that 30,000 people took part out of a population variously estimated at between 150,000 and 250,000.[34] A regiment of soldiers recently returned from East Africa was sent to restore order but quickly lost control. The Alake fled for his life to a Catholic mission hospital. Another prominent chief was captured and killed by a mob that included his own son. They carried his head with them for the remainder of the rebellion.

Alan's involvement began in late June when a train carrying 8,000 pounds in currency (worth about $1 million today) under an escort of 12 police was stopped and attacked by the Egba rebels. The train retreated to a station down the line, where the police dug in to await reinforcements. Rebels followed them, threatening not only the train but also the nearby water pumping station for Lagos. As a captain with battle experience, Alan was chosen to lead

Figure 3.1 After Egba Uprising, Nigeria, 1919. *Source*: Private Collection of Alan Dixon.

a contingent of troops to relieve the trapped police. His company traveled part-way up the line before moving on foot to avoid ambush.

The rebels were armed with "Dane guns," long flintlock muskets that fired small pieces of wire and metal to create horrible wounds—relics of the slave-trading eighteenth century. "At close range and in thick bush they are more deadly than rifles," Alan would write. As Alan's company made its way toward the besieged train station, it encountered several rebels with their deadly guns. "[They] fought with great courage against hopeless odds, creeping up through the thick bush to fire their Dane-guns at short range into a line of troops advancing in single file along a bush path and then running off to reload their cumbersome weapons," he recalled.[35]

Fortunately, Alan knew how to steady the nerves of his soldiers (see figure 3.1). Within two days, his party had made it to the station without casualties. His relief effort could only reinforce the garrison, however. "The rebels frequently came out on the railway line and sniped at the British forces," an official history recounted. "They also used the forest as cover to continue harassment of the British-led troops, and at times would continue their sniping after dark."[36]

As luck would have it, several more detachments of Nigerian forces returned from East Africa and were immediately rerouted to the station. "For a few days more the situation was tense[,] but the rebellion was crushed without much difficulty when the reinforcements arrived," Alan wrote.[37] Like the chance presence of the HMS *Cordelia* at St. Kitts 22 years earlier, the fortuitous return of the troops from East Africa may have saved his life. "Had this rising taken place a few months earlier," he would recall, "The situation would have been very grave." As it was, the rebels "had no chance against the well-armed veterans of the Cameroons and East Africa."[38] In all, 2,600 soldiers were engaged in crushing the Egba uprising. Only 100 government troops were killed or wounded, while the rebels suffered deaths and wounded of about 1,000. A total of 85 rebels were later convicted.

The Egba uprising left Alan with a deep suspicion of rule by traditional chiefs. In the few instances where tribal affiliations remained strong, rule by chiefs might make sense; indeed, he wrote, "I believe that for such people there is no better school in which they can learn the art of self-government."[39] Economic and social change, however, meant that the legitimacy of chiefs was waning. Local government needed to be civic and universal. "You cannot set the clock back in Africa, or anywhere else, and you cannot expect the educated African to be satisfied with a Native Administration run by men in whom he has no confidence—illiterate men whom in his heart he despises," Alan would tell new colonial service recruits many years later: "We must not merely set up autocratic chiefs through whom we can govern, because such rule is just as direct as any rule that a District Officer could administer—and probably less efficient."[40]

The effects of World War I on colonialism were profound. The postwar settlement at Versailles asserted that all colonial powers had a "sacred trust" to advance the interests of subject peoples. The universal citizenship that had called upon the loyalty of subject peoples in World War I now owed them universal rights in return. As one scholar pithily summarized: "The main effect on the British Empire was to encourage national feelings that were expressed, entirely sincerely, in terms of great attachment to Britain and yet turned out to have the effect of helping to dissolve the empire."[41]

In 1917, the British government promised to push India toward "self-governing institutions with a view to the progressive realization of responsible government."[42] The liberal governor of French Indochina likewise promised in 1919 to create a "modern state" with a "constitutional charter" that would eventually become "an autonomous country."[43] This new thinking carried over into debates about the territories seized from the German and Ottoman empires. Giving them back was a nonstarter. Liberal voices wanted the territories placed under some form of temporary international administration. A compromise emerged: they would be administered by colonial powers under a "mandate" given by the newly created League of Nations. The mandates would be more open to international scrutiny than colonies: annual reports would be submitted, visiting inspection teams would be sent to monitor conditions, and subject peoples would have the right to petition the League over any matter of concern.

The assignment of mandate territories largely followed the spoils of war. A Permanent Mandates Commission began work in 1921. Alan would later praise the work of the commission, in contrast to the later United Nations. The most effective critics on the commission, he wrote, were from the European colonial powers. The British representative from 1923 to 1936 was Alan's former boss as governor of Nigeria, Frederick Lugard. "From his great experience, he was the representative best qualified to criticize," Alan would write. The collegial nature of the commission, in contrast to the fractious character of the later UN system, was, in Alan's view, the key to its success: "There was in the commission a greater desire to help the people of the territories under mandate and an intelligent realization that this could not be accomplished by continuous abuse of those responsible for their administration."[44]

The seizure of German colonies would prove a sore point in that country, especially as British officials published lurid books on alleged atrocities and misrule in them. The Germans replied point for point, arguing that their mistakes were no worse than those in British colonies. There is at least one aspect of German colonialism that Alan would endorse. Many years after the war, one of the main contributions of German colonialism came to fruition: the discovery of a cure for sleeping sickness. The insect-born disease had originated in nomadic cattle-herding populations whose movements had spread the disease for hundreds of years before the colonial era. The intensification and modernization of agriculture that accompanied the rise of global markets caused the disease to break out of its previously geographically limited boundaries and kill large numbers. Between 1901 and 1907, it killed between 200,000 and 300,000 people in Uganda alone. "The sleeping sickness problem over-shadows everything else in my work here. The disease rages unchecked[,] and hundreds are dying every month," wrote the governor of Uganda in his diary. Many of the sick fled to Catholic mission hospitals to avoid being thrown into the jungle by their kin to be devoured by leopards. On a visit to one such hospital in 1906, the governor noted that the 110 patients included many children: "Unaware of their impending doom, the little black mites played and romped to their heart's content in the shade of the banana grove[,] and only the enlarged glands at the base of their necks showed that their fate was sealed."[45]

The cooperation among colonial powers, including Germany, to find a cure through the multinational Sleeping Sickness Commission in the years leading up to the war was a demonstration of the solidarity that many hoped would prevent war in the colonies. After the war, the Germans continued work in their laboratories and in 1921 found a cure. They offered to reveal the formula in exchange for the return of their colonies, but France and Britain demurred. Instead, the French reverse-engineered the drug, issuing their own version in 1924. Treatments in French West Africa alone in the 1920s numbered in the hundreds of thousands. To put that into perspective, assuming very conservatively that the German discovery of a cure for sleeping sickness saved one million people by the time the disease began to retreat in the 1930s, that is one person for every letter in this book.

Later writing on such colonial-era health interventions would be heavily freighted with what one tropical medicine scholar called "the hermeneutics of suspicion" that reduced every achievement to a devious maneuver to consolidate colonial rule.[46] Alan would point to such health interventions as a sincere and critical achievement of colonialism. "Sleeping sickness and yaws, yellow-fever and malaria, and numerous other diseases have been reduced in their incidence, or abolished altogether in some instances," Alan would write.[47] "Hospitals built by colonial authorities and the work of British medical men and nurses in the public health services in the colonies have reduced mortality and improved the health of millions."[48]

One result was rapid population expansion, outpacing food supply. "With the best of intentions, the members of the colonial medical services have been largely responsible for creating one of the world's most pressing problems: the fact that food production has difficulty in keeping up with the demands of an increasing and hungry population."[49] The British, he would insist, are justly proud of their contribution to the control of malaria, which accentuated this food problem. "Medical work in colonial territories has been beyond praise and can hardly be blamed for one of its results—the difficulties facing the underdeveloped countries due to the rapid increase of population."[50]

One further consequence of World War I that would profoundly shape Alan's later career was his brother Emile's conversion to communism. Revolutionary movements had been sparked in both China and Russia as a result of losses suffered in World War I. The British decision to allow Japanese forces to take the lead in seizing the successful German colony at Qingdao in north China brought an angry social response in China, discrediting its nascent democracy and fueling the rise of a communist alternative. The new Russian-run organization that controlled communist parties abroad, the Comintern, funded the creation of an international anti-colonial movement centered in Berlin, the League against Imperialism and for National Independence, led by a German confidante of Lenin.

In Britain, the fringe anti-colonial movement now had a major international sponsor in Moscow and the Comintern. Cecil left his position in government to join the Labour Party and its joint research center with the national trade union, although he was skeptical of the violence of the Russian revolution and its anti-colonial rhetoric. It was Emile who was more taken with events in Russia. He graduated from Cambridge in 1912 and married Elinor Enfield, who was active in the English food co-op movement. They joined the Communist Party of Great Britain, which was founded in 1920 with the equivalent in today's money of $3 million in aid from Moscow, some of it smuggled into Britain in chocolate-encrusted diamonds. The party never had more than about 5,000 members despite its claim to represent the "masses." But its internal coherence was strong. Members were expected to marry other members, and those of Scottish descent were held in special awe because of their leading role. Emile and Elinor were a model couple of the party. Alan joked that Emile fertilized the red roses at his north London home with shredded copies of the CPGB's *Daily Worker*.

The three Burns brothers were thus setting off in divergent directions in the postwar period. Alan was emerging as a liberal imperialist, intent on both the importance of colonialism and its responsibilities. Emile, having spent the war-years agitating for social reform in an impoverished London, had turned to Soviet Marxism as the historic force for good, and with it a virulent anti-colonialism. Cecil stood uneasily between them, rejecting both the fanaticism of revolution and the pretensions of colonialism. It was unclear whose cause would win the day.

NOTES

1. CCC, p. 29.
2. Hesketh Bell, *Glimpses of a Governor's Life, from Diaries, Letters and Memoranda* (1946), p. 207.

3. CCC, p. 244.

4. "Medals for the oversea contingents," *The Times*, July 1, 1911.

5. Octavio Paz, *The Labyrinth of Solitude: Life and Thought in Mexico* (1962), p. 103.

6. CBAA, p. 195; CP, p. 37.

7. "Inspections of colonial troops," *The Times*, June 20, 1911.

8. Roger Tangri, "Some New Aspects of the Nyasaland Native Rising of 1915," *African Historical Studies* (1971), p. 308.

9. HON, pp. 222, 228.

10. HBWI, p. 702.

11. Cecil Delisle Burns, *International Politics* (1920), p. 57.

12. Rudin, op. cit., p. 419.

13. CCC, p. 246.

14. "ACB to Katherine Burns," personal letters, September 11, September 27, October 16, and November 11, 1914, private collection; Alan Burns, personal diary from World War I, private collection.

15. CCC, pp. 246–47.

16. Howard Gorges, *The Great War in West Africa* (1916), p. 148.

17. Frederick James Moberly and Committee of Imperial Defence, *History of the Great War Based on Official Documents: Military Operations: Togoland and the Cameroons, 1914–1916* (1931), p. 137.

18. Gorges, op. cit., p. 148.

19. Julian Corbett, Henry Newbolt, and Committee of Imperial Defence, *History of the Great War Based on Official Documents: Naval Operations: To the Battle of the Falklands, December 1914* (1920), p. 275.

20. CCC, pp. 246–47.

21. Moberly, op. cit., p. 137.

22. CCC, p. 247.

23. Gorges, op. cit., p. 160.

24. Moberly, op. cit., p. 148.

25. Gorges, op. cit., p. 160.

26. Charles Dobell, "Cameroons Campaign, Army Despatch," *London Gazette (Supplementary)*, May 31, 1916, p. 5420.

27. Gorges, op. cit., pp. 161–62.

28. Ibid., p. 166.

29. HON, p. 229.

30. FBCE-G, p. 8.

31. Following sections from CCC, pp. 249–50.

32. John Ausman, "The Disturbances in Abeokuta in 1918," *Canadian Journal of African Studies* (1971), p. 47.

33. CCC, p. 249.

34. Harry Gailey, *Lugard and the Abeokuta Uprising: The Demise of Egba Independence* (1982), p. 38.

35. CCC, p. 248.

36. Gailey, op. cit., p. 90.

37. CCC, p. 248.

38. HON, p. 235.

39. CCC, p. 204.

40. Ibid., pp. 321–22.

41. Trevor Lloyd, *The British Empire, 1558–1995* (1996), pp. 276–77.

42. Richard Danzig, "The Announcement of August 20th, 1917," *Journal of Asian Studies* (1968).

43. Albert Sarraut, *Grandeur et Servitude Coloniales* (1931); Christopher Goscha, *The Penguin History of Modern Vietnam* (2017), p. 118.

44. IDOC, p. 116.

45. Hesketh Bell, *Glimpses of a Governor's Life* (1946), pp. 112–13, 120.

46. Pascal James Imperato, "Review of 'Lords of the Fly: Sleeping Sickness Control in British East Africa, 1900–1960,'" *African Studies Review* (2005), p. 167.

47. IDOC, p. 68.

48. CBAA, p. 133.

49. Ibid., p. 119.

50. IDOC, p. 293.

Chapter 4

Koko Town

Alan's first assignment in Nigeria in 1913 was to travel up the Benin River to relieve a customs supervisor who had gone mad. The remote Koko Town station was little more than a sleepy dockside used to offload cargos for overland journeys, "a single street along the right bank of the river, with a bungalow for the Supervisor of Customs, a mud-walled rest house, customs offices, a few trading 'factories' and the houses of the merchants, and practically nothing else," Alan recalled.[1]

The incumbent who greeted him was "decidedly odd" and "very suspicious" as Alan handed him his discharge papers. "I was unable to give him any proof that satisfied him that I was in fact the person mentioned in the official letter, and in these circumstances he refused to acknowledge me or to take me to his house." The supervisor shunted Alan off to the mud-walled "rest house," which Alan accepted, "leaving it until morning to decide what my next move should be."

That night, torrential rains arrived, and the man sent a note to Alan saying he could sleep on the veranda of the official residence. Just as Alan dozed off, the man came to him by candlelight "in a highly excitable condition" wanting to discuss various matters. At one point, he produced two photographs of apparently different European women and asked Alan if he would like to see "his wife." When the bleary-eyed Alan responded, "Which one?" he retorted indignantly: "Sir, do you suggest that I have two wives?" The next morning, without saying a word, the expired overseer leaped onto the downriver mail steamer with only a canvas bag, leaving Alan in charge. The Colonial Office eventually declared him unfit for duty even though he obtained testimony from a London doctor as to his sanity: "I am not a lunatic! I have a certificate that I am sane!"

Living for months in remote outposts, the "old coasters" who fashioned colonial rule found solace in drink and mistresses in equal measure. They regarded colonial service, Alan wrote, as "a bachelor's paradise, where a man could dress as he pleased, drink as much as he liked, and be easy in his morals without causing scandal."[2] Sexual liaisons between colonial officials and native women were "particularly frequent in those tropical lands where there are few white women, or where the general standard of sexual morality was low."[3] Alan was sympathetic. The old coasters had done the pioneering work of establishing ties with native groups and, partly as a result, "they travelled more and saw more of the people in their villages; they visited and were visited by Africans more freely" than later generations of colonial officials.

In response to the prurient declamations of later critics about places like Koko Town, Alan was fond of citing Kipling's 1890 poem "Tommy" in which a rank-and-file soldier admits that "single men in barricks [*sic*] don't grow into plaster saints": "Their work . . . seldom suffered from these indulgences, and one could perhaps adapt a line from Kipling by saying that single men in lonely stations 'don't grow into plaster saints.'"[4] Fictional accounts of depraved men in remote stations, like the hit 1923 Broadway musical *White Cargo*, might stir the scolding passions of reformers on the home front, but they were far from realistic. "At no time did I see anything in any way resembling the life portrayed in *White Cargo*," Alan wrote. "And if these men of a previous generation were not plaster saints at any rate they did their work well, and it was they who laid the foundations on which their successors were building."[5]

White Cargo was based on the 1912 novel *Hell's Playground* written by the adventuring daughter of a Pittsburgh millionaire, Ida Vera Simonton.[6] She spent sixteen months travelling alone in French Congo (Gabon) in 1906 and 1907, becoming a legend in her own right for scheming to become the queen of local tribes that, as one scholar noted, had never had a single ruler, "let alone one from Pittsburgh."[7] *Hell's Playground* centers on a young British aristocrat, Cecil Huntingdon, who comes to French Congo to make his fortune, hoping to save his family estate and marry his "intended" in England, the noble Marjorie. "It's the divvil's own time you'll have out here to be true to her," comments the steamship captain as they near the coast. Huntingdon seems to concur as he catches the first whiff of the tropics: "Africa certainly breathes sex."[8]

In the novel, the white traders and French colonial officials are all "physical wrecks, from their affairs with native women," yet dare not bring their European wives or children to Africa. At first, Huntingdon remains true to his intended, establishing himself as a successful trader. His health deteriorates as his business thrives, however, and during one severe bout of fever, an elegant Gabonese woman nurses him back to health. The old coasters are jealous of her attentions and spread the rumor that he has taken a mistress. When the rumor reaches Marjorie in England, she breaks off their engagement. Huntingdon is enraged. "The white race had dealt him his death blow and he was done with it forever." After a long and erotic build-up involving crocodile eggs, palm wine, and a glimpse of a "perfectly molded breast," he makes love to the Gabonese woman. "He had indeed cast his lot with Africa."

In the French version of the story, Huntingdon would have settled down to sire a brood of mixed race *citoyens* and be elected a Gabonese delegate to the French National Assembly. In French colonies, official policy actively promoted the taking of a native wife or girlfriend (the latter known in France as a "colonial marriage") on the grounds that it reduced prostitution, improved bonds between the races, and would promote the integration of a Greater France. The French awarded their highest literary award for colonial writing in 1925 to a French mining executive who wrote a novel, *Mambu and Her Lover*, about his extramarital affair with a native woman in French Africa.[9]

In the early days, British colonial conventions were likewise tolerant of native mistresses. Many whites who regarded inter-racial marriage "with horror," Alan noted, viewed "illicit intercourse, and even permanent concubinage, in the case of a white man and a black woman . . . with tolerance."[10] British policy changed after a series of scandals in Kenya in the early 1900s, when a British district officer was discovered with a harem of twelve native women, while one of his colleagues was found to have purchased three girls for forty goats. Black Kenyans found the scandals amusing, but back in "Victorian" Britain, they were just scandalous. In a circular of 1909, known as "the immoral relations memo," the secretary for colonies threatened "disgrace and official ruin" for any new recruit who was found to have "entered into arrangements of concubinage with girls or women belonging to the native populations." A less threatening memo was sent to the old coasters, who were warned of "gravest condemnation" and a "vigorous reprobating" if they did not give up their native lovers. (The West Indies was one of the few places where the immoral relations memos did not apply given their impracticality there.)

One scholar believes that by caving into domestic puritanical pressures in Britain, the immoral relations memos "remoralized the empire in a way which may in the long run have fatally undermined it."[11] Top-flight administrators could be hounded out of office with nothing more than an anonymous complaint of "immoral relations," while the emphasis on the separation of races may have contributed to the rise of nationalism in some colonies. So when the upright and pious Alan Burns stepped from the weekly mail boat onto the heavy timbers of the Koko Town customs dock in 1913, he was enacting the remoralization of empire that had become the central justification for his presence there, as well as a source of imperial decline.

Alan's four months in Koko Town were supplied with enough amusements to keep him from succumbing to the allure of the bottle or of perfectly molded breasts. About twenty-five miles upriver was the district headquarters, where he played tennis once every two weeks. His "comparatively abstemious habits" did not sit well with the district commissioner who each evening presided over the "Scotch Club" overlooking the river where "each man's boy brought his master's deck chair, glass, bottle of whisky and soda water, and each man drank as much as he liked." Only when Alan explained to his superior "that I could not play hard tennis if I had done some hard drinking the evening before" was he excused from the club's transactions.[12]

The tippling district commission was happy to delegate many of his downriver duties to Alan. One of these involved making regular visits to the irascible Chief Nana Olomu. Chief Nana, as he was known, had been recognized as the local ruler of Koko Town by the British in 1885 but had abused his status to terrorize surrounding villages, block trade, and build himself an armed fortress with machine guns and cannon emplacements. The British stormed the fortress in 1894, freeing five thousand slaves, and deported Chief Nana to a comfortable exile in the Gold Coast. In 1906, the contrite chief was allowed to return, although he left behind six of the sixteen children he had fathered in the Gold Coast, wanting them to be raised as Englishmen.

Back in Koko Town, the irrepressible chief, who was adept with hammer and saw, built a new trading village extravagantly named America. There he received visitors in presidential fashion. For Alan, Chief Nana was an example of the "old and illiterate" chiefs who, despite their faults, "knew and understood their people, especially the country people who formed the majority of the population, the peasants who worked the land." Compared to post-colonial tyrants, these authentic chiefs "were very wise, with the wisdom of experience, the knowledge of traditional law and custom, and the tolerance of opposition."[13] A long-time British friend of Chief Nana, who had advised him to surrender back in 1894, lobbied Alan to restore his full trading rights in recognition of his "laudable conduct as a loyal subject since his release" and "the example he has set of industrial and orderly progress."[14]

Alan found that Chief Nana "was so pressing in his hospitality that I could not avoid drinking the warm, sweet champagne which he produced when I visited." The chief certainly "bore no ill-will towards the British who had defeated and exiled him."[15] As two local historians argued, Chief Nana's concerns had always been economic, not political—attempts to backcast him as a proto-nationalist engaged in "resistance" to colonialism are absurd—and he was happy to make new allies with whichever colonial official showed up on the Koko Town customs dock.[16] Nana had accepted "wives" from all the clans he traded with and solved one dispute by offering "two canoes filled with goods and a seemly slave girl."[17] In times past, it would have been normal for Nana to supply Alan with his own "girl" as part of a similar arrangement. The girl would have appeared at Alan's bungalow after hours and be gone by sunrise. But by now, at least, the British Empire frowned upon such assignations. Alan thus conducted his oversight of Nana at a moment when warm champagne was probably all that was offered, and in any case all that would have been accepted by the redoubtable Alan.

In this sense, Alan's brief four months in "the bush" was less like the sexually charged and absinthe-soaked life of the French *douane* in *Hell's Playground* and more like the maidenly and moderate life of district officer "Mr. Commissioner Sanders" of Nigeria brought to life in the wildly popular *Sanders of the River* novels of journalist Edgar Wallace that first appeared in 1911. In the novels, Commissioner Sanders always rebuffs sexual advances from native women. When his resolve weakens, his faithful Hausa manservant Abidoo appears in timely fashion to rescue his master from peril, including in one episode where Commissioner Sanders is at grave risk from two women performing "the dance of the three lovers."

In the view of the old coasters, sexually promiscuous and culturally informed lives were a more genuine motivation for colonial service. The moralizing and improving new generation of Commissioner Sanders was seen as a bunch of prudes who would undermine the empire. When another junior officer in Nigeria was recalled to Lagos, he complained bitterly: "[F]or my sins I have been posted to the Secretariat, to half-sexed work for which I have no training and no inclination."[18] Alan had some sympathy for this "anti-Secretariat complex which one finds in stations away from headquarters." The bodily sins of the old coasters might be easy to reproach, he noted, but the luxurious life at headquarters was no less a problem: "The fleshpots of headquarters spoil him for future life in the districts."[19]

In the course of his long colonial career in Africa and the Caribbean, Alan would be regaled with a fair share of flopping breasts and bare buttocks on public occasions—especially at the frequent *durbars* that had become a pageantry of native life throughout the empire. On one occasion years later, when his boat approached a river village, the women appeared "with the breasts discreetly covered" only to discover that it was "only the governor" rather than a Christian priest, at which point they "removed the hastily donned upper garments."[20] With his own staff, he would issue several rebukes for immoral relations. But he never stinted to note that improving morality was a universal challenge since reality at home was hardly a model of probity: "Some Negro dances may be indecent, but so is some of the stage and ball-room dancing of the whites," he would write. Bawdy conversations among African men were "no more pornographic" than those of Europeans, and "there is probably not as much indecency and sexual immorality in a tropical Negro town as there is in many European and American cities."[21]

Katie had been in New York City for four years when Alan's first tour of duty ended in early 1914. Despite the long separation, their bond had strengthened. One happy consequence of the immoral relations memos was that the Colonial Office began to increase salaries, leave times, and travel allowances so that junior officers could marry their intendeds. Against that background, Alan and Katie decided to fix their date.

Alan had bought a house for his mother near sister Essie's convent school at St. Leonard's-on-Sea in the south of England in 1910. When he arrived for his first leave in 1914, before the war, his mother was not well. Katie arrived from New York City in March. His mother died in April. A month later, with Alan's leave rapidly disappearing, he and Katie were wed. Photos from their wedding day show them in the peak of youthful optimism, hale and hearty (see figure 4.1). Less than five weeks later, Alan shipped out for Nigeria and his wartime duty. On the inside of his war diary, he asked "anyone finding this book" to post it to "Mrs. Alan Burns." Fortunately, this was not necessary. When Alan returned from his wartime combat for his second leave in

Figure 4.1   Wedding Day, St. Leonard's-on-Sea, 1914. *Source*: Private Collection of Alan Dixon.

England in 1915, he had a keener sense of the fragility of life. The couple returned to Nigeria together.

Even with official encouragement to get married, colonial officials who brought their spouses to the colonies were still viewed as a nuisance. Small salaries and a lack of accommodations were vexing. The old coasters, meanwhile, believed that wives in the colonies "interfered with their husbands' work, and prevented them from travelling on duty," Alan recalled.[22] The husband might not travel when his wife was ill or unhappy, as was frequently the case. It was not surprising, Alan would write, that "the presence of the increasing number of white women who now accompany their husbands to tropical colonies, very desirable as it may be from one point of view, should tend to create a barrier to friendly social intercourse between the races which did not previously exist."[23]

Alan had by now developed a view that on balance it was better for colonial officials to have their spouses with them despite the challenges. "Too often the European woman has to decide whether to be separated from her husband," serving in the colonies. "The separation is unnatural and the cause of much suffering and unhappiness and it adds to the financial difficulties of men who are never overpaid." Without a spouse, colonial officials took to drink or mistresses or went mad. "The officer who has his wife with him (unless she is entirely unsuitable as a wife) lives a better and happier life, and eats better food, than he can possibly do as a grass-widower. I attribute my own good health, after so many years' service in West Africa, to the fact that my wife was with me nearly every tour."[24]

Katie brought with her all the joys and comforts of a stable marriage and a settled home life. As someone raised in the colonies like Alan, she also relished the challenges of native life. She was wont to strike up friendships with Nigerians and to plunge into the streets unaccompanied. She was independent and equal in their marriage, and no less enthusiastic about the local community. Lugard, among other giants of colonial affairs, found her immensely congenial—perhaps more so than her taciturn husband—closing one letter to Alan with the words: "Please give my love (no less!) to my dear Mrs. Burns."[25]

In order to bring Katie to Nigeria, Alan had to obtain special permission since there was a shortage of married quarters. A senior officer was sent to a bachelor's accommodation, stirring resentment. "Throughout the tour we lived in constant fear that, owing to the shortage of quarters for married men, the wife of so junior an officer would have to be sent back to England." The arrival of a "Missis" brought sulks also from the house staff. In homes where there was no wife, Alan wrote, houseboys neglected "their work as soon as he" left "for the office" while the cook served "up meals which no wife would tolerate." When Katie arrived, Alan's head boy quit in a huff because of her "insistence on cleanliness" and "interference with their accustomed slack routine." The servant soon returned, though, explaining: "My friends tell me all Missis be the same trouble."[26]

Attractive women like Katie were a common temptation for men in the colonial service when their husbands had gone to bush. Taking one's wife on tour was usually impractical, Alan noted, but it was "equally unsafe to leave her in a lonely station while one traveled." As a result, "men who had to travel frequently through their districts would hesitate to leave their wives alone in isolated stations."[27] In Kenya, one memoir noted, "the husband might go off on safari and the temptation was stark." The problem of daytime romances got to such a pitch that a familiar joke went: "Are you married or do you live in Kenya?"[28]

Even in the relative safety of Lagos, Katie was the recipient of admiring overtures from lonely officers. In 1916, a minor British judge who was her distant relation sent her a rapturous note.[29] "I wish to come and pay my respects to you, and assure you how pleased I am to discover a new cousin in so charming a lady," he wrote. "Now that we have found each other I hope that you will look upon me as the cousin that I am and that you will command my services at any time as one of the men of your family and our family. I want to know my newly-found cousin better." Katie was too much in love with Alan to succumb to daytime romances in Lagos. The fact that she kept the letter shows the mirth with which it must have been shared by the couple.

Once Katie arrived, Alan spent more of his social time at the gatherings of "small chop" (hors d'oeuvres) parties at fellow officers' houses. The gatherings were good to "break down cliques," which were "so harmful in stations," Alan wrote. One senior official with whom Alan had frequent, if civil and constructive, disagreements, would make a point of phoning Katie anytime there was a quarrel to invite them to dinner: "My wife could always tell by the receipt of this invitation that there had been a row in the office." Yet the mixing could be dangerous if the feuding carried on: "in a small community, where one meets socially in the evening the same people one works with during the day, this is disastrous."[30]

Black Nigerians, including the government advisor Kitoyi Ajasa and the legislator Henry Carr, would often join Alan's parties, where they were "always welcome." His friendship with the erudite Carr would blossom to the point that they began to plan the writing of a book together on race relations in the colonies. "I had happily reached such a degree of mutual understanding with some of my African friends that we could discuss frankly the difficult and delicate questions of race and colour."[31]

Another favorite past-time for Alan was playing "auction bridge" at the colonial Lagos Club (known as the "gin tank" locally). He played in the evenings after tennis with increased determination, keeping track of his earnings. On a whim during one home leave, he suggested to the *Daily Telegraph* "with some effrontery" that he would make an excellent bridge correspondent. They accepted, and between 1922 and 1924, he wrote a weekly column for the newspaper under the penname "A.C.B." The bridge articles earned him a tidy sum, especially when they were published in book form as *Auction Bridge for Beginners* in 1924.[32] All told, Alan earned 200 pounds, or $15,000 in today's money, writing on bridge.

Despite the book, Alan never really liked the game, especially when people took it too seriously. "I am thought always to be keen on the game, and to be a good player, both of which assumptions are incorrect." One woman made several disastrous plays before she "sweetly informed me that she had learned all her bridge from my book." His favorite letter came from a facetious friend: "Since I've read your book, I've lost eleven pounds at bridge, but my wife, who read it less diligently, has lost only two pounds. Hanson, who has never seen the book, is three pounds up."[33]

Katie's enthusiasm for colonial life had come into play to support an earlier publishing foray by Alan. As a staff member attached to the colony's head office or secretariat, Alan found, as in the courts of St. Kitts, that there was a lack of basic information. "I soon realized the need for some handy volume which, if it could not itself contain all the necessary information about Nigeria, could at least indicate where that information was to be found." His superiors disagreed, so Alan and Katie decided to write and publish a book on their own, hoping to build a nest-egg. Using the equivalent of $3,000 in today's money, including the equivalent of $800 for a typewriter, the couple labored by evening on a handbook of Nigeria, which appeared in 1917. It covered everything from geography and demography to business and statistics, with an extensive section on government, laws, and personnel.[34]

Books in the tropics rapidly succumbed to mold and insects, but Alan and Katie could not afford the special paper that guarded against this. One cruel reviewer of the first edition noted: "The chief merit of this little work is that it is *not* bound in a solution that renders it impervious to the ravages of insects." Mostly, however, the *Handbook* was welcomed. The director of a prominent West Africa trading firm commended Alan even though "I feel certain that there will not be very much profit in it and feel somehow that you would not expect it."[35] As it turned out, the *Nigeria Handbook* was a roaring success. The first edition broke even, and the next three editions earned the couple the equivalent of $48,000 in today's money. So successful was the *Handbook* that the colonial government bought the rights to it in 1924 at Lugard's insistence for the equivalent today of $114,000 — "as it should have done from the first," Alan noted.[36] With the proceeds, Alan and Katie could start a family.

Seven more editions of the *Handbook* would be issued, the last in 1953. Alan's authorial imprint would remain. His growing interest in the flora and fauna of West Africa, for example, took up more space in each edition. A young Nigerian reviewer of the eleventh and final edition of 1953 complained that plants and animals took up ninety-eight pages compared to just six pages for the health system. A more revealing aspect of the *Handbook* was its objective tone. Alan was never one for blustery propaganda, believing that colonial rule could speak for itself. By the 1950s, as the colony prepared for independence, this neutral tone was seen by the Nigerian reviewer as a lost opportunity. The *Handbook*, he wrote, should showcase more "progressive Nigerians" trying to follow the modernizing trajectory compared to the growing clamor of nativist appeals that would send the country backward: "It must be borne in mind that a reference book of this nature . . . has other values than the purely factual . . . After all, there are attractive people in Nigeria who like to believe they are marching with the times and taking their place in the society of advancing nations," the reviewer wrote.[37] Thirteen years later, the reviewer would serve as spokesman for the breakaway republic of Biafra as Nigeria plunged into a catastrophic civil war.

When Katie and Alan returned to England in 1916, they agreed that she should remain there for the duration of the war. She took a job as a clerk in the Ministry of Shipping and travelled on weekends to St. Leonard's-on-Sea where sister Essie's convent school had been turned into a hospital. In 1919, Katie returned to Nigeria a second time, a passage considerably safer than during the war and now also paid for by the Colonial Office. With the war over and the proceeds from the *Handbook* giving them some security, the couple felt confident enough to start a family. Katie was pregnant in early 1920 and returned to England. Alan had told Essie on a lark that if it was a girl, he would name her Benedicta after the heroine in Essie's first novel, *The Grand Duchess Benedicta*. In September, Benedicta Burns was born.

If there was any question more vexed than spouses in the colonies, it was children. West Africa was considered the least hospitable place for colonial children because of the climate. "In practically all colonies except those in West Africa, children thrive up to 6 or 8 years of age," a colonial manual advised.[38] Alan concurred, writing that given all the health risks from malaria, prickly heat, insects, and unsafe food, "governments should do nothing to encourage parents to bring their children to West Africa."[39] The result was that colonial civil servants in Nigeria had to face what one book called "that cruel separation" from their children as well as "the awful choice" of whether the wife should remain in Britain with the children or put them into a nursery in order to be with her husband.[40] Many colonial officers abandoned their careers when children arrived.

Alan returned to England in 1922 to see the daughter he barely knew. Katie then faced the "awful choice" and opted to be with Alan. They deposited "Dickie," as Benedicta was known, in a nursery and returned together to Lagos. The reunion was short-lived. By early 1923, Katie was pregnant again and returned to England to prepare for their second child. With prospects of another long separation from Katie and from his two children, Alan began to inquire about a transfer back to the Caribbean. "The fact he could have his wife with him, and the child[ren], is no doubt an important factor in his mind," Nigeria's chief secretary, Alan's direct boss, wrote to the Colonial Office in support. "His ambitions are set in that direction and if they were gratified I have no doubt that the selection would be justified." The current governor, one of Katie's many admirers, also wrote in support: "Mrs. Burns would greatly assist her husband" in the many roles expected of the spouse of a top official in the Caribbean, he testified.[41]

The Bahamas was at the time looking for a second-in-command, the colonial secretary. It was difficult to fill the post, because the Bahamas was expensive and the salary miniscule. The attorney-general lived in a second-rate hotel, while the top judge lived in a former mortuary for infectious disease victims. Three candidates turned the job down before it was offered to Alan.

Lugard, then serving on the League of Nations Mandates Commission but still making mischief in Lagos, wrote to Alan that his promotion had been received with "very mixed feelings" at Government House. Yet "more proper and more unselfish considerations presently prevailed" because it was so obviously good for Alan's career: "It puts your foot definitely upon the ladder of further promotion in the Colonial Service," he promised, "and, when I am retired and forgotten, I shall watch your career with sympathy and interest."[42]

With the success of the *Nigeria Handbook*, Alan had begun work on a history of Nigeria. He offered to hand the research to Lugard, who in 1922 had published *The Dual Mandate in British Tropical Africa* that became a bible for colonial administrators. Lugard was being asked to fill in as Governor of Ceylon and told Alan he would not have time for the manuscript. Like Alan, he was being torn from his first love, and his sentiments spoke for them both: "There are times, and many of them, when the prospect of having to abandon all my work in Africa goes near to break my heart."

The commiserations were shared by Alan's house staff. One of his most loyal and long-serving houseboys, Joseph Agbake, begged to be allowed to follow him to the Bahamas. Alan refused, explaining, "I did not think he would be happy so far from his family and friends, and that I could not afford to pay for his passage from Nigeria to the Bahamas and back."[43] So in September 1923, Alan bid farewell to Nigeria, returning to England to be with Katie in her pregnancy. Their second daughter, Barbara, was born in

November, and Alan boarded a ship for the Bahamas in early 1924. Katie would follow with the girls months later.

Alan had barely opened the shutters on his new digs in the Bahamas when a knock at the door announced Joseph Agbake's arrival. Determined to remain in Alan's service, he had signed on as a steward on a cargo steamer and worked his way across the Atlantic, landing in New York in the dead of winter. He then found work on a southbound steamer calling at the Bahamas, where he jumped ship and tracked down his old boss. Alan was grateful to have Joseph back, a constant reminder of the Nigeria he had left behind.

It is hard to imagine a more eventful eleven years since Alan sat with the governor of Dominica watching an azure sunset over the Caribbean and decided that his future lay in Africa. He had fought in World War I, led a military assault on Egba rebels, married his intended, published two books, become father to two children, and earned his way into the good graces of some of the empire's most storied leaders. Now he was returning to the comparative ease of a small Caribbean Island chain, with his career on the upswing and his family life settled. The island paradise would prove more challenging than anything he had seen.

NOTES

1. CCC, p. 35.
2. Ibid., p. 42.
3. CP, pp. 117–18.
4. CBAA, p. 131.
5. CCC, p. 42.
6. Ida Vera Simonton, *Hell's Playground* (1912).
7. Jeremy Rich, "Ida Vera Simonton's Imperial Masquerades: Intersections of Gender, Race and African Expertise in Progressive-Era America," *Gender & History* (2010), p. 326.
8. Following citations from Simonton, op. cit., pp. 31, 187, 331, 350.
9. Louis Charbonneau, *Mambu et Son Amour* (1925).
10. CP, pp. 117–18.
11. Ronald Hyam, "Concubinage and the Colonial Service: The Crewe Circular (1909)," *Journal of Imperial and Commonwealth History* (1986), p. 182; also see Ronald Hyam, *Empire and Sexuality: The British Experience* (1990).
12. CCC, p. 37.
13. CBAA, pp. 126–27.
14. George Neville, "Nanna Oloma of Benin," *African Affairs* (1915), p. 167.
15. CCC, p. 37, 38.

16. Kemi Rotimi and Olukoya Ogen, "Jaja and Nana in the Niger Delta Region of Nigeria: Proto-Nationalists or Emergent Capitalists?" *Journal of Pan African Studies* (2008).

17. Obaro Ikime, *Merchant Prince of the Niger Delta: The Rise & Fall of Nana Olomu, Last Governor of the Benin River* (1968), p. 46.

18. Stanhope White, *Dan Bana: The Memoirs of a Nigerian Official* (1966), p. xv.

19. CCC, pp. 49–50.

20. Ibid., p. 136.

21. CP, p. 126.

22. CCC, p. 41.

23. CP, p. 28.

24. CCC, pp. 27, 42–43.

25. "ACB to Frederick Lugard," personal letter, November 3, 1924, private collection.

26. CCC, pp. 41–43.

27. CCC, p. 41; CBAA, p. 128.

28. Charles Allen and Helen Fry, *Tales from the Dark Continent* (1979), p. 119.

29. "Hal Berkeley to Katherine Burns," personal letter, June 19, 1916, private collection.

30. CCC, pp. 59, 52, 42.

31. CP, p. 12.

32. A. C. Burns, *Auction Bridge for Beginners* (1924).

33. CCC, pp. 69–71.

34. A. C. Burns, *The Nigeria Handbook: Containing Statistical and General Information Respecting the Colony and Protectorate* (1917).

35. "James Pickering Jones (Lagos Stores) to ACB," personal letter, November 22, 1917, private collection.

36. CCC, p. 41.

37. Cyprian Ekwensi, "Review of 'The Nigeria Handbook,' 11th Edition," *African Affairs* (1954), p. 259.

38. Charles Jeffries, *The Colonial Empire and Its Civil Service* (1938), p. 125.

39. CCC, p. 43.

40. Allen and Fry, op. cit., pp. 110, 123.

41. CO 23/293/40, "Colonial secretary (Bahamas) vacancy: Notes and candidates," October–November 1923.

42. "Frederick Lugard to ACB," personal letter, February 26, 1924, private collection.

43. CP, p. 144.

Chapter 5

The Bootleggers' Ball

In July 1924, Bahamian naval police spotted a small cargo ship, the *Florence*, anchored at Gun Cay, a sandy sliver about fifty miles from Miami. The ship's captain claimed he had run out of oil. When police boarded, they found a hold full of Cuban whisky that had not been declared. Further inquiries revealed that the owner of the Bahamas-registered *Florence* was an American, in contravention of local laws. Barely two months into his new job, Alan, as acting governor, found himself in a political and diplomatic squall.

The United States had enacted Prohibition in 1920. A roaring trade in smuggled liquor had promptly brought untold riches to British colonies in the Caribbean. Rum-running, or bootlegging, involved importing liquor legally into a British colony like the Bahamas and then re-exporting it to "the high seas." The rum-runners would sell their wares at floating markets just outside of U.S. territorial waters to smugglers who did the dangerous work of landing it. There was nothing illegal about the trade on the British side as long as the merchants paid local import duties and did not violate shipping laws. "The American coastguard officials were almost helpless to stop smuggling from such a convenient base as the Bahamas," Alan recalled, "especially as American public opinion was almost entirely on the side of the bootleggers and many of the officials themselves were in the racket."[1]

In times past, the *Florence* might have been handed back to the bootlegging crew with a small fine. Coming at a time of rising American power, however, there was a new sensitivity to views in the United States.[2] The American frustration with Bahamian bootleggers was not just about Prohibition. Rather, it reflected a new Wilsonian sense of ascendancy over European colonies. Winston Churchill, in his new role overseeing British government finances, advised West Indies governors to make a show of prosecuting such instances. "The case appears to be precisely [like] one of those referred to in

Mr. Churchill's confidential despatch," Alan wrote to the Colonial Office.[3] He thus imposed a whopping penalty equivalent to over $100,000 in today's money in fines, duties, and expenses on the boat's owner. London cited Alan's decisive act as evidence of its sincerity toward the United States. "Mr. Burns seems to be doing a very good best in difficult circumstances," the British foreign secretary noted.[4]

There was another force to consider: the growing sense of self-determination among colonial peoples. In the local view, people like Alan were brought in and paid by the local legislature to do the will of the Bahamian people, not to play diplomatic games for London. The bootlegging business was a boon for the Bahamas, and Alan had no right to constrain it. The *Florence* case "caused considerable local interest, and the action of the executive" was "freely criticized from all sides," Alan wrote to his superiors.[5] "Sympathy for the master and owner of the vessel has been openly expressed not only by the general public but even by some of the Customs officials."

Among the most vocal critics was Etienne Dupuch, editor of the *Nassau Tribune* newspaper. Dupuch's great-grandfather had fled to the Bahamas from post-revolutionary France in 1840, where he became a member of the House of Assembly following the same Catholic emancipation act that had allowed Alan's forebears to take up government positions in St. Kitts. Dupuch's father launched the *Nassau Tribune* in 1903, promising to agitate "for the establishment of popular privilege, for the uplifting the ennobling of our fellow creatures, for the improvement and education of the people."[6] Having married a black school teacher, his populist tone was soon closely associated with the colored and black populations. "It is a well-run journal, much more alive and interesting to read than its staid and highly respectable rival [*The Nassau Guardian*]," Alan wrote of the *Tribune*.[7]

When the penalty on the *Florence* became known, Dupuch was quick to publish a critical news story. Lubricant oil for ships was in short supply, consistent with the captain's excuse, it noted, while police had not actually observed liquor being sold over the side.[8] His stinging criticisms of Alan's handling of the *Florence* were repeated in the colonial legislature, among police and customs officials, and even in cabinet. The issue flared for several weeks as Alan stood his ground. Eventually, the boat's "Bahamian" owner quietly agreed to pay the fine. "A trial of the case might have revealed the fact that the vessel is the property of an American citizen," Alan noted.[9]

Alan was summoned back to London for a meeting with the Foreign Office to discuss the *Florence* case. He agreed that the Bahamas would purchase a special patrol boat to watch its waters more closely. When the colony's legislature, the House of Assembly, heard of the pledge, it flew into a rage and refused to allocate funds. If the Machiavellis in the Foreign Office wanted a patrol boat to smooth relations with the United States, a Colonial Office staffer wrote defending the Bahamian House's stance, then "the moral obligation of providing it" rested "with H.M.G."[10] Alan advised against this, predicting that the use of London money to impose the boat on the Bahamas would be unpopular. A Foreign Office official sniffed, "The Bahamas owe their independence to the protection afforded by this country and [the foreign secretary] . . . is not aware that this country derives in present circumstances any advantage from the connection."[11] The secretary for the colonies shot back his "emphatic dissent from the doctrine . . . that any portion of H.M.'s dominions possessing the right of representative government should be constrained to subordinate its own interests to those of the Mother country in return for the protection afforded by H.M. Navy." Such a doctrine, he wrote, would be "wholly subversive of existing practice" and likely to foment a revolt, as had happened in 1776: "The consequences of applying a policy of coercion to colonies possessing a constitutional status with that now enjoyed by the Bahamas are a matter of history."[12]

Instead, the Colonial Office urged Alan and his staff to persuade the House of Assembly that limiting the bootlegging trade would be prudent. A continuation of bootlegging, a senior official wrote, would "force the annexation cry to the front in the U.S.A." Bahamians might relish the battle, but "whatever the determination of this country not to cede British territory, there would be no support whatsoever for a vicious quarrel with the U.S.A. in defense of the right of the Bahamas to smuggle liquor." British opinion would demand that the colony's legislature be suspended in favor of direct rule. "If they want to be defended, they must take care that their actions are defensible."[13]

The control of rum-running would dominate Alan's four years in the Bahamas. The Foreign Office would delete all mentions of the trade in Alan's annual reports—"committing *suppressio veri* [falsehood by the omission of truth] at the instance of the F.O. Machiavelli," as a Colonial Office staffer explained.[14] Alan secretly fed news copy to the *Tribune* in which "a government official" denied the slanders on the colony showing up in the Miami and New York press.[15] "This government is doing everything in its power to assist the United States authorities in putting a stop to the illicit liquor traffic. In return it is receiving nothing but discourtesy," he complained on one occasion. With only fifty-four thousand souls, the Bahamas was tiny, no more than a small town in Nigeria. But it was a political pressure cooker. Alan would need all his wits to prevail here.

Like a whirligig set spinning on the floor, Alan began his posting in the Bahamas by visiting every one of the colony's populated islands, most of which had never seen an elected representative, much less a senior colonial official. A "flying boat" took him to harbors, and whenever possible, he hired a Ford Model T car to pound over the dirt roads. The peregrinations won applause, including from Etienne Dupuch. "We wish some of the members of the House of Assembly would take the same interest in the islands—even their own island—as Mr. Burns is manifesting,"[16] he wrote. "Courteous and pleasant on all occasions, a man of commanding figure, with a face that wins immediate confidence, and unusual vigor, he has won general popularity, eclipsing that of many of the older officials."[17]

The support of local elites was essential because of the arcane structure of government in the Bahamas. Unlike other colonies, there was no "government party" in the House of Assembly, which controlled the purse strings, made appointments to government agencies, and could block government bills. The House "was always suspicious" of the governor and "determined to assert its independence," Alan noted.[18] If a senior civil servant were reprimanded, "that officer immediately complained to a local 'M.P.' who then proceeded to make himself highly disagreeable." The "ideas of discipline of a properly-run Colonial Service, such as Nigeria,"[19] Alan lamented, were not to be found in this boisterous colony. "I had to adjust my mind to an entirely different form of colonial administration from anything I had known before."[20]

Normally, Alan would have been given a symbolic seat in the rubber-stamp upper house. But "it seemed to me that I could be of more use in the House of Assembly, which held the real power, and that I should find membership of that House more interesting and amusing."[21] As a West Indies native, Alan saw himself as no less entitled to represent locals than the other assemblymen. "You know, the Colonial Secretary is not an Englishman, but a West Indian," it was whispered among the English expatriates.[22] Despite their many battles to come, Dupuch would recall Alan as "a brilliant man, who had grown up [in] the West Indies and understood the Bahamian politician better than the average Englishman."[23]

To that end, a sympathetic member agreed to resign his seat before the 1925 election and "was good enough to speak flatteringly of me and to assure the electors that I would represent them efficiently."[24] Dupuch's *Tribune* offered its "unconditional support" for Alan's candidacy: "Every inch of the road he has travelled he has distinguished himself as a man of action and ability and enjoys the confidence of all who have come in contact with him," the paper enthused.[25]

The Bahamas retained its ancient tradition of open balloting, where electors stood around a chalkboard and called out their votes. The system was believed to screen out disreputable candidates since elites could sanction anyone who voted for a demagogue. As a result, elections were a time for "money, unlimited rum, and a great deal of fun," Alan recalled, especially because the franchise was unusually broad for the time, encompassing fifteen thousand male voters, about two-thirds of adult males. When Alan was asked for bribes, "I replied that I did not propose to pay anything and that I thought my constituents would be lucky to have such a good representative." The electors "were so taken aback that they agreed with me."[26] Alan became the elected member for New Providence Western District. In the same election, Dupuch was returned in a constituency named Crooked Island.

Alan's election to the House marked the beginning of three years in which "he so completely dominated the official and political life of the Bahamas that his period here is still spoken of as 'the Burns regime,'" Dupuch would recall.[27] "He has been in close touch with the feeling of the House and his opinion therefore carries much weight," the first governor he served noted.[28] So impressed were his fellow House members that they voted to increase his salary as colonial secretary by a third in 1926 and to allow him to qualify for a Bahamas pension after only three years (rather than the normal ten). The law was jokingly referred to as "the Alan Burns Act." "I do not always agree with the Colonial Secretary but I do think he is giving the colony good and efficient service," the bill's sponsoring member declared. The bill was seconded by a Mr. Toote.

The "Alan Burns Act" set off a Trollopian play of English manners. The Colonial Office strongly disliked it because of the populist undertones. Alan too argued that a policy of setting a chief officer's salary based on their popularity was "thoroughly bad" especially "in a small community . . . [where] an unscrupulous officer could easily intrigue with members of the legislature with a view to having his salary raised."[29] Dupuch was the only member of the House to protest, marking the first crack in his love affair with the Burns regime. The workload at Alan's office had "increased least of any public department" he asserted, while "the movers expect something in return and the public might almost be justified in most unkind and severe suspicions." Dupuch added caustically that since Alan "carries with him the best recommendation for appointment to a governorship" elsewhere in the empire "we wonder if Mr. Burns will consider the love this colony bears him and say 'Oh no! I can't leave my dear little children in the Bahamas.' No. He will go, and this colony will be saddled with a pension for many, many years."[30]

In the end, Dupuch was over-ruled by his fellow members. Alan, meanwhile, "gratefully accepted the much needed money" against his better judgment. "Perhaps [Dupuch] and I were wrong in our views, and I was right to accept the larger salary," he wrote sheepishly.[31] With two young daughters at home, and his expenditures running about 40 percent ahead of his income in these years, he felt he had little choice. But over time, the windfall would grate at his conscience. "Although this was not due to any intrigue on my part, the public probably believed that it was." The bill was "a bad precedent," he admitted, one of the few ethical mistakes of his career.

Alan was the de facto governor of the Bahamas, because the two governors he served had little interest in the colony and were usually either ill or on vacation. "It has been obvious for some time that the Colonial Secretary and not the Governor is 'the Boss,'" Dupuch wrote.[32] This caused the first tempest between the two men when Dupuch wrote a withering attack on the first doddering governor. "In the quiet and comfort of his office chair, he may be hatching schemes for the betterment of [government] institutions and the colony generally, and we look forward to the time when they will no longer remain concealed in his 'fertile' brain," the jesting editorial began. This would dispel the charge that the governor's chief concern was "an unhealthy interest in the winter visitors" which had arisen as a result of his being seen most often on "drives through the city to the golf links and bathing beaches." With his "enviable grasp of conditions, of the people in this colony and their aspirations" he would be recognized by future generations which would "realize his real worth as we do not know it yet." Meanwhile, the colony would "live in hope that some higher voice" would "summon him to service elsewhere or retirement."[33]

"The town blew up," Dupuch recalled. "Apparently a governor had never before been criticized in the press of the colony."[34] A clutch of clerics declared the editorial an "outrage upon good taste."[35] Dupuch shot back, lamenting that this rare show of Christian unity had arisen not to combat some moral wrong but in a "lame defense" of a governor. Alan was duty-bound to protest. He summoned Dupuch to complain of the "quite unwarranted and offensive attack."[36]

Dupuch defended himself: "This is a democratic age. . . . The governor of this colony is no more and no less than a public official. He is paid a salary from public funds, he has duties to perform like any other public official, and if those duties are neglected it then becomes the duty of every self-respecting newspaper . . . to voice its criticism with the hope to remedying matters."[37] Most of the House membership agreed, and eventually an esteemed editor of the pro-establishment *Nassau Guardian* jumped ship and wrote in his defense. Alan let it pass. He was, in the end, on the same side as Dupuch and was frustrated working under governors whose main interests seemed to be golf and swimming.

By 1927, Dupuch's sights were aimed squarely on Alan. "The big guns now keep a black book and anyone who comes under their disapproval is listed there," he gossiped.[38] He called Alan "the Ghost of George Washington,"[39] and an editorial in the *Tribune* warned that "if [Bahamians] desire a one-man government then they had better abolish the legislature."[40] When the second governor was appointed, Dupuch wrote that "One of [his] first talks will be to impress upon Mr. Burns that it is the governor's and not the colonial secretary's prerogative to head and lead the government of this colony, and it is just possible that the Bahamas government may continue to function even should [Burns] be removed to another and more exalted sphere."[41] The *Tribune* alleged that Alan had used the inter-regnum to bring "his scheming of the last few years to a grand climax" because of bills he pushed through the House to limit immigration and to set up a civil service commission. The two bills prompted Dupuch's most colorful indictment:

> The entire administration of Mr. Burns has been notable for its recklessness born only of egotistic youth and inexperience, an entire disregard for authority, procedure, tradition, good taste, and law itself. We know of no official that has won the measure of general confidence and popularity as has been enjoyed by Mr. Burns. We know no man who so quickly and so completely reversed the position through egotism and selfishness by making even the most trivial disagreement with his opinion a personal issue, vindictiveness, and recklessness.[42]

Dupuch did not spare the docile members of the House: "most of whom are quite satisfied to sit with smugly folded hands while [Burns] swings the pendulum the way he will."[43] House members, in his view, had "consistently bent the knee in adoration of the false god of imported officialdom."[44] Alan did not help his cause by questioning the grey matter of local elites. He derided the "less intelligent members of the House" for their opposition to a government development scheme, and then dug himself deeper with an "apology" to one member: "If I did mean anyone in this House, I certainly did not have reference to the honourable member." As Dupuch wrote: "The genuine views of the Leader of the Government often escape unintentionally in this way and create wounds that no sugar coated balm can heal. It would not be surprising if some people inferred that Mr. Burns regards some of the members of the House as being too ignorant to occupy the positions which they have the honour to fill."[45]

When Katie arrived in the Bahamas in 1924, she caused a stir among the conservative European community with her full flapper regalia, including revealing hemline and exposed shoulders.[46] It was in the Roaring 1920s that the Bahamas had become a libertine dream. The bootlegging millionaires spent liberally at the Bucket of Blood nightclub, while punters could play roulette and poker at the Bahamian Club. A letter in the *Tribune* described the dissipation at the Lucerne Hotel in Nassau: "Dancing to the accompaniment of a full 'jazz' orchestra, loud hand clapping, some singing, and occasional shouting and screaming."[47]After one notorious party, Dupuch wrote of "a rowdy, noisy, and disgraceful orgy" where "the latest dance abomination, 'the Charleston' was danced by barely half clad women in a vulgar and sometimes indecent manner."[48] The Bootlegger's Ball, held at the hotel in late July, attracted tourists from the United States and Canada, carrying on for twenty-four hours, until the Irish "security guard" chased the crowds away with the guns he kept in his hip pockets.[49] "All the energies of legislature and people alike were bent on the important business of relieving the tourist of his money, and I am bound to say that the tourist cooperated fully in this matter," Alan recalled:

> The tourists reveled in the winter sunshine, the perfect sea-bathing, the fishing, and, especially during the reign of prohibition, in the unlimited amount of liquor they could obtain. . . . Coloured orchestras played banjos and ukuleles in the moonlight, and sang to entranced audiences songs full of local allusions. There was dancing every night in the hotels, and at all times there were highballs and cocktails, followed by more highballs. . . . It was a glorious playground.[50]

Alan's reports caught the attention of the British foreign secretary: "The situation revealed by Mr. Burns' despatches is really a rather disgraceful one," he wrote.[51] Americans were on the prowl for the relatively cheap property in the Bahamas.[52] Alan was frequently asked to meet with prospective buyers, where open bribes were on offer. "On one occasion, when I was listening patiently to two Americans who were seeking a concession for real estate development in New Providence, one of them suggested that I might accept some shares in the enterprise. Before I had time to reply, the other interrupted with the remark that 'you can't do that sort of thing in a British colony.' I have often wondered whether this was genuine or a preconcerted and subtle form of flattery."[53] One real estate transaction took Alan and Katie on a trip to Miami. When they returned, their seaplane struck debris in the harbor and sank from the stern.[54] Alert local fishermen came to the rescue.

One consequence of the roaring economic fortunes was that the colony's reserves of gold and silver used to back the local currency expanded at a rapid rate. One night in 1926, two local staff of the audit office blew their way into the vault holding the reserves and made off with the equivalent of about $1.2 million today. "When [the vault] was built no one dreamed that it could contain so much money or anyone would be so depraved to break into it," Alan wrote to the Colonial Office explaining the crime.[55] The part-time Commissioner of Currency had rarely inspected the reserves, complaining that it took time away from sailing. The disappearance of the gold and silver prompted *Nostromo*-like quests to outlying islands and wild tales of sightings of the missing specie, which was never recovered. Two local fishermen swung from the gallows for luring an American businessman to a remote island with promises of the treasure before chopping him up with an axe and stealing his money.

The reserves robbery brought into sharp relief the tensions between the penny-pinching local legislature and the Colonial Office, which had to replace the metals. The House refused to approve funds for a new vault or for imported guards. In response, the Colonial Office suggested keeping the new reserves with the local branch of the Royal Bank of Canada, the colony's government banker, since it was "open to some doubt whether the 'guard' (presumably a native policeman) could be depended upon to be proof against the temptation to connive in [another] contemplated robbery."[56] Alan suggested the new vault be built under the police station.[57]

In the end, Alan convinced the House to pony up for a second-hand vault purchased from the Royal Bank of Canada, which was encased in concrete at the old site. "The incident has done a certain amount of good by proving to the House of Assembly that it is a poor policy to have cheap officials," Alan sighed. Yet his ensuing attempts to reorganize the treasury and audit departments were met with foot-dragging by the incumbents and cavils from the ever-critical Dupuch, who called Alan a "monumental egotist" who was "an unfortunate victim of a misplaced confidence in his own abilities."[58] "When one sees the attempts being made to establish an autocratic government in this city at the present time," Dupuch opined, "one can readily realize how any decent-minded, manly citizen can—and should—become a Bolshevik and worse."[59]

The Bahamas was settled by the British in the 1600s, replacing the Spaniards who had arrived following Columbus. In 1834, when slavery was abolished, ten thousand black slaves in the Bahamas became free alongside six thousand whites and coloreds. The annual Emancipation Day parade was a celebration for blacks and whites alike, both of whom took pride in the elimination of slavery and in the universal brotherhood of man in the British Empire. A photo survives of Alan standing with one Emancipation Day band, reflecting his ease in the mixed-race communities of the Caribbean (see figure 5.1).

When Alan arrived, the population was growing mainly due to immigration from Haiti which had thrown off its colonial "yoke" a century earlier and promptly descended into chaos.[60] The "oppressed" Bahamas, by contrast, was free, orderly, humane, and prosperous. Dupuch reported that most of the journalists in Haiti were in jail. British colonialism attracted foreign investment and prosperity, while also laying the institutional foundations for the development of a distinctly Bahamian civic culture and national identity. Alan would note: "It is useful to compare conditions in present and former colonial territories with those in countries which have never 'suffered' from colonialism. In these latter countries capital has been shy of the risks involved under inefficient and unstable government."[61]

Figure 5.1 With Emancipation Day Band, Bahamas, ca. 1926. *Source*: Private Collection of Alan Dixon.

Such voluntary immigration from noncolonial to colonial states, or internally from less intensively to more intensively colonized areas, was for Alan always the prima facie evidence of the legitimacy of colonial rule. The "almost constant revolution" of Haiti, he would write, contrasted with the ordered liberty of the colonial Bahamas as well as other British possessions in the Caribbean.[62] Critics of colonialism, Alan would write, "fail to compare the conditions in these territories with the conditions existing in neighboring independent states."[63] At around this time, the League of Nations was conducting an inquiry into slave-holding by black elites in the "free" African state of Liberia and the atrocities they committed against native tribes refusing to submit to their rule.[64] Alan was fond of quoting a Liberian diplomat who spoke of the advantages of colonialism: "It is the difference between the home of a man who has had to accomplish everything by his own sweat and toil and that of a man who has enjoyed a large inheritance," the diplomat explained.[65]

Colonial rule was however paid the compliment of greater scrutiny and higher expectations by outsiders, especially the "anti-colonial" Americans. As Alan wrote to London:

If, as I believe, the good opinion of prominent Americans is of value to the Empire, it is most unfortunate that the Bahamas, which lie so close to the shores of the United States as to be practically the shop-window of the Empire, and which are visited by a larger number of leading Americans than any other colony, should be in such a condition as to create an unfavourable impression on those who are not able to correct that impression by a visit to other Colonies.[66]

The most immediate concern was public health, since, as one committee noted, Americans who were taken to local hospitals were "prone to regard the Colony as a sample of administration under the British flag."[67] Alan's efforts to boost spending were rejected by the stingy House of Assembly. At one point, Alan threatened to withdraw all British doctors and nurses if more spending was not forthcoming. An outbreak of typhoid fever in 1926 finally frightened the House into action. Alan's proposal to invest in closed sewers was passed without debate. The emergency also allowed Alan to get rid of an incompetent superintendent at the Bahamas General Hospital—not without Dupuch complaining loudly about his use of "principles of Red Russia" to attain the goal.[68] Before the outbreak, the plan had been thwarted by the House. "A certain section of the press took up [the superintendent's] defense and exhorted the inhabitants to sink their personal differences and unite in defense of the 'native' officials against a tyrannical Government," Alan informed London.[69] Dupuch called the plan "autocratic and high-handed": "The plain fact of the matter is that the Colonial Secretary doesn't believe there is a single competent local man in the colony and would dearly love to oust them all and thus help reduce the ranks of the unemployed in the home country regardless of what our own people suffer."[70] The typhoid outbreak silenced Dupuch, who voted for the change on the advice of his physician, Dr. Quackenbush.

Alan also won the House's approval for a public health survey of the colony. The effort was intended mainly as a public relations exercise. Yet the man sent to conduct the survey, William Beveridge, was no pushover. A crusading social reformer, his social insurance and universal healthcare schemes would shape the post–World War II British welfare state. After a four-week visit to the colony, he published a damning report in 1927 about substandard housing, overcrowding, lack of cleanliness, inadequate medical facilities, and mismanagement of disease.[71] Fearing a loss of tourism, the House voted more funds.[72] British colonialism proved effective in stirring the people into self-awareness and action.

Alan's favorite "colonial" achievement in these years was also his most prosaic: the creation of the first accurate map of the Bahamas. As in Nigeria, Alan found the absence of basic information on the colony an irritant and took actions to remedy the ignorance. The map produced by the surveyor's department included facts on every island in the Bahamas, as well as a useful guide to the colony's harbor lights, streets signals, street signs, and place names. One of the unexpected results was the discovery that the land first sighted by Columbus in 1492 was probably an island in the Bahamas. Alan introduced a bill into the House to have the island renamed San Salvador as the explorer had named it in his diaries.

A half century later, colonial map-making would be seen by anti-colonial critics as a wicked endeavor linked to colonial acquisition and conflict. The curious assumption is that the maps that would have emerged absent colonialism—presumably drawn up by some combination of ambitious indigenous chiefs and scheming Western freelancers—would have ushered in self-government, peace, and progress. In addition, it is remarkable how rarely critics of colonial cartography consider the extent to which the maps were welcomed by subject populations. "The lack of information about their own home by the best informed Bahamians has often made these people appear ludicrous in the eyes of foreigners," Dupuch wrote in the *Tribune*, enthusing about Alan's new map with uncharacteristic warmth. "We have no hesitation in saying that this is one of the most—if not the most—permanently useful and beneficial things [Burns] has accomplished since [his] arrival in the colony . . . and as everybody knows he has by no means been idle."[73]

On a scorching July day in 1928, a prisoner was being subdued for disorderly conduct at the Nassau prison. About ninety fellow inmates rushed to his defense. The ringleaders were arrested and put into an unsecured infirmary to await interrogation. The next morning, they broke out and emptied the cells. The warders fled, leaving the prison in the hands of the rebels. A fire truck was sent, but its hose produced only a fine spray, which the rioters used to cool themselves off before attacking the fire brigade, which scattered. When news of the riot reached Alan, serving as acting governor, he formed a contingent of police and proceeded to the prison. It was exactly ten years since he led a similar contingent to suppress the Egba rebels in Nigeria:

> We entered the main building of the prison; here the damage done by the prisoners was considerable, everything possible had been broken and the doors of the cells had been forced open. At this stage, a prisoner on one of the upper galleries of the building threw an axe at me, but another prisoner warned me in time to get out of the way. Further prisoners then surrendered and were removed, but a band of armed men retreated into a corner of the yard and defied us to come and take them, while some of them placed ladders against the walls of the prison and prepared to escape. The yard was, unfortunately, full of heaps of stones and broken bottles which were used by the prisoners as missiles; one struck me on the helmet and several of the police were injured.[74]

Alan's experiences going back to his childhood convinced him that early action against rioters saved lives.

I again called out a warning to the prisoners, who were now approaching closer and endeavouring to outflank the small party with me; every prisoner appeared to be armed with an axe or a machete. Finally, some of them, armed with axes rushed forward on our small party, and I instructed the sergeant of police to fire; he fired two shots and one man was killed instantly. I called out that one man had already been killed and that more would be shot if they did not surrender. Resistance immediately ceased and I ordered the prisoners to come forward one by one with their hands raised; they did this and they were all handcuffed.

Alan's first letter to the colonial secretary reporting the riot ran to eight pages. "I greatly deplore the death of the prisoner, for which I accept full responsibility," he ended. "I am confident that I did not give the order to fire a moment earlier than was necessary and that if I had delayed giving that order further bloodshed would have been inevitable and a very serious situation would have arisen." The colonial secretary wrote a personal note to Alan praising his "promptitude, courage, and leadership" and added: "You acted with vigour, resolution, and decision, refraining with calm deliberation from giving the order to fire until you found it absolutely necessary to do so."[75]

The use of force was always tricky, Alan would recall. Shoot too early, and you were blamed for unnecessary force. Shoot too late, and the suppression would require much greater loss of life. "Often, when a mob gets completely out of hand, and firing is deferred until too late, a great many people have to be shot before the situation can be controlled," he would write.[76] Elsewhere in the British Caribbean, it was "remarkable how often rioting occurred . . . and how seldom effective action was taken in time."

It is easy enough to exercise a balanced judgement when sitting in the safe seclusion of one's office, far from the maddened crowd and with plenty of time in which to think. It is a different matter to face a mob with only a handful of armed [police], some of whom have perhaps already been knocked out by stones, with the knowledge that the [police] party must be overwhelmed if the mob is allowed to get too close, and that, if the party were overwhelmed, further outrages would follow. So the man on the spot, generally a hot spot, with little time to think his problem out, but pretty sure that he will be blamed for whatever action he takes, and hating the thought of taking a human life . . . has to decide on the exact moment when he should shoot. He may be right or he may be wrong in his decision, but I for one would hesitate to condemn an error of judgement in such matters unless I had been there to see for myself at the critical moment and was therefore competent to criticise.

In the case of the Nassau prison riot, Dupuch and the *Tribune* heralded Alan's firm response, indeed wished it had been firmer: "Had severer measures been taken at the very outset, the riot would have been settled in a few minutes," Dupuch wrote, noting that "it is only in the Bahamas that such patience would have been displayed by officials in handling this situation." Dupuch complained that the Nassau prison was "a place of peaceful retirement and quiet reflection," which was why so many prisoners reoffended.[77] Both men understood that a liberal political order must rest upon a firm implementation of the law.

In later anti-colonial histories, the Nassau prison riot has been cited as an example of "resistance" to colonialism and the response as an example of "colonial violence." In the words of one historian, police actions in such cases were intended to "maintain the apparatus of imperial government" and to keep "the political economy it supported intact" even if "more abstract questions of law, procedure, and accountability constrained police activity."[78] One work on the Bahamas described the colonial police as "a paramilitary force" whose role was "maintaining the existing social and economic order."[79] Alan would have accepted these characterizations without sharing their disapprobation. Imperial government in the Bahamas and the political economy of law-based market capitalism that supported it was legitimate and beneficial. Allowing self-interested criminals to disrupt this order would have been unpopular and disastrous. The use of force by colonial police was "violent" only in the sense that all use of force is violent by definition. The popular and reasoned support for the police actions showed that, unlike later critics, the law-abiding people of the Bahamas understood the difference between the legitimate and illegitimate use of force.

A commission of inquiry into the Nassau prison riot held fifteen sessions in August and September. More than half of its twenty-seven witnesses were prisoners. One of them, a prisoner serving a life term who had tried to mediate the dispute with Alan, was given an early release. A fifty-page report was published in October and printed widely for distribution in the colony. All this for a single prisoner shot dead after attacking police: the high liberal standard of the British Empire that people like Dupuch expected. For Alan, this example of the rule of law and accountability was a key legacy of colonialism. "It is not in economic expansion, social improvements, or political progress, noteworthy as these may be, that the vindication of our stewardship entirely lies," he would write. "It lies rather in the achievement of persuading indigenous peoples to realise the meaning of justice between man and man, and the inculcation of the spirit of respect for the rule of law and an independent judiciary, where the lowest and the poorest stand equal with the highest and the richest. This is the real worthwhile legacy of the British Empire."[80]

When Alan reported the Nassau prison riot to the Colonial Office, his telegram ended: "This has nothing to do with constitutional troubles."[81] The cryptic assurance was a reference to his attempts to reform the creaky system of independent boards and part-time officials in the Bahamas that had made the prison vulnerable to the insurrection. This in turn resulted from the colony's ancient constitution that vested so much power in the querulous House of Assembly. As the secretary for the colonies commented: "We cannot reform the Bahamas prison until we have reformed the Bahamas constitution."[82]

At one level, the constitutional problem was a simple clash between the appointed colonial executive and the partly elected legislature. Alan believed that the "ignorant and suspicious" House and its appointed boards held too much power, while the imported officials and executive held too little. "The colony could not be run by local officials, who lack education and training" and yet the imported officials "are systematically abused in the [House] and made to feel unwelcome."[83]

The danger, as Dupuch warned his fellow populists, was that democracy from below would prompt executive rule from above, pointing to British Guiana (today's Guyana), where the governor had recently seized power from a thoroughly corrupt and incompetent legislature.[84] Bahamian legislators, Dupuch wrote, should not "butt their head against the steel-reinforced position of the British Government. . . . This colony has all to lose and nothing to gain by persisting in an antagonistic spirit."[85]

As he had done over hospital reform, Alan threatened to withdraw imported officials if the administrative system were not reformed to give more power to the executive. "If the people of this colony are to be permitted to continue misgoverning themselves under their ancient constitution, they should not have the assistance of officials selected by the Imperial Government who are powerless to effect any real check on existing abuses," he wrote. Alan reckoned that when faced with the choice, the people would prefer the imports: "The majority of the public would view with profound misgiving the prospect of our removal."[86]

The tensions reached a breaking point in 1928 when Alan forced the House to accept an amendment to a spending bill before sending it to the governor for his signature. Not wanting to appear bullied, the House passed a second law with the amendment included. The result was the passage of two nearly identical bills and twice as much spending as intended. When the governor indicated that he would sign both bills, the House speaker, a walking reference book on the colony's parliamentary tradition,[87] withheld one of them,

claiming precedent in a similar action in 1772. The governor promptly dis-
solved the House for its stupidity and left on summer vacation. Alan was left
to clean up the mess.

When the same speaker was chosen in the newly elected House of 1928,
Alan exercised the royal prerogative and refused to recognize him until he
apologized for the bills fiasco. It was a reminder to the House of "how far
it had overestimated its own powers," Dupuch commented.[88] Alan defended
the dignity of the crown while respecting the choice of the House. When the
humbled speaker took his chair, the *Tribune* reported, "no one was seen to go
up and congratulate him."[89] Those involved in the fiasco, it added, had "lost
the respect and confidence of this community by their ill-advised conduct."[90]

One result of the 1928 election was an increase in the number of nonwhite legislators from nine to eleven of the twenty-nine seats. Alan wanted
to accelerate this change by introducing secret voting. But in this, he faced
opposition both from London and from the Bahamian white middle classes
who wanted to keep open voting as a check against poor black populists.
While the "present system is theoretically indefensible," the Colonial
Office wrote, "to abolish it would result in return of the black or coloured
members for nearly every constituency in the islands. . . . The resulting fear
of the black and colored ascendancy could lead to an immediate demand
[by whites] for Crown Colony Government."[91] Preventing white flight was
critical to social justice and well-being for the black population. In this
instance, London may have showed more political savvy than the younger
Alan. The secret ballot eventually came in 1949, universal male suffrage
in 1959, and universal adult suffrage in 1962. By then, the black Populist
Party had become a font of good sense and wisdom. It won power in the
House in 1967 with promises of continuity. Independence came in 1973
and caused barely a blip in the country's fortunes. The Bahamas was able
to steadily develop its self-governing institutions without ethnic tensions
causing a crisis. Today, Bahamians are among the richest and freest people
in the Caribbean. Haiti continues in turmoil.

One of Alan's last acts in the Bahamas was a preview of his return to Africa.
In September 1928, just before leaving the Bahamas, he approved a visit to
the colony by the black nationalist Marcus Garvey. This was the first of many
times that Alan would confront the question of how to respond to radicals
intent on laying waste to colonialism.

Garvey was a native of Jamaica who called himself "Provisional President
of Africa." He appeared in black communities in Britain and the United States
as well as the Caribbean sporting a military hat tipped with white feathers,
black trousers with gold stripe, gold epaulettes, a gold sword, and white
gloves. His plan was to bring all black people back to Africa, which would

be unified as a single republic under his rule. His supporters believed that he had invented a perpetual motion machine to fuel the return.

In practice, Garvey was a buffoon—philandering, hyperbolic, unorganized, and criminal.[92] After serving four years of a five year sentence in the United States for fraud, he was deported to Jamaica in 1927. This prompted discussions among colonial officials about whether an existing policy allowing him free movement within the empire should change.[93] The governor of the British Honduras chose to deny him a visa, noting that the Garvey movement there was "split by dissension and recriminations as to embezzlement of funds" and that "there is fair ground for hope that it will break up before long." The Colonial Office met Garvey to explain the decision in order to deny him "an opportunity of posing as a martyr." In general, London advised letting him alone.[94]

The governor of Jamaica, who had recently been governor of Hong Kong, compared Garvey to the Chinese nationalist Sun Yat-sen. Those who denied him entry, the governor wrote, "have strengthened his hand as he is making capital out of the fact that the white people are afraid of him 'which shows the strength of my cause' etc. etc."[95] The Jamaican government engaged in heated constitutional debates about whether Garvey could stand for election—very quaint by the standards of post-colonial governments, who simply murdered or jailed people they did not want in politics. In the end, it agreed that it could not make up laws to disqualify people from standing for office or entering a country simply because of their politics.

Alan too maintained a liberal attitude toward Garvey. The newsletter of Garvey's Universal Negro Improvement Association, *Negro World*, had been sold in the Bahamas since 1924. Alan approved a visa. He later reflected that colonial officials "almost invariably adopt the point of view of the local inhabitants and become the most ardent supporters of their aspirations," which averted "decisions which dependent peoples would have resented."[96] Indeed, Alan's visa for Garvey was more liberal than many black and colored Bahamians preferred. When news of the visa became public, the *Tribune* ran a scathing editorial about Garveyism.[97] His ideas were "preposterous and without foundation,"[98] Dupuch charged. Garvey—with "his body of peers and knights and grand ladies"—knew far less about Africa than he claimed, having never been there.

The great irony, Dupuch argued, was that Garvey's schemes were imaginable only because of the institutions and infrastructure of European colonialism. "We seriously doubt that even Mr. Garvey would relish the idea of being dropped into any part of [Africa] with empty hands and no institutions of any kind."[99] It was difficult to have confidence in Garvey's plans for an African empire given the "startling series of colossal failures and mismanagement" of the UNIA.[100] Let Garvey build schools like the colonialists in order to prove his worth, he wrote, not political platforms.[101] A month before his arrival, a large crowd turned out to hear Garvey's jilted former wife denounce him as a bigamist and gangster. She noted that UNIA thugs had recently killed a Ghanaian princess in a church in Miami whom Garvey had said should be "silenced" because of her opposition to his Africa plans.[102]

Garvey disembarked in the Bahamas on November 19th, 1928. In his speech that evening in Nassau, he rekindled his famous oratory skills and irascibility. "At one moment he extolled the merits of the white man and condemned the Negro as a lazy good-for-nothing specimen. At the next moment, he declared that the same lazy good-for-nothing man had reached the point where he was capable of managing his own affairs, and his white brother, who fathered him all the way to the present moment, should be relieved of the burden," the *Tribune* reported.[103] Garvey thanked Alan for his visa and announced that the Bahamas would serve as a model for the "future development of the [black] race."

True to his reputation, Garvey used the speech to settle a score. Amid all the financial irregularities and follies of his movement, one of the greatest had been the purchase of a rust-bucket ship to bring blacks to his imagined republic in Africa. The man who overpaid for the ship and became its "captain" was a black Bahamian. Garvey suspected he received kickbacks. It was Garvey's attempts to recover from that financial disaster that ultimately put him in prison in the United States. Although the "captain" was by then living in the United States, Garvey ended his speech with a withering attack on him, calling him a "damned scamp." The comment went down like a lead balloon, seemingly an attack on the probity of all black Bahamians, already smarting from Garvey's attacks on the black race. "Mr. Garvey tried to shield himself at the expense of the reputation of a man even in the man's own home town," the *Tribune* reported.[104]

Alan ordered three senior police officers and several more in plain clothes to watch the gathering. The crowd was "very orderly and in good humor" according to the police report, and his "very scathing remarks concerning his own race" were greeted with "much amusement."[105] In all, it was "perfectly harmless behavior" that other colonies would do well to allow. If Alan learned anything from the Garvey visit, it was that patience and sympathy were probably more effective responses to bombastic anti-colonial figures than repression. It was easy to dismiss Garvey as a rogue. Yet behind the excitement of Garveyism was a more serious and reasonable desire for racial uplift and equality. "There is a natural and understandable desire on the part of tropical peoples to secure their independence, and to be treated as equals by the nations of the world," Alan would write. "Most of the leaders, and most of their followers who are not merely hypnotized by the oratory of demagogues, are chiefly anxious to attain, with independence, the recognition of racial equality that they feel is denied to them as colonials. To underestimate this factor of the problem is to misunderstand the whole position."[106]

Alan's proving years were at an end. He had "languished for five years" in the islands, he recalled, and was desperate to be summoned elsewhere.[107] He did not stand in the 1928 election so that he would be free to leave. That year, he was offered a senior position in Nigeria, which he hurried to accept. News of the promotion seemed to touch a soft spot in Dupuch:

> Quite apart from our differences of opinion, there is no disputing the fact that Mr. Burns was a man of remarkable personality, unusual ability, and rapid action. He was very much ahead of most of the men he came into contact with in this colony and twisted most of them about his fingers like so many children. He was very positive and quick in arriving at a decision and people who approached him on business were not kept long in doubt. Mr. Burns got action one way or the other immediately. But as strongly and sometimes as bitterly as we may have differed from him, we liked and admired the man. Nothing will stop the progress of a man of Mr. Burns' type. He is going to climb the ladder and before he stops will reach the top. In wishing him success, we have no hesitation in saying that we shall miss having him to fight with.[108]

The Bahamas encouraged in Alan a growing liberal spirit toward the role of the local politicians and press. "Many rude things were said of me," he recalled, "but I hope I gave as good measure as I received and no one was a penny the worse."[109] He would tell young recruits many years later: "Do not be put off because you are criticized or opposed by colonial politicians or by the colonial press. What you must do in such cases is to grin and bear it, and try by your own good manners to shame the others into better behavior."[110]

In later years, Alan and Dupuch would meet in London and laugh about their hot-headed days in the Bahamas. "We agreed that we had both been young and foolish, and became very good friends," Dupuch would write.[111] Alan agreed, noting: "I bore no ill-will towards him or his newspaper. I very often agreed with his views on local politics, and when I did not I always found his views an interesting adversary."[112]

In this respect, Dupuch the rabble-rouser of the colored and black population was more Dupuch the loyal and sagacious guardian of colonial rule, "preaching the gospel of caution and compromise," as he wrote in the midst of the double bills crisis.[113] After the Garvey visit, the local UNIA chapter testily challenged the *Tribune* to "com[e] down from the fence on which you are perched and encourage the masses to aspire after national independence."[114] Later critics too would denounce Dupuch's caution and moderation. He "oppose[d] black power politics so adamantly that he ended up supporting

Bay Street" and even "changed his views on imperialism, developing a highly personalized ideal of the British Empire and Crown," one historian wrote.[115] Because of Dupuch's duplicity to the cause of black power, in this historian's view, "restiveness against colonialism and the wave of democratic sentiment that [World War I] stimulated in other colonies bypassed the Bahamas." While British Guiana was falling into disorder as a result of such "restiveness against colonialism," the Bahamas continued to prosper. Its independence would be built on sure foundations, which Alan helped to build. It saved the Bahamas from tragedy. Other places would not be so fortunate.

NOTES

1. CCC, pp. 85–86; CO/23/344, "ACB to secretary for colonies Leo Amery re: U.S. coast guard," December 27, 1926.

2. Andrew Norris, "Rum Row: The Sinking of the Rum Runner I'm Alone," *Tulane Journal of International & Comparative Law* (2015).

3. CO/23/295, "ACB to Thomas," October 4, 1924.

4. CO/23/344, "Chamberlain to Amery," March 24, 1927.

5. CO/23/295, "ACB to Thomas," October 4, 1924.

6. Etienne Jerome Dupuch, *Tribune Story* (1967), pp. 19–22.

7. CCC, p. 91.

8. "Bootlegger vessel seized by customs," *Nassau Tribune*, August 16, 1924.

9. CO/23/295, "ACB to Thomas," October 4, 1924.

10. CO/23/244, "Case Notes on liquor smuggling," March 15, 1927; CO/23/344, "Case notes on liquor smuggling," April 29, 1927.

11. CO/23/344, "Under-secretary for foreign office Robert Vansittart to C.O.," April 19, 1927.

12. CO/23/344, "Notes on liquor smuggling," April 29, 1927.

13. CO/23/344, "Sir Gilbert Grindle on liquor smuggling," April 14, 1927.

14. CO/23/297, "Minutes on Bahamas annual report for 1925, Darnley," March 17, 1926.

15. CO/23/344, "ACB to Amery," December 27, 1926.

16. "Colonial secretary visits Exuma," *Nassau Tribune*, November 29, 1924.

17. "Return of the governor," *Nassau Tribune*, October 29, 1924.

18. CCC, p. 266.

19. CO/23/297, "Notes on appointment of stipendiary and circuit magistrate," June 8, 1926.

20. CCC, p. 266.

21. Ibid., p. 267.

22. "Here and there," *Nassau Tribune*, April 16, 1927.

23. Dupuch, op. cit., p. 76.

24. CCC, p. 267.

25. "The Hon. A.C. Burns the 'man of action' in the field," *Nassau Tribune*, December 17, 1924.

26. CCC, p. 271.

27. Dupuch, op. cit., p. 76.

28. CO/23/296, "Cordeaux to Amery," June 11, 1925.

29. CCC, p. 89.

30. "Political notes," *Nassau Tribune*, March 6, 1926 and March 10, 1926.

31. CCC, p. 90.

32. "The colonial secretary and the Treasury," *Nassau Tribune*, April 24, 1926.

33. "Our governor; his sins of omission," *Nassau Tribune*, July 25, 1925.

34. Dupuch, op. cit., p. 34.

35. "Letters to the editor," *Nassau Tribune*, August 1, 1925.

36. CCC, pp. 91–92.

37. "Editor's note," *Nassau Tribune*, August 1, 1925.

38. "Here and there," *Nassau Tribune*, July 13, 1927.

39. "The ghost of George Washington leads government of the Bahamas," *Nassau Tribune*, February 29, 1928.

40. "More irregularities," *Nassau Tribune*, June 30, 1928.

41. "Opening of the legislature," *Nassau Tribune*, January 12, 1927.

42. "Peace, happiness, and success," *Nassau Tribune*, March 16, 1927.

43. "A champion!" *Nassau Tribune*, February 11, 1928.

44. "Our pleasant surprise," *Nassau Tribune*, March 28, 1928.

45. "Legislative notes," *Nassau Tribune*, February 3, 1926.

46. Interview with Christine Barrett, June 16, 2016, Macroom, Ireland.

47. "The noise at the Lucerne Hotel," *Nassau Guardian*, February 3, 1926.

48. "The city of dreadful night; orgy at Lucerne; drunken Americans," *Nassau Guardian*, September 11, 1926.

49. Gail Saunders, *Race and Class in the Colonial Bahamas, 1880–1960* (2016), pp. 124–25.

50. CCC, pp. 83–84.

51. CO/23/344, "Chamberlain to Amery," March 24, 1927.

52. CO/23/296, "Cordeaux to Darnley," August 8, 1925.

53. CCC, p. 88.

54. "Real estate," *Nassau Guardian*, August 1, 1925.

55. CO/23/297, "ACB to Darnley," May 23, 1926.

56. CO/23/297, "Darnley to ACB," May 21, 1926.

57. CO/23/297, "ACB to Darnley," May 23, 1926.

58. "The colonial secretary and the Treasury," *Nassau Tribune*, April 24, 1926.

59. "Political Notes," *Nassau Tribune*, February 23, 1927.

60. Keith Tinker, *The Migration of Peoples from the Caribbean to the Bahamas* (2011); Bertin Louis, "The Haitian Diaspora in the Bahamas: An Alternative View," *Wadabagei: A Journal of the Caribbean and Its Diasporas* (2011).

61. CBAA, p. 114.

62. CP, p. 83.

63. IDOC, p. 293.

64. League of Nations, *International Commission of Enquiry into the Existence of Slavery and Forced Labour in the Republic of Liberia* (1930).

65. Wayne Phillips, "Liberian upholds colonial benefit," *New York Times*, March 24, 1957.

66. CO/23/368, "ACB to Freeston, Notes on Bahamas system of government," August 30, 1927.

67. CO/23/297, "Minutes of Sanitation Committee meeting," June 15, 1926.

68. "One man government," *Nassau Tribune*, April 16, 1927.

69. CO/23/297, "ACB to Amery re: removal of Stanley Albury," October 20, 1926.

70. "Representative of Colonial Office investigates the Bahamas," *Nassau Tribune*, September 3, 1927.

71. William Beveridge, *Report on the Public Health and on Medical Conditions in New Providence, Bahama Islands* (1927).

72. "Dr. Pearce at the Old Colony Club speaks on sanitation in the Bahamas," *Nassau Tribune*, February 4, 1928.

73. "Maps of the Bahama Islands," *Nassau Tribune*, November 24, 1926.

74. CCC, p. 250; CO/23/391, "ACB to Amery re: Nassau Prison riot," July 28, 1928.

75. CO/23/291, "Darnley to ACB re: Nassau Prison riot," November 30, 1928.

76. CCC, pp. 251–52, 242.

77. "The prison riot," *Nassau Tribune*, July 29, 1928.

78. Martin Thomas, *Violence and Colonial Order: Police, Workers and Protest in the European Colonial Empires, 1918–1940* (2012), p. 327.

79. Howard Johnson, *The Bahamas from Slavery to Servitude, 1783–1933* (1996), p. 168.

80. CBAA, p. 199.

81. CO/23/391, "Telegram from Officer Administering the Government of the Bahamas," July 26, 1928.

82. CO/23/391, "Freeston re: Nassau prison riot," November 9, 1928.

83. CO/23/368, "ACB to Freeston, Notes on Bahamas system of government," August 30, 1927.

84. "Retrospection," *Nassau Tribune*, December 7, 1927.

85. "Downing Street bomb," *Nassau Tribune*, July 29, 1928.

86. CO/23/296, "ACB and Logan to Cordeaux," August 14, 1925.

87. Harcourt Gladstone Malcolm, *A History of the Bahamas House of Assembly* (1921).

88. "Is the end yet?" *Nassau Tribune*, August 22, 1928.

89. "Political Notes," *Nassau Tribune*, August 4, 1928.

90. "Hit and run," *Nassau Tribune*, August 4, 1928.

91. CO/23/390/3, "Freeston to Grindle," July 27, 1928; Saunders, op. cit., p. 116.

92. Edmund David Cronon, *Black Moses: The Story of Marcus Garvey and the Universal Negro Improvement Association* (1955); Colin Grant, *Negro with a Hat: The Rise and Fall of Marcus Garvey* (2008).

93. CO/318/391/12, "Case notes re: Garvey visit," February 1, 1928 and March 3, 1928.

94. CO/554/78/8, "Case notes re: Garvey visit," April 5, 1928, and April 10, 1928.

95. CO/318/391/12, "Stubbs to Wilson," February 24, 1928.
96. IDOC, p. 301.
97. "The 'President General of Africa,'" *Nassau Tribune*, November 10, 1928.
98. "Here and there," *Nassau Tribune*, November 14, 1928.
99. "Here and there," *Nassau Tribune*, November 24, 1928.
100. "Hail Mahommet!!" *Nassau Tribune*, November 21, 1928.
101. "Here and there," *Nassau Tribune*, November 17, 1928.
102. "Negro 'king' coming in murder inquiry," *New York Times*, March 21, 1928.
103. "Here and there," *Nassau Tribune*, November 21, 1928.
104. "Hail Mahommet!!" *Nassau Tribune*, November 21, 1928.
105. CO/318/391/12, "Police Office Nassau to Colonial Secretary (ACB), Notes on Garvey visit," November 23, 1928.
106. OPT, p. 9.
107. HON, 1st edition, 1929, p. 11.
108. "In the Public Eye: The Honourable A.C. Burns," *Nassau Tribune*, December 1, 1928.
109. CCC, p. 268.
110. Ibid., p. 322.
111. Dupuch, op. cit., pp. 76, 17.
112. CCC, pp. 91–92.
113. "Downing Street bomb," *Nassau Tribune*, July 29, 1928.
114. "Climbing monkeys," *Nassau Tribune*, November 24, 1928.
115. Saunders, op. cit., pp. 105, 120.

Chapter 6

River Diving on the Benue

In 1930, the sixth child of a black Protestant missionary was born in an Igbo town about 250 miles east of Lagos.[1] He recalled the "extraordinary luck" of being born into colonial Nigeria where "the pace of change . . . was incredible." He wrote, "I am not just talking about the rate of development, with villages transforming into towns, or the coming of modern comforts, such as electricity or running water or modes of transportation, but more of a sense that we were standing figuratively and literally at the dawn of a new era." After secondary school, he won a place at a new university in Nigeria founded by University College London. "As a young man, surrounded by all this excitement, it seemed as if the British were planning surprises for me at every turn, including the construction of a new university!"

One of the books he read while at university was *Mister Johnson*, a 1939 novel by a former colonial district officer, Joyce Cary.[2] The novel drew on Cary's experiences managing the strains of modernity in western Nigeria. "Every reform we brought also caused dislocations or evils of some kind; and this was inevitable," Cary recounted.[3] The novel provided a way for the young Igbo student to understand similar convulsions in his own village: "Cary was good, he was sympathetic, he knew Africa."[4] After graduation, the young man began to write his own version of *Mister Johnson*, told from a Nigerian perspective. When it appeared in 1958, *Things Fall Apart* was a sensation. The author, Chinua Achebe, became the father of modern African literature.

In their writings, both Cary and Achebe captured the disorientation that came with rapid development in the 1930s and 1940s. Both believed that colonialism was an agent of change that must inevitably come. Indeed, as one wag wrote, the Nigeria that Achebe recounted seemed more like a place where "things were coming together" than falling apart.[5] Achebe saw the colonial period as a "habitable community,"[6] one African scholar noted, where the strains of modernity were moderated and redirected by colonial institutions. A year before he died, Achebe even ventured a "heresy": "The British governed their colony of Nigeria with considerable care," he wrote. "There was a very highly competent cadre of government officials imbued with a high level of knowledge of how to run a country."[7]

Cary and Achebe shared other passions as well, not least their advocacy for self-government, which Cary expressed in his 1941 book *The Case for African Freedom*.[8] Yet both men brayed at the suggestion that they were "anti-colonial," a false dichotomy thrust upon their works by later critics whom Cary likened to authors of children's stories: "A cat is on the mat. The Empire is naughty. Primitive savages are good—but European civilization is corrupt."[9] As Achebe would explain: "I am not one of those who would say that Africa has gained nothing at all during the colonial period. I mean, this is ridiculous—we have gained a lot."[10]

Like Achebe, Alan became an avid reader of Cary's books. *Mister Johnson* was Alan's favorite because of its poignant portrayal of the hapless African clerk, whence the title. "Men of this type were not unusual in some of the smaller up-country stations" where Cary worked, Alan wrote in the *Times*. Cary "was sincere in his sympathy for the Africans, without sentimentality, and regarded each as an individual, good or bad, or more generally, as in all of us, a mixture of both." The only distortions in Cary's novels, Alan pleaded, were his depictions of the top officials in Lagos: "Not all senior officials are such careerists—or so foolish—as Cary paints them."[11]

During his five years as the deputy colonial secretary of Nigeria, Alan presided over his fair share of "surprises" for Nigerians (see figure 6.1). The most festive was the opening in 1932 of the Benue river bridge, which linked northern Nigeria to the colony's main port in the south. The half-mile span was the longest bridge in Africa at the time and the biggest investment the British had made in the continent. It was completed thanks to the work of the river-dwelling Tiv people, who donned primitive diving suits of compressed air to build the underwater foundations. "They would compress and decompress as rapidly as the air-cocks of the man-locks would allow, and could not be induced to see the point of doing otherwise," the resident engineer remarked.[12]

Alan thought the money spent on the bridge "could have been employed more usefully on social improvements."[13] But in general, he viewed such investments as incontestably beneficial for colonial peoples. "But for British exploitation, in the better sense, the present and former colonial territories would be even poorer and more backward than they are today."[14] The Tiv men who earned income by working on railroad projects began offering cash dowries for their wives instead of the usual offer of a female from their own extended families. To legitimize this change in marriage customs, the British

Figure 6.1   Alan and Katie with Household Staff, Lagos, 1932. *Source*: Private Collection of Alan Dixon.

helped the Tiv to create a group-wide decision-making body among the fifty-four clans, which became the Tiv Tribal Council in 1932, the year the bridge opened. The first head of the council was a decorated war veteran of the West Africa Frontier Force.[15] River diving for the Benue bridge had caused things to fall apart. It had also allowed them to come together again.

More broadly, rapid development allowed men like Chinua Achebe to attend new universities, acquire new knowledge, and write books for a global audience. That in turn stoked a rising self-consciousness and a desire for self-rule. For Alan, this had been the plan all along. "It has been the policy of British colonial administrations to build up a national consciousness which would one day make it possible to give independence to a united country," he would explain.[16] The growing rumblings for "African freedom" from the likes of Cary and Achebe indicated success, not failure, in Alan's view. What was at stake in these years was whether Nigerian society could come together faster than colonial rule would fall apart.

Alan was in such a rush to report for his new job in 1929 that he left the proofs of his *History of Nigeria* unexamined in London. The publisher expected a loss. Yet it sold like pies. "Difficult to put down," said one review. "A model of what such works should be," said another. A French official cribbed notes from the detailed exposition of indirect rule "which we have adopted with much success in Morocco."[17] The book would go through eight editions over the next fifty years and earn Alan the equivalent of $300,000 in today's money.

Alan's was the first history of Nigeria *as such*, and it was pro-colonial without apology. The British had installed "an ordered administration . . . between the long-suffering peasantry and their hereditary tyrants" who "were no longer permitted to amuse and enrich themselves with war and slave-raiding."[18] Indeed, the British reviewers of the first edition felt it was too harsh on the British. One upbraided Alan for missing various "great men" in Nigerian colonial history and for ignoring railway construction and research on malaria. Another disliked his excessive attention to the depredations of the British involvement in the West African slave trade and the insufficient attention to the peace-making and economic development of the Royal Niger Company: "Mr. Burns' apologia in his last chapter comes too late: the mischief has been done."[19]

The *History of Nigeria* was the first time that Alan worked through a historical reconstruction of colonialism. His interests were moving from the specific to the general and from the professional to the public. Years later, his defense of colonialism would extend to all European colonies: "With all its imperfections, European government in Asia and in Africa has given to the native inhabitants of the tropics greater personal liberty and economic opportunity than they have ever enjoyed before," he would conclude.[20] Put in terms of the great what-might-have-beens, Alan, like Cary and Achebe, judged that ordered rule by a relatively liberal state was almost always better than premodern rule by a traditional enemy or indigenous tyrant. "I can assure you that no one exploits the African so effectively as members of his own race, and no one has better protected the African from tyranny than the so-called imperialists who govern the colonies. I am proud that I have been one of them."[21]

The *History of Nigeria* set out the argument for colonialism's legitimacy alongside its benefits. The first edition merely noted that the British occupation came easily. As Alan noted in a later speech, "For people who had never known anything but tyranny and terror, the mild rule of the British was a pleasant change."[22] Later editions would incorporate the testimony of the leader of a small northern tribe whom Alan appointed as a native district head in 1934 and who would rise to become premier of northern Nigeria at independence: "There was no ill-will after the occupation. We were used to conquerors and these were different; they were polite and obviously out to help us rather than themselves," he wrote.[23]

A key event described in *History of Nigeria* was the native response to the rebellion in the northern village of Satiru in 1906. It was led by a blind

Islamic cleric and part-time ventriloquist whose acolytes believed he could produce kola nuts from his person and levitate on his prayer mat. His rebels razed a village, killing all fourteen of its men. They then massacred twenty-five government troops who came for a parlay. The major emirs of the region rallied around the British, providing horses, supplies, and troops (as their native counterparts had done on the French side) to suppress the rebellion. After the rebellion was defeated, the outlawed cleric's head was put on a stake by native soldiers, and his encampment was cursed by the local emir. The British then obtained a ruling from Islamic judges in Mecca refuting the occult claims of the rebels. "Throughout this critical period the loyalty of most of the chiefs and people was remarkable," Alan wrote.[24]

Later scholars would concur that the crushing of the Satiru rebellion was the point when British rule became firmly entrenched in the north. The "over-whelming loyalty to the British" showed that "colonial rule was ultimately founded on the cooperation of those who for a variety of reasons sought, and exploited for their own ends, the cooperation of the invaders," one historian noted.[25] Yet as time passed, the Satiru rebels, like other rebels during the colonial era, were increasingly described as freedom fighters—"a militant wide-ranging organization" formed in response to the "deprivation of sover-eignty," in the excited prose of one scholar.[26] Others viewed the Satiru rebels as proto-Marxist revolutionaries whose rebellion "revealed class tensions."[27] The support of local chiefs was explained away as insincere: "Probably they were convinced of the long-term futility of even a major rising,"[28] one book speculated.

More generally, these later histories of Nigeria would downplay the entire colonial period, except as an illegitimate object of resistance. Historical unity was to be found not in the British amalgamation of the country but in more distant sources like the medieval iron smelters of Mandara, the slaving states of the central region or the men-only masquerades of the northern Igbo. The colonial period was now described as "a fleeting episode" and Alan's book as "tainted colonial historiography."[29] Every instance of unrest and dissent was now recast as anti-colonial resistance, "nationalist history in search of a nation" as two historians called it. The Egba uprising in which Alan had kept the peace was "an opportunity to break the yoke of foreign rule," one history claimed.[30] Another ventured that "heavy resistance met British incursions at almost every turn."[31]

What was at stake with these competing histories of Nigeria was whether colonialism should be seen as a unifying and legitimate force or as a divisive and illegitimate one. Older writers—whether British or Nigerian—would render the colonial period in varied hues, noting both aspects. "Let us give the devil his due: colonialism in Africa disrupted many things, but it did cre-ate big political units where there were small scattered ones before," Achebe would note.[32] Alan's *History* also stressed this coming together under colonialism. If you removed the "habitable community" of the colonial state, it was not clear what exactly would attract the loyalty of Nigerian peoples. When the third edition of the *History* appeared in 1942, a reviewer noted that its lessons about the unifying force of the colonial state were being quickly forgotten by "some of the more vocal politically minded southerners" in Nigeria.[33] Ironically, those southerners would include Achebe, an Igbo whose beliefs in a meritocratic society would put him at odds with the group-based demands of others and thrust him into the center of a pitiless civil war after independence.

Colonialism taught disparate groups how to live together. The British quite consciously "imposed" on subject peoples the civic institutions that had brought peace to European peoples, for, as Alan noted, "it would have been wrong not to offer to such peoples the institutions which we believe to be the best."[34] Yet without sufficient time to take root, those institutions and norms would be ejected amid the pressures of modernity.

Alan foresaw that the fate of colonialism would turn on the question of timing. "If colonial territories are given self-government before they are fit to govern themselves, the result must be inefficiency, anarchy and chaos," he would warn.[35] "In the chaos that might result from inefficient administration, the living standards and the health of the inhabitants would certainly suffer" because people would be "exposed to exploitation by a handful of their better educated compatriots or, at best, to the bungling of untrained and incapable politicians."[36] This was why the emirs of northern Nigeria had rallied around the British defeat of the Satiru rebels in 1906. It was why the Egba rebellion had been so easily crushed in 1918. It was why the Tiv Tribal Council won widespread assent in 1932. It was the fundamental lesson of the *History of Nigeria*.

Alan's life quickly reverted to form in Nigeria. Katie had been with the girls in England since 1927. Again, she opted to leave them at boarding school to be with her husband. The Missis returned to her realm. So too did the loyal Joseph Agbake. Alan had paid Joseph's passage back from the Bahamas to Nigeria, telling him that his services were no longer needed. Once Joseph heard of Alan's appointment, he made his way to Accra where Alan's Nigeria-bound ship stopped. He sweet-talked his way on board and burst unceremoniously into Alan's cabin to begin arranging things for offloading at Lagos. Alan did not even bother to protest.

Alan's reunion with his two close Nigerian friends, the government advisor Kitoyi Ajasa and the legislator Henry Carr, by now the top civil servant for Lagos, prompted him to launch a new mixed-race social club. The Lagos Dining Club, as it was called, was composed of an equal number of European and African couples who met for dinner once a month at a hotel. "At first, the evenings tended to be rather stiff, but later as we got to know one another better, the stiffness wore off and the evenings became very pleasant," Alan recalled.[37] The *Nigerian Daily Times* called the dining club "the best service which could be rendered in this country towards the removal of racial misunderstanding."[38] Racial prejudice was not something to be steam-rolled by punitive laws and righteous denunciations, Alan believed, but by everyday interactions and trust-building.

It was from the dining club that Alan's other social innovation emerged. In their previous stint in Nigeria, Alan and Katie had begun a book club in their home since the governor would not allocate funds for a public library. Writing on official stationary and promising that the government would furnish a building, Alan sought a grant from the Carnegie Foundation of New York for a public library in Lagos. Carnegie agreed and provided a $6,000 grant. The Lagos Library opened in 1932, making it one of just a handful of nonspecialist libraries in Africa open to all races.[39] "One of Burns' accomplishments was to bring educated Westernized Africans into the ruling circles as much as possible," wrote one scholar of the library. "Too shrewd to discriminate on the basis of skin color, Burns knew that the very small elites of Europeanized Africans and Europeans in Africa had interests in common."[40]

Along with the drawing of maps, the creation of libraries is another colonial endeavor that has been scorned by later critics as devious and wicked.[41] Having first imposed an alien conception on the outer geography of place, the colonialists next implanted an alien conception on the inner geography of the mind. Such libraries were intended, the critics allege, to create a pro-colonial native elite that would perpetuate European rule and train a literate workforce to boost colonial profits. All those elderly lady volunteers affixing labels and dusting stacks are transformed by such works into powerful agents of imperial reach as they assist Africans to sign out copies of Baudelaire. "The violence of the library" and "conceptual contamination" are stock phrases.[42] The effect of colonial libraries was "to dismember the dynamism and effectiveness of the oral tradition," one alarmed Nigerian scholar complained. "Library colonialism remains one of the most hidden but deadly instruments of neo-colonialism," he warned. On those quiet shelves "the malignant influences of Western civilization are diffused among literate Africans like invisible bubbles of air."[43]

If the Lagos Library was intended to perpetuate British rule, it was a clumsy effort. Of the six thousand volumes in it by 1934, half were novels, poetry, and drama, and most of the nonfiction was travel writing. The collection "was heavily slanted towards fiction and designed purely for the entertainment purposes of its subscribers," a historian wrote. "It was a place for the British and indigenous elite to be entertained and to stay informed

about the world around them rather than to be educated in an academic or
scientific capacity."[44] The hours spent putting the library into operation, Alan
recalled, were "amply repaid by the joy of opening cases and handling the
numbers of volumes which arrived."[45] One excitable American graduate student described the Lagos Library as "an entertainment bunker in a barrage of
reformist attacks on colonial privilege."[46]

By 1934, about 10 percent of the members (39 out of 396) were African.
Ajasa and Carr were the first African members, and Carr sat on the governing board. Carr in particular has been vilified by later anti-colonial writers as
a "collaborator."[47] The black radicals who crossed swords with him during
this era—including the first president of an independent Nigeria—seemed
as much irked by his erudition as by his support for colonial rule. His own
private collection—18,000 volumes of invisible air bubbles—was the stuff of
legend and later became a public library unto itself. "All the Europeans who
knew Dr. Carr regarded him with great admiration," Alan wrote.[48]

Other critics complain that colonial libraries did too little brainwashing
rather than too much. "Burns must have been very persuasive," one critic
contended, because "no library of this type could be expected to serve any
wider social purpose." All that time unpacking newly arrived wooden crates
"could have been used to more effective social and national purpose," the
critic complained.[49] Yet such cavils ignore the library's main purpose: the
provision of intellectual and social diversion for colonial officials and their
spouses. By 1935, the library had lending branches at twelve towns outside
of Lagos where colonial officers could borrow books. For modern social
critics, such endeavors are yet further proof of the mendacity of an enterprise claiming "wider social purpose." But if Achebe is right that Nigeria's
success as a colony owed to the excellence of its colonial administration,
then keeping those colonial administrators mildly amused with books was
of critical importance. It is for this same reason that Alan argued that more
attention should be paid to the upkeep of gardens in colonial bungalows.[50]
In their small way, gardens, clubs, and libraries contributed to the excellence of the colonial administration on which advances like poverty reduction, child survival, and the rule of law depended. Soaring rhetoric about
"social justice" from colonial critics could never compete with a competent
public service.

By bringing the Carnegie Foundation to Nigeria, Alan's project had an
indirect impact as well, since Carnegie would later build the national library
system without which, one scholar wrote in 1970, "the present situation . . .
might have been bleak indeed."[51] The experts in library development who
later swarmed into West Africa, often on Carnegie-funded missions, "spent
much of their time criticising the work of those who had had, of necessity, to
make bricks without much straw," Alan sighed.[52]

There is a final contribution of the Lagos Library that should not be underestimated. Colonial libraries were often refuges for young scholars participating in the re-discovery and preservation of indigenous culture. One such man was a South African–born district officer of Welsh heritage, Gwilym Iwan Jones, who served as the first treasurer and honorary secretary of the Lagos Library. From his post in eastern Nigeria, Jones was in thrall to the region's social and cultural practices. His stints in Lagos were spent in Alan's library compiling his notes and poring over photographs. G. I. Jones was as adventurous as his name suggests, spending weeks at a time on safari. His photographic record of housing styles, social rituals, masquerade performances, bronze sculpture, musical instruments, and clothing would culminate in *The Art of Eastern Nigeria*, his seminal book after leaving the colonial service to become a lecturer at Cambridge.[53] "Some may try to condemn him, and his work, as a scholar whose major field researches were carried out in colonial times," wrote an art historian whose graduate studies were mentored by Jones. "His writings will outlive that, for they provide a rich commentary on the art of eastern Nigeria, for a time that would have been largely unknown to us otherwise, by an intelligent and just observer and a keen photographer."[54]

For Alan, this role of libraries in expanding and preserving knowledge of native cultures was central to the colonial purpose. "We do not try to assimilate the colonial peoples, nor to turn them into imitation Scotsmen—or even Englishmen—but to help them to develop a higher civilization of their own, soundly based on their own traditional institutions and culture."[55] Colonial civil servants like G. I. Jones, Joyce Cary, and Alan Burns had more of a claim to be authentic voices of Nigeria than later legions of critics, whether African or European, whose safaris never extended beyond the faculty lounge. In his many acts—writing a history of Nigeria, forming a mixed-race dining club, founding a library, administering a law-based government—Alan became a true Nigerian.

Rapid economic and social change was creating fertile ground for radical ideas. The Soviet Union had in 1927 created a League Against Imperialism, based in Berlin, that encouraged national leaders in European colonies to turn on their rulers. In a 1927 pamphlet *British Imperialism in West Africa* written for the joint research center of the British Labour and Communist parties, brother Emile's wife Elinor had written of how an "articulate leadership" of the "working class" in colonial areas was coming to "recognize as their oppressors not the individual white man but the [colonial] government."[56] Emile made sure that anti-colonial forces in Britain heaved closely to Stalin's party line in Moscow, purging free thinkers on charges of being "intellectuals."[57] He even made a point of depositing his autobiography at the Comintern archive in Moscow, hoping that one day he would be heralded as a hero of the Soviet Union.[58]

Capitalist development was indeed a disruptive force. At the secretariat in Lagos, Alan and his colleagues repeatedly thwarted attempts by British firms to acquire freehold land for plantations in Nigeria because of the social disruption it would cause. Alan even forced one European firm to close its business of selling oils, spices, and nuts in rural areas where women traditionally controlled the markets: "They did not realise how much the women would resent being deprived, not only of the opportunity of making a little money but also of their enjoyable occupation, nor did they realise how dangerous angry women can be," Alan recalled. "They were striking at the roots of social life in Nigeria."[59]

That lesson had been vividly demonstrated by the so-called Women's War that had erupted in 1929 shortly after Alan and Katie arrived in Nigeria. Like all areas of the colony, the Igbo areas of the southeast had experienced losses alongside gains as markets developed and opportunities changed. The small market society of West African women was losing out to an integrated national market that could supply more and better items for less. The counterparts of the newly enriched Tiv river divers spending cash for brides were the newly impoverished women traders of Owerri and Calabar provinces unable to sell their inferior goods (the Owerri women regularly adulterated their palm oil with water and potash[60]). Their discontent was expressed on all manner of issues: taxation, market tolls, water fees, land use planning, and corrupt native officials. Local British officers initially held regular parlays with them, promising no taxation of women, the removal of corrupt "warrant chiefs," and a revision of market tolls. But the movement spiraled out of control and looting began. When a group of women stormed a government building, the order was given to open fire. The final toll was fifty-seven women dead and another thirty-one injured.

At its deepest level, the Women's War (or Aba Riots as they were called at the time) was not so much about the colonial government or even the market economy. It was a more fundamental disquiet about the wrenching transformation of premodern village life. The women, three scholars wrote, wanted to return to a time before roads, buildings, and other "material manifestations" which they felt were "estranging all from the greatest spiritual forces."[61] The Oxford lecturer Margery Perham, who stayed with Alan and Katie while visiting the affected areas, concluded: "It is produced by the sudden strain thrown upon primitive communities by the strong, all-embracing pressure of European influence."[62]

A wide-ranging inquiry was held, including testimony from 123 Igbo women and the publication of voluminous records. The inquiry's final report faulted police for opening fire too soon. It fell to Alan, as acting chief secretary, to respond. While accepting the recommendations relating to government reforms, he insisted that no police would be punished. The fact that he kept a copy of his "very difficult speech" to the legislature in 1931 suggests he felt it was one of his finest moments.[63] The echoes of his remarks on the Nassau prison riot are clear:

> It is extremely difficult, when riots occur, for those officers who are responsible for the restoration and maintenance of order to estimate accurately the temper of the mob, and it is not improbable that errors of judgement might occur. . . . The Government considers they did their duty in circumstances of great danger, circumstances without precedent, and circumstances of great difficulty with courage, patience and restraint.[64]

Not surprisingly, later historians have elevated the Aba riots to a mythic status with their apparent confection of socialism, feminism, and anti-colonialism. It was a revolt against "masculine" things like currency, warehouses, and product standards, three American scholars enthused, and thus "a historical high point in West African resistance to colonialism."[65] One Nigerian historian called it a "turning point" when "a new generation of anti-colonial activists was emerging to fight not only for local improvements within the colonial system but also for complete independence for the whole of Nigeria from British rule."[66]

Yet very few of the million or so women in the affected areas took part, and many of those that did admitted they were press-ganged into joining. Most local people sided with the colonial government. No one seriously argued that land use planning and warehouses were "alien" or "men-only" conceptions unsuited to Nigerians. Rather, the lesson from the riot was that the colonial government was badly needed to moderate the pace of change. "Not very long after the disorders has ceased, my wife and I drove through this area by car," Alan recalled, "and were everywhere greeted in the most friendly way."[67]

When his initial appointment was nearing an end in 1934, Alan pleaded to remain in Nigeria in hopes of becoming chief secretary. But his provenance kept following him. Every time a position in the Caribbean came up, his name would appear in Colonial Office dockets. It so happened that a governor was needed in the Central American colony of British Honduras, a swampy colony of Mosquito Coast pirates and Indiana Jones adventurers that was in a ruinous state. The colony had traditionally "received a greater proportion of the incompetents in colonial service than any other West Indian colony," one scholar noted.[68] The previous governor had simply fled. Alan's name came up for discussion.

With a population of only fifty-eight thousand—no more than a railway depot in Nigeria—and a governor's salary and pension lower than elsewhere, British Honduras had few attractions. Assignment to this colony was a sacrifice, and, as one historian noted, "the minimum tour of duty seldom expired without the officer feeling that his transfer was overdue."[69] At the age of forty-seven, Alan might not escape from the "darkest slum" of the empire a third time. He might become one of those pathetic governors who spent most of his time writing colonial memoirs in his study. He "must have been an exceptional man to be chosen for so responsible a post in such a crisis in its affairs" a later historian would write. "He could have expected nothing but hard work among a dejected people, whom nothing short of a miracle could restore to solvency."[70]

Alan complained that it was a demotion. Friends encouraged him to accept the errand. "Once you have got your foot on the gubernatorial ladder I have little doubt that you will climb to the top of it, and that one day Nigeria . . . will be glad to recapture our lost friend as H.E. The Governor for a long and prosperous term," wrote a friend who served on the Lagos Library board.[71] When the news broke in Lagos, the laments were genuine. "He has made more contributions towards an understanding between man and man than any officer similarly placed can boast of," the *Nigerian Daily Times* commented.[72] Kitoyi Ajasa wrote to Alan as someone who had lost a best friend. "We cannot hope to have our European friends always with us. But the wrench is so awfully hard."[73]

When Alan left Nigeria, colonial rule there was strong and legitimate. Not for another two decades, with the passing of the generation of Ajasa and Carr, would this period of collaborative change under the pressures of modernization be threatened by nationalists. Colonialism could spare Alan Burns in Nigeria, where things were coming together. It needed him in British Honduras, where things had fallen apart.

NOTES

1. Chinua Achebe, *There Was a Country: A Personal History of Biafra* (2012), pp. 20, 39, 27.

2. Joyce Cary, *Mister Johnson* (1939).

3. Chinua Achebe, *Hopes and Impediments: Selected Essays, 1965–1987* (1988), p. 99.

4. "An Interview with Chinua Achebe," *The Manchester Guardian*, February 28, 1972.

5. Douglas Chambers, "'There Was a Country': Achebe's Final Work," *Journal of Asian and African Studies* (2013), p. 753.

6. Mpalive-Hangson Msiska, "Imagined Nations and Imaginary Nigeria: Chinua Achebe's Quest for a Country," *Journal of Genocide Research* (2014), p. 413.

7. Achebe, *There Was a Country*, p. 43.

8. Joyce Cary, *The Case for African Freedom* (1941).

9. Joyce Cary, *The African Witch* (1936), Carfax edition (1951), p. 11.

10. Gordon Killam, *The Novels of Chinua Achebe* (1969), p. 5.

11. Alan Burns, "Joyce Cary's Nigeria," *The Times*, September 2, 1959.

12. William Ewart Thomas, "The Construction of a Bridge Over the River Benue at Makurdi, Nigeria," *Selected Engineering Papers* (1934), p. 20.

13. CCC, p. 110.

14. CBAA, p. 113.

15. David Dorward, "The Development of the British Colonial Administration Among the Tiv, 1900–1949," *African Affairs* (1969), p. 325.

16. CCT-G, p. 5; IDOC, p. 76.

17. Fred Shelford, "Review of 'History of Nigeria,'" *Journal of the Royal African Society* (1929), p. 104; Edward Source, "Review of 'History of Nigeria,'" *The Geographical Journal* (1929), p. 84; Henri Labouret, "Questions Africaines," *Annales d'Histoire Economique et Sociale* (1931), p. 103.

18. HON, pp. 307, 308.

19. E. Hyslop Bell, "Review of 'History of Nigeria,'" *Journal of the Royal Institute of International Affairs* (1929), p. 656.

20. CP, pp. 49–50.

21. CPCW-G, p. 6.

22. FBCE-G, pp. 7–8.

23. Ahmadu Bello, *My Life* (1962), pp. 18–19.

24. HON, p. 198.

25. Rowland Adevemi Adeleye, "Mahdist Triumph and British Revenge in Northern Nigeria: Satiru 1906," *Journal of the Historical Society of Nigeria* (1972), p. 210.

26. Ibid., p. 194.

27. Paul Lovejoy and Jan Hogendorn, "Revolutionary Mahdism and Resistance to Colonial Rule in the Sokoto Caliphate, 1905–6," *Journal of African History* (1990), p. 242.

28. Elizabeth Isichei, *A History of Nigeria* (1983), p. 371.

29. Bernth Lindfors, "Chinua Achebe: A Puzzling Pioneer," Keynote delivered on May 3, 2014, at the 2014 Chinua Achebe Colloquium held at Brown University, Providence, Rhode Island.

30. Isichei, op. cit., pp. xi, 396.

31. Toyin Falola and Matthew Heaton, *A History of Nigeria* (2008), p. 108.

32. Killam, op. cit., p. 4.

33. Leonard Lewis, "Review of 'History of Nigeria,'" *Africa: Journal of the International African Institute* (1945), p. 99.

34. CBAA, p. 161.

35. FBCE-G, p. 16.

36. CBAA, pp. 68, 74.

37. CCC, p. 107.

38. "The Lagos Dining Club," *Nigerian Daily Times*, May 19, 1934.

39. Glenn Sitzman, *African Libraries* (1988), pp. 82–87.

40. Olden, op. cit., p. 405.

41. Elizabeth Fitzpatrick, "The Public Library as Instrument of Colonialism: The Case of the Netherlands East Indies," *Libraries & the Cultural Record* (2008).

42. Zubairu Wai, "On the Predicament of Africanist Knowledge: Mudimbe, Gnosis and the Challenge of the Colonial Library," *International Journal of Francophone Studies* (2015), pp. 277, 281.

43. Adolphe Amadi, "The Emergence of a Library Tradition in Pre- and Postcolonial Africa," *International Library Review* (1981), p. 70, 164–65.

44. Sterling Coleman, "Empire of the Mind: Subscription Libraries, Literacy & Acculturation in the Colonies of the British Empire," Florida State University, Department of History, doctoral dissertation (2008), p. 116.

45. CCC, p. 106.

46. Coleman, op. cit., p. 117.

47. Emmanuel Ayandele, *The Educated Elite in the Nigerian Society* (1974), pp. 75–77.

48. CCC, p. 108.

49. John Harris, "Libraries and Librarianship in Nigeria at Mid-Century," *Ghana University Department of Library Studies Occasional Papers* (1970).

50. CCC, p. 102.

51. Harris, op. cit.

52. CCC, p. 106.

53. Gwilym Iwan Jones, *The Art of Eastern Nigeria* (1984).

54. Simon Ottenberg, "In Memoriam: G. I. Jones, 1904–1995," *African Arts* (1995), p. 21.

55. CCC, p. 323.

56. Elinor Burns, *British Imperialism in West Africa* (1927), pp. 64, 63.

57. John McIlroy, "The Establishment of Intellectual Orthodoxy and the Stalinization of British Communism 1928–1933," *Past & Present* (2006); Andrew Thorpe, "Comintern 'Control' of the Communist Party of Great Britain, 1920–43," *English Historical Review* (1998).

58. Fredrik Petersson, *Willi Münzenberg, the League against Imperialism, and the Comintern, 1925–1933* (2013), p. 559.

59. TCCC-G, p. 5.

60. Susan Martin, *Palm Oil and Protest: An Economic History of the Ngwa Region, South-Eastern Nigeria, 1800–1980* (1988), pp. 110–11.

61. Marc Matera, Misty Bastian, and Susan Kingsley Kent, *The Women's War of 1929: Gender and Violence in Colonial Nigeria* (2012), pp. 236, 238.

62. Margery Perham, *Native Administration in Nigeria* (1937), pp. 218–19.

63. CCC, p. 275.

64. "Acting Chief Secretary Reports on Aba Commission," *Nigeria Legislative Council Debates*, 9th Session, 1931.

65. Matera et. al., op. cit., p. 2.

66. Isichei, op. cit., p. 135.

67. CCC, p. 253.

68. Peter Ashdown, *Race, Class, and the Unofficial Majority in British Honduras, 1890–1949* (1979), p. 74, fn. 52.

69. Cedric Grant, *The Making of Modern Belize: Politics, Society & British Colonialism in Central America* (1976), p. 356, fn. 62.

70. Stephen Caiger, *British Honduras: Past and Present* (1951), p. 162.

71. "Edward Henry Lionel Beddington (Africa and Eastern Trading Company and United Africa Company) to ACB," personal letter, May 18, 1934, private collection.

72. "The Lagos Dining Club," *Nigerian Daily Times*, May 19, 1934.

73. "Kitoyi Ajasa to ACB," personal letter, January 4, 1936, private collection.

Chapter 7

Our Man in Belize

In 1903, a medical officer in British Honduras, Thomas Gann, was asked by the colony's governor to investigate a suspected Mayan ruin reported by woodcutters along the southern Rio Grande River. While tending to his medical duties, Gann had become an expert on the Mayan civilization that had been at its peak in Central America from roughly AD 300–1000. He was passionate about preserving the sites, because when discovered by locals, they tended to be either looted for trinkets or demolished to build houses. The descendants of the Maya had little idea that these stony mounds and ledges were from their ancestors. The black and Creole populations viewed them as a form of dark magic to be avoided. The only previous European to study the ruins made copies of everything he found, fearing the originals would be looted or destroyed.[1]

Gann arrived in the southern town of Punta Gorda in April and, accompanied by the British district officer, travelled to the mouth of the Rio Grande with several boatmen. Two dinghies were loaded with equipment for the upstream passage. After negotiating a series of small waterfalls, the party left the river at the woodcutters camp and beat its way through the jungle. After a mile, the scene appeared: a 900-foot by 210-foot raised platform "faced on all sides by nicely cut stone" and "surrounded on all sides by virgin bush." A series of smaller platforms lay nearby. Gann was mystified: "One cannot but wonder whence the builders came? What was their history? And, above all, how it is that they have so completely disappeared?"[2]

More than a decade would pass before Gann returned to the site, which he named Lubaantun, the Mayan word for "fallen stones." To the southwest, he found a royal palace that included a playing field for the Mayan ball game that he described as "a cross between rugby football and free fight."[3] After the second expedition, he published a book—*Mystery Cities: Exploration*

and Adventure in Lubaantun[4]—that fired the imaginations of explorers
everywhere. The showing of a Mayan relic at an imperial fair in London in
1924 brought "much prestige to the colony by proving the great antiquity of
its cultural history," an Anglican missionary wrote. "British Honduras had a
Past; she could hang ancestors on her walls."[5] One English explorer claimed
to have found a "crystal skull" with magical powers at Lubaantun. It would
inspire generations of tall tales, including the 2008 movie *Indiana Jones and
the Kingdom of the Crystal Skull*.[6]

The British Museum carried out the first full-scale excavations of the site in
1926 and 1927. Its assiduously documented digs created the first systematic
knowledge of the Maya and turned London into the center of Mayan research.
As the head of the British Museum explained:

> This expedition was an attempt on the part of this country to help a British
> colony to investigate its own past history. It seems to me that this is a duty
> which lies upon the country in one form or another, not only in British Honduras
> but elsewhere. There are parts of the world in which we have special political
> responsibilities, and it is important, it seems to me, for the credit of this coun-
> try as a civilizing agency and as civilized people, that we should show that we
> are interested in the history, the antiquities, the archaeology of these various
> countries.[7]

A plaque at the Lubaantun site today asserts that "Gann's motives were questionable and his methods were horrific as he often blasted the tops of temples
with dynamite" and asserts that the sites "would have unquestionably fared
better without Gann's 'excavations.'" To be sure, Gann's methods were crude
by modern standards. Yet as a later researcher wrote, "if Gann had not opened
those mounds, looters would have done so, or the mounds would have been
bulldozed to supply road metal or to level land for plantations, fates which
have befallen so many archaeological sites in Belize."[8] Colonial excavations
created the first sustained and systematic engagement with the archaeological
past in many countries, a past that might otherwise have been forgotten, if not
lost entirely. The cultural history of the Maya is inextricably wrapped up in
its discovery and interpretation under British colonialism.

Critics have also reproved Gann for working as the chief intelligence
officer for Britain and the United States in the colony after he retired from
medical service. "Not only was the good doctor Our Man in Belize, he was
also Their Man in Belize," two American historians noted with surprise.[9]
Gann was a perfect spy, because the Mayan sites were often found in the
borderlands near hostile Guatemala and Mexico, whose treatment of Mayan
sites and peoples was atrocious. Indeed, most of the Maya in these areas
of British Honduras had fled from forced labor and anti-Catholic pogroms

across the borders. The British not only "discovered" Mayan culture, in many cases, but they saved Mayan lives. Gann's archaeology and his espionage were of a piece. His final book in the year he died, 1938, was titled *Glories of the Maya.*[10]

Enter Alan Burns, "Our Man in Belize" for the Colonial Office. When Alan and Katie arrived in 1934, "Maya fever" was at a peak. "Throughout the colony finds are made from time to time of buried Mayan houses, pottery, flint implements, obsidian knives, jade ornaments and figurines and face masks of stone or clay," Alan wrote.[11] In his initial visits around the colony, he not only visited, or stumbled upon, Mayan ruins but also got to know the descendants of the Maya, numbering about seventeen thousand at the time, a quarter of the population. They were "the best agriculturalists in the colony," he noted, and ruled themselves peaceably through eccentric chiefs who imposed minor punishments "without much regard for the law but generally to the satisfaction of the villagers." Compared to the sharp-mouthed critics of Belize Town, the capital, Alan found the Maya a noble and pleasant people.

Alan recognized that Mayan history offered a potential source of meaning and unity for a place that had long been dismissed as nothing more than a timber settlement. "We see that the people have their bread but too often forget to let them have some butter with it, and they certainly never get any jam," he wrote.[12] To that end, he looked back on the terms of the British Museum digs of 1926 and 1927. One condition was that *half* of the finds should be returned to the colony if it ever started a museum. Alan wrote to London, asking that the museum honor the pledge. "We do not want our full half but would be grateful for a small compact collection which they might make up for us from their spoils."[13]

In taking this initiative, Alan was part of a new, broader view of colonial trusteeship. The Treaty of Versailles of 1919 had required Germany to return a sacred skull to East Africa, the first notable repatriation of a cultural relic in colonial times. In the 1930s, the colonial government of British Ceylon (today's Sri Lanka) repatriated the throne, footstool, scepter, ceremonial sword, and cross belt of the last king of the island's precolonial Kandy kingdom. Alan did not claim that the Mayan relics were "stolen," an anachronistic word for items that regularly changed hands through force, only that they were discovered and preserved and that the next logical step would be for some of them to be returned where appropriate. A senior member of the Colonial Office was skeptical: "Personally, I think this 'local collections' business can be overdone," he grumbled. "The archaeologist who already has to wander right round Europe in some cases to get a comprehensive knowledge of [the Maya] cannot be expected to go to Belize; for practical purposes, except for accidental or occasional visits, anything sent to a place like Belize is as good as lost to science."[14]

Alan did not deny that access to, and preservation of, the relics were key concerns. At the time, travel to British Honduras took weeks, and there was no adequate power supply or running water. So, he endeavored to start a small museum that was up to the task. Good fortune intervened. The Carnegie Foundation's Washington-based Institute of Archaeology and Anthropology was actively competing with the British Museum in the Americas at the time, seeing itself as the natural center for the study of cultures like the Maya.[15] The Carnegie field officer in British Honduras took a liking to Alan's "nationalist" project. The officer supported the inclusion of funding for a museum as part of a library grant that Alan had submitted. A local timber merchant donated a building next to Government House that was large enough to host both museum and library. With promises of proper ventilation and upkeep, Alan's little museum was approved. The director of the British Museum promised "a good representative series of pottery fragments and stone implements" as well as "a series of casts, from molds taken in the bush" of stone stelae.[16] Alan asked the museum to prepare labels for the selected items "to save us from our stupidity."

The arrival of the ship carrying the crates was a high point for Alan in an otherwise gloomy five years in British Honduras. Out came cave stones covered in petroglyphs, shells used in personal adornment, funerary statues, ceremonial flints, painted ceramic vessels, and casts of tall stone stelae among the trove. For good measure, the British Museum threw in reproductions of Greek statues and other non-Mayan items. The museum became so popular that the library's reading room was cut in half in order to accommodate more exhibitions. "I must confess that I found greater interest in the organizing of this museum than I did in the general administration of the colony," Alan wrote, "and it may well be that the foundation of this institution will prove of greater benefit to British Honduras than any of my normal administrative actions."[17]

In the coming years, it was the ruins of the British Honduras more than the ruins of the Maya that would demand his time. Yet the two remained linked, as if the ancient civilization exercised some occult sway over Alan's work. The remains of terraced fields from the Mayan kingdoms were the inspiration for Alan's efforts to expand agriculture. The road projects he launched frequently led to the discovery of Mayan sites. The museum also led to a critical friendship between Alan and Lord Moyne, a storied British politician, Churchill confidante, and colonial problem-solver. Moyne sailed into town aboard his yacht the *Rosaura* in 1937 after carrying out excavations on a pre-Columbian burial site at the nearby Bay Islands of Spanish Honduras. He was delighted when Alan showed him the museum, and he promised to deposit some of his finds there. When Moyne returned in 1938 heading the latest royal commission on the West Indies, he presented burial urns and clay pottery with painted designs.[18] Through this link, Alan became known to Churchill, whose bond to Moyne had been forged during a long voyage aboard the *Rosaura*. A year after Moyne's gift-giving, Alan was summoned home by Churchill at Britain's darkest hour.

Until that critical moment, the museum would provide Alan with solace amid the intractable administration of colonial rule. "Whenever I receive the official despatches from the Colonial Office," he told a friend, "I walk across the lawn to the museum and look at the Maya writings. I don't understand them either."[19]

V. S. Naipaul, the Trinidadian Nobel laureate of Indian descent, described British Honduras as a "wretched British colony, coastal timberland poached from what had been the Spanish empire, peopled with slaves and servants, and then more or less abandoned: New World debris."[20] The capital, Belize Town, was built on a stagnant mangrove swamp with decayed vegetable matter as its principal sub-soil. Mud and mosquitos occupied a lot of mental space. People sat outside with their feet wrapped in pillowcases since the colony was "just one continual itch and scratch," Alan recalled.[21] There were only twenty-seven miles of paved roads in British Honduras when Alan and Katie arrived, mostly just paths hacked through the jungle. The only links to the outside world were a twice-a-week boat to New Orleans run by the United Fruit Company and once-a-month packet service to New York. Swimming was dangerous because of sharks, and golfing was an adventure: "The Belize golf course had more than [one hundred] holes, all but nine of them made by crabs," Alan observed. The golf course was abandoned during Alan's time after an airplane skidded off a nearby runway and into the club house, destroying everything but a ping-pong table.

The colony's forest-based economy had declined in the 1920s when demand for both mahogany and chewing gum chicle collapsed. The coup de grace came with a violent hurricane in 1931 that flattened Belize Town, killing a thousand people and depositing the harbor dredger on top of the court house.[22] The town was awash with unemployed. Relief schemes were curtailed in order to balance the budget. Alan's predecessor offered the hungry five cents a day to break rocks, which the populist newspaper called "a disgrace."[23] A report on the colony issued by London shortly before Alan and Katie arrived was a counsel of despair, suggesting a retrenchment of government and more forestry.[24] It recommended the abolition of the local defense force, as if London would not mind if Guatemala, which had long claimed the colony, made good its threat.

In early 1934, an "unemployed brigade" was formed by a local barber, Antonio "Tony" Soberanis, who made lengthy speeches at Battlefield Park in the capital, which commemorated the seizure of the territory from the

Spanish by British settlers and their slaves in 1798. A "messianic and vociferous" figure, according to one historian, Soberanis' disquisitions were "often incoherent and eschatological and couched in bombastic English and thus dismissed by the Establishment as the ramblings of a lunatic."[25] A month before Alan and Katie sailed for the colony, the "Tony Movement" brought sawmills and coconut factories to a standstill and looted the public works department. Police were called in, wounding one protestor and arresting seventeen. Soberanis' colleagues sprung him from the police station by throwing two enormous snakes into the building, causing constables to flee through the windows. "The crowd of spectators roared with laughter," a newspaper reported.[26]

When Soberanis learned of Alan's appointment he told his supporters "what a hell of a time he would give the new governor," and that Alan "would meet the devil and all his angels."[27] The new governor was "urgently needed" the *Belize Independent* beseeched. "Everything is wrong with the economic condition of the colony and because this is so we are beset with evil on every side."[28]

Throughout October, Alan met in London with the former governor and anyone connected with the colony. He was heading into a crisis and wanted to be prepared. "I have formed the impression from all I have heard that the local situation is serious," he memoed the Colonial Office. People would expect him "to produce an immediate cure for all their ills, economic and political" and while the inevitable disappointment was ordinarily harmless, "conditions are not now ordinary in British Honduras."[29] Surging unemployment and poverty would "lead to civil disturbances unless something" was "speedily done."[30] Recalling the Benue bridge project in Nigeria, he begged for money to begin new roads and bridges that could be worked up into an overall development scheme. Having learned its lesson from the first riots, the Colonial Office agreed: "B.H. really is a case for something more than the indifferent smile," a staffer commented.[31]

When Katie and Alan's ship arrived, the honor guard for the welcome ceremony was late, and the officers were "untidy in appearance and improperly dressed." Alan found "an atmosphere of slackness and inefficiency" that was "a disgrace to the administration."[32] The streets of Belize were "fouled not only by the rubbish and the mango seeds that are thrown carelessly about, but by the language which is used, I regret to say, even by small children."[33] The worst surprise came when Alan and Katie walked into Government House:

> The ugly, square building was almost beyond description: one large room was furnished with garden chairs in every state of disrepair; these chairs were infested with termites and have since been condemned. Two of the tables had lost a leg each and had to be propped against the wall, while one of the settees

harbored a nest of mice. The furniture in the upper hall consists of old packing cases covered with chintz; it has not been possible to replace this "period" furniture. When there are visitors staying in the house the supply of clean linen becomes a problem which can only be solved by methods which would be embarrassing if they were not so amazing.[34]

Katie was never happy here. Economic depression had brought an abrupt end to the colonial high-life. The newly ennobled "Lady Burns" worked with single mothers to create a savings scheme that she supplemented with her own money. She pressed local merchants for food packages for the poor. The days of tennis and dancing in the Bahamas were long gone. Katie's garden at Government House and her bets on local ponies were among the few diversions. The gubernatorial car sank into mud the first day it was used and had to be abandoned. Dickie and Barbara were brought out once until Katie decided to send them back to boarding school in England. Things got so bad that when local protestors threatened to circulate a petition demanding Alan's removal, he told them that Katie would be the first to sign, and that he would forward it to the Colonial Office with his strongest recommendation. The protest leader "departed on his errand shaking his head sadly and obviously in grave doubts as to" Alan's "sanity."[35]

The truth is that these were the most difficult years in the couple's life. The mandarins in London often wrote as if they had sent Alan to a wasteland: "Burns has a very difficult row to hoe in Belize," a Colonial Office staffer wrote.[36] The secretary for colonies was asked to append encouraging personal notes to all correspondence to "keep him cheerful in surroundings where every such help is needed."[37] Alan was "Our Man in Belize" in every sense of the word: dependable, loyal, and willing to accept the hardship posting without complaint. Yet his mandate was seemingly impossible.

Alan threw down the gauntlet as soon as he arrived, congratulating police on their handling of Tony the Barber's riots and warning protestors they were "doing nothing but harm to themselves."[38] In a colony with so many people descended from slaves, it was important "to use . . . freedom in the proper way and not to abuse it."[39] He took to the road (and river) to visit the remote corners of the colony, visiting places that had never seen a colonial administrator, much less a governor. He was "not the sort of governor to let the grass grow under his feet," the Colonial Office observed.[40] When a group of farmers arrived by boat from the south seeking an audience over tax arrears, Alan ushered them into Government House and promised relief. They left "highly gratified and with happy expressions upon their lips," reported the *Belize Independent*, the opposition newspaper.[41] After that, Alan maintained an open door policy. No one should riot if they had not bothered to visit Government House. The *Belize Independent* at first sang his praises for having "already significantly demonstrated that he" was "capable of steering us in the right course."[42]

There were reasons for optimism. New rice mills and sugar factories were opening, and planters were gaining access to land to grow beans, bananas, and corn. New houses were under construction, and agricultural extension officers were generating interest among farmers. The Colonial Office called Alan's first report "the most cheering document" they had "received from British Honduras for years."[43] Still, Alan believed the recovery was fragile and that without a splurge of public investment, the Battlefield orators would continue to attract adherents: "The people have behaved in the circumstances, with admirable restraint but their tempers are rising and matters must come to a head within a few months unless something is done." The belt-tightening prescribed by the official report before his arrival was penny-wise but pound-foolish. "A disastrous epidemic, or an equally disastrous explosion of public feeling, would probably cost far more in the long run than expenditure on public works."[44] His warning frightened London into action: "If Burns (with his knowledge of West Indies) writes as he does in this despatch, you may be sure that he is not exaggerating[,] and it is up to us to give him all the help we can."[45]

Almost on cue, Soberanis led the biggest labor protest yet at a government project at Stann Creek in the south six weeks after Alan's arrival. About four hundred members of the "unemployed brigade" brought a railway to a standstill, encouraging workers to demand higher wages. Alan sent police reinforcements to disperse the strikers and instructed the head of the railway to refuse to employ them. "The peace and order of the colony shall be maintained at all costs," he warned.[46] By this time, Alan's reputation preceded him: "Burns will undoubtedly act with vigor," the Colonial Office assured the cabinet.

Soberanis skipped town before police arrived. Alan instructed his staff to watch his every move in the following months. Their chance came in late 1935 when Soberanis tried to start another strike in the north of the colony. Alan told the local prosecutor to bring charges on seven counts, including sedition and threatening public safety. He imposed a curfew on protests and sent a Creole district commissioner to serve as magistrate, because he did not want the trial to be "a black-white affair."[47] By now, his dislike of the man was palpable. "I hope that 'Tony' will be put away for a good long sentence, and that the Chief Justice does not release him on appeal. It is intolerable that my time, and the time of others, should be wasted on his doings."[48] Alas, colonial law applied to governors as well as commoners. Without enough witnesses to testify, and with a magistrate determined to be fair, all the charges were dropped or the sentences suspended. Soberanis walked free.

Feeling emboldened, Soberanis petitioned to hold a demonstration on the grounds of Government House. When Alan refused, Soberanis derided him as "despotic" and "wicked and malicious."[49] Alan's counterpart in Jamaica— facing similar unrest—had succumbed to a heart attack, and the *Belize Independent* warned that "our fragile administration with Governor Burns may have a worse ending."[50] A few months later, Soberanis staged a satire at the Battlefield set in the fictional colony of Little Paradise in which protestors confronted a Governor Barnes. It was called "When Crooks Meet Crooks" and ended with the chorus's singing "good riddance to bad rubbish" as the drunken governor staggered off stage.[51]

Alan dismissed the Tony Movement as "professional agitators" who "shrank with horror from any offer of employment. . . . Not only were the agitators irresponsible, but they were also very ignorant and stupid. Their nightly vapourings on the 'Battlefield' contained very little except abuse," he sniffed.[52] They were paid, Alan believed, by the local chicle magnate Robert Turton, the same man who contributed the building for his library and museum. A part owner of the Wrigley Chewing Gum Company of Chicago, Turton's aim in Alan's view was to toss out the Brits in order to expand American influence.[53] Yet Turton was also a responsible legislator and a keen mind. If the colonial government was to retain the loyalty of such men, Alan believed, it would need to show that it was a more dependable steward of the colony's future than the Battlefield orators. The way to do that, he believed, was with roads.

In early 1935, the American millionaire William Vanderbilt II put into Belize for yacht repairs. Alan and Katie joined him aloft in his yacht's seaplane for a one hour excursion. There, Alan saw in monotonous green the stunning absence of a road network.[54] When he returned to his office, he sketched out plans for a national road network. "As you will see, I am neither an artist nor a cartographer," he wrote to his staff of the scribbling.[55]

While the need for roads had long been recognized, expansion had been thwarted by the local forestry industry, which relied on rivers and whose leaders kept a tight grip on power. For Alan, this was the critical blockage: "Without roads, I can see no future for British Honduras other than one of bankruptcy, accompanied with a steady and accelerating decline in the physical and moral welfare of the inhabitants," he wrote glumly to London.[56] Roads would bring diversified agriculture and new settlements. "I consider agriculture to be the last hope of British Honduras and the construction of roads to be the only hope for agriculture. Failing this, the country must deteriorate."[57] An expansion of agriculture would also broaden political power, "for economic freedom is an essential preliminary to political independence," he asserted.[58]

Local critics, he predicted, would contend that "the roads should be built in some other direction, that they should run a mile or two miles more to the east or to the west, and that the bridges" were being "placed in the wrong position." Such second-guessing would not be tolerated. "I will not allow any criticisms at this stage to divert me from my purpose."[59]

Alan's appeals for loans and grants from London jibed with a fundamental shift toward economic development in the British Empire. A Colonial Development Fund had been created in 1928 which dispensed over £8 million (about $1 billion in today's money) to over 800 projects between 1929 and 1939, half of it as outright grants.[60] Alan became known as the "begging governor" for his constant requests.[61] When consideration of one request was delayed, he called it "a confession that the Government considers British Honduras as past hope and foredoomed forever to bankruptcy and despair."[62] During his term, loans and grants to the colony from the fund amounted to $990,000 (about $15 million today), accounting for a third of government revenues. "It is up to us to give him all the help we can," the Colonial Office explained.[63] The *Belize Independent* observed that "the whole of Sir Alan's term might be said to have been practically spent in directing the expenditure of free grants."[64]

The roads required deft diplomacy. The completion of Alan's trunk road to the west would have met a long-standing Guatemalan demand for access to the Caribbean for its northern region. Alan kept the border open to traders despite occasional incursions by Guatemalan soldiers, and the Guatemalans did not menace the road crews as they neared the border. Alan's only regret was that a paved border crossing was never completed, because London refused to allow him to talk directly with the president. "I feel certain that with a man of this sort some reasonable compromise could have been arrived at if the matter could have been discussed in a friendly way."[65]

No such proscription applied to Mexico, even though it had declared itself a communist country in 1935 and was in the process of nationalizing British oil assets. Alan became close friends with the general in charge of the bordering state, where he frequently went for lunch (see figure 7.1). Even as their masters feuded, Alan and the general became close friends. When the general stayed with Alan and Katie at Government House, he "apologized for not wearing a dinner jacket in the evening; this bourgeois garment had been banned by the President." The unlikely friendship "was of some benefit to our two countries," Alan pointed, not least because of the speedy completion of the road north.

During Alan's time roads, bridges, sewers, water towers, electricity systems, port facilities, latrines, and sanitary markets were constructed. Like libraries, maps, and archaeology, the expansion of infrastructure has found its way into the cross-hairs of later critics as yet another wicked colonial undertaking. It was intended to subdue restive populations rather than bring

Figure 7.1 Official Lunch in Chetumal, Mexico, 1936. *Source*: Private Collection of Alan Dixon.

genuine economic development, the critics charge, "the employment of idle hands lest the devil find work for them," according to one scholar.[66] A Marxist historian lamented that Alan was "successful in mobilizing middle-class reformers and British funds in his drive to subdue mass politics."[67]

It is true that both Alan and the Colonial Office were concerned about unemployment. On one occasion, London released funds "to prevent disturbances due to unemployment" after Alan had warned of "a serious situation."[68] Alan informed local newspapers when emergency funds were available for small public works—sidewalks, retaining walls, canal resurfacing, bridge painting—"with a view to relieving unemployment."[69] He made a point of publicizing every major grant from the Colonial Development Fund in order to show up the Battlefield orators. "The ground has been cut from under their feet," he reported after one large grant was announced.[70]

But if his aim was mere pacification, the projects were not so efficient. The unemployed who failed to win jobs on relief projects or road crews often rioted. The details of the projects also became a topic of local debate and, in the view of the *Belize Independent*, caused "bitter hatred for British administration."[71] If the British were merely trying to tamp down unrest, the use of repression would have been more effective.

Instead, Alan's motivation was to kick-start sustained growth and in the process to wean the colony's middle classes off the idea that London owed them a living. The clarifying moment came in 1936 at the opening of a bridge over the entrance to the Belize River in the capital that replaced a ferry service. "There is something I need to say to the people of British Honduras that badly needs saying," he began, Katie and Dickie at his side:

> This bridge has been designed by competent authorities qualified to express an opinion upon bridge designs. We can therefore afford to ignore the uninformed and sometimes extremely foolish criticisms that have been directed against it. Let me make it quite clear that I welcome intelligent and constructive criticism, but not the criticism that is actuated by malice, as so much criticism unfortunately is. . . . It was by my direction that it was designed as a one-way bridge and for this I accept full responsibility. I have been amazed at the attitude of mind of those who have criticized this decision. If a car on one bank of the river had to wait while half a dozen other cars crossed the bridge, the saving of time would still be very considerable as compared with the old ferry which has been sufficient for you for so many years. But I know that it is only for a love of talking and a love of finding fault that these criticisms have been made. And I am quite sure that if the bridge had been made forty feet wide, it would still have been criticized, possibly because it was constructed only of concrete when marble would have been so much better.[72]

If there was a moment when Alan Burns, colonial civil servant, became Sir Alan Burns, defender of European colonialism, this was it. The personality so evident here would remain his trademark. Why apologize for colonialism when it was so obviously better than the alternatives? The scolding at the Haulover Bridge continued:

> This bridge has been built by the taxpayers of the United Kingdom . . . and I for one consider it a generous gift to the people of this colony. . . . If the people of this colony want a better bridge they can pay for it. . . . I am glad and thankful to admit that what I have said and what I am going to say does not apply to all. There are, thank God, some thoughtful people in the colony. . . . But I have thought it necessary to speak in this fashion because I have been surprised and disgusted by the apparent lack of appreciation by some of the people of the British Honduras. . . . This money has come not out of the hat of a conjuror or from some other mysterious source but from the pockets of long-suffering British taxpayers. I could wish that this fact would be appreciated by the people of British Honduras at its full significance. My wife will now perform the opening

ceremony and I propose then to drive across the bridge. I, for one, shall be thankful that I need no longer cross the river by means of an antiquated ferry.

As time passed, His Excellency's "pointed speech" at the Haulover Bridge would be seen as a clarifying moment in British Honduras history. For the *Belize Independent*, it showed his "defiance of any criticism from the masses" and an attitude of "arrogance rather than service."[73] But for most in the colony, including "the masses," it was a gamble that showed his mastery of the local political situation. The Battlefield radicals were silenced by his appeal to good governance and prudent decisions. "No one will deny that Governor Burns is one of the best governors that have ever come to British Honduras. His accomplishments are so evident that it is unnecessary to name them," another writer for the *Belize Independent* would assert, citing roads and bridges at the top of the list.[74] By the time Alan and Katie left, the colony's 27 miles of all-weather roads had grown to 250 miles either completed or under construction. Soberanis' attempts to stir up unrest sputtered even as unemployment remained high.[75] Objective public goods coupled with a robust public defense of colonial rule had cut the ground from under their feet. A new motoring public appeared that had better things to do than listen to tirades in Battlefield Park. "The people of Belize [Town] are slowly learning, through the medium of the improved roads, that their town is not the whole colony, and the effect on their mentality is a good one," Alan wrote to London, noting surging imports of cars and fuel. "These people are discovering the country for themselves with the enthusiasm of explorers."[76]

Alongside infrastructure came new social spending. Alan's partner in this effort was Vivian Seay, a social reformer who headed the local black nurses' association and served as a sort of den mother to the colony as a whole. When "Nurse Seay" spoke, people listened. With Katie as patron of her various charities, she worked assiduously for mothers' education and social relief. The nurses' association was a key part of Alan's major social innovation while governor: the public funding of child welfare clinics where mothers would learn about infant health and nutrition. Seay authored a proposal sent to London in Alan's name for a land settlement program for women and advised him on teacher training.

Alan and Seay—the white governor and the black social worker—were of one mind that social uplift, not street protest, was the key to political advance. "If education in British Honduras is to consist of a number of ignorant and untrained teachers instructing undernourished children, it seems to me difficult to expect anything very much in the way of citizenship from the inhabitants," Alan wrote in one grant request coauthored with Seay.[77] When Alan awarded Seay a medal of honor, he contrasted her "service to the country" with the "talkative critics" who contributed nothing. "Speechmaking has become an epidemic which the nurses should cure," he joked.[78] Latter-day critics accuse Nurse Seay of "reproducing class and race hierarchies and perpetuating colonial rule," in the heated prose of one armchair reformer. Her efforts to distribute food aid to poor mothers were intended to "thwart class revolt," while her cardinal sin was to have become a "close collaborator" with Alan, in the words of an American scholar.[79] An alternative view is that Seay and the colony's black and mixed-race middle classes were more prudent stewards of the country's future than the Battlefield apostles. They recognized the palpable danger that the Tony Movement represented, not just to the nascent economic recovery of the colony but to the ordered stability of colonial life. The "negative aspects and tenor" of the Battlefield plans were "distasteful and even repulsive to the middle-class Creole elite," one historian noted.[80] Alan believed that the attacks on him from the Battlefield "may indeed have done me good by winning for me the support of decent people who might otherwise have been lukewarm."[81]

Back in London, Alan's efforts attracted high-level admiration. "I have been watching Burns's work very closely, and I am convinced that at last we have got in Honduras a man of sound judgement and real keenness," the secretary for colonies wrote. "I have felt pretty hopeless about Honduras in the past, but if it is ever to be pulled 'round, I think Burns will do it."[82]

By the 1930s, most colonial governments were under pressure to set out a plan for self-government if not outright independence. India was the furthest along, and African, Asian, and Caribbean nationalists wanted to follow. Good government was losing its appeal amid the allure of self-government. British socialists and communists, including Alan's brother Emile, were calling for the empire to be handed over to the League of Nations. The *Belize Independent* columnist and Battlefield general Luke Kemp told his readers that they should follow the advice of Emile, "reputed to be the greatest exponent of the Marxist (communist) doctrine in England" and treat colonial rulers like his brother as temporary "aliens."[83] "It is the 'great brains' that ran this colony to the rocks. Now we ask that men we feel are honest be given a chance," Kemp demanded.[84] Universal suffrage was needed, because national unity would "be as strong as the political latitude granted to the entire population."[85] When colonial officials complained about the desultory singing of *God Save the King* on one occasion, Kemp riposted: "I am quite sure the English taxpayers and the Secretary of State for the colonies would be shocked at the result of a plebiscite in British Honduras as to whether a change to the *Stars and Stripes* would be desired."[86]

London had imposed direct rule on British Honduras after the 1931 hurricane to speed recovery. Alan returned the colony to partial self-rule in 1936 with the election of 5 of the 13 seats in the legislature. He gave women the vote for the first time. Even so, the number of votes cast in the 1936 election was a meager 1,300 (less than 5 percent of the adult population), compared to 1,900 in the election before direct rule. Many people had fallen below the income or property thresholds, while others simply could not be bothered to register or vote. Most of the votes, about 1,200, were cast for the two seats in Belize Town. Of the other three seats, two were acclaimed. One returned a candidate whose nomination papers had been signed by a road crew. Robert Turton, the chewing gum nationalist, won the northern chicle district by sixty-five votes to forty-four.[87] Given Alan's legislative experience in the Bahamas and his "great ability as a speaker," the *Belize Independent* bemoaned, the government bloc in the legislature—consisting of six officials and two appointees—was "so well clothed with power that their position" was "nigh impregnable."[88] Alan was "a Mussolini" for the way he "swept aside" opposing views in legislative sessions.[89]

As in the Bahamas, London argued that any attempt to loosen voting qualifications would cause a backlash from white elites fearing mob rule. Luke Kemp, for instance, wanted only blacks and Creoles to be given the vote under his "natives first"[90] plan. The Maya would be relegated to a secondary role while whites would be disenfranchised or even expelled.[91] Kemp wrote that "fascism or Nazism is a superior form of government" to colonial rule "for food, shelter, and medical treatment are within the reach of citizens and it is only the small minority that suffers unjustly."[92] Soberanis and Kemp appealed for "closer association" with military-ruled Guatemala despite its comparative poverty and instability.[93] Law and order "would be so under any flag," Kemp wrote.[94]

Just as Haiti provided a sobering reminder to citizens of the Bahamas of the dangers of popular government, Guatemala, which had thrown off the colonial "yoke" in 1821 and similarly descended into a century of chaos, did so for British Honduras. When Alan arrived, the conditions of the working class in Guatemala were far worse than in British Honduras, and labor leaders there were simply killed by the government. For the colony's middle classes, a populist politics that led to control by Guatemala or by a native fascist regime would spell disaster. When Guatemala mobilized troops on the border in 1938, even the *Belize Independent* scurried for cover: "British Honduras must ever remain a British colony."[95]

For Alan, demands for political advance were rooted in demands for social dignity. "The one problem at the bottom of all their troubles, and the ones for which they passionately seek a solution, is how they are to obtain from the white world that recognition of social and political equality which has, up to now, been denied them," he would write. When the German boxer Max Schmeling defeated the black American boxer Joe Louis in the first of their two fights in 1936, Alan recalled, "The gloom among the coloured inhabitants of British Honduras was worthy of a major national disaster." Colonialism had, for better or worse, brought "social restrictions and personal insults" to subject peoples which prevented them "from recognizing or admitting" its great benefits. "The inevitable effect of this is that the unthinking mob . . . will follow the noisy and irresponsible persons who freely express their hatred of the white man and promise the people fantastic and impossible things."[96] The task was to expand democracy without handing over power to demagogues. Holding ultimate power in the hands of the governor for as long as possible, Alan would later write, was critical because it "ensured that British humanitarian and liberal principles should prevail, for the benefit of the underprivileged and often illiterate classes, against the selfish policies of the members of the old Assemblies."[97]

Alan drove this lesson home in his reform of the Belize Town Board. Since its founding in 1912, the board had been treated as the de facto democratic legislature of the colony because of its elected majority (eight out of fourteen seats). Board members typically debated issues far outside their purview, and the board was diligently covered in the local press. But it was also dysfunctional, constantly in turmoil over committee battles and mutual recriminations. It failed to collect most of its taxes and most of its elected members were in arrears on their own taxes.[98] One local merchant called it "effete, dishonest, and a menace to the progress of our City."[99] Without consultation or explanation, Alan cut it down to five elected and five appointed members for the 1936 election.

The act by *Il Duce* caused outrage on the Battlefield. But locals noticed that municipal affairs were working better and that day-laborers on town projects were being paid on time. A new "Sanitary Brigade" kitted in khaki replaced the slovenly food market and street inspectors of the defunct board. In 1938, Alan suspended the board altogether pending a reorganization. He made himself chairman of an interim board and was seen on the streets inspecting clogged drains and filthy latrines. Kemp eventually admitted that "90 percent of the citizens of Belize wanted the defunct board to be abolished" and congratulated Alan on "a master step."[100] Alan had proven his point: when faced with a choice between good government and elected government, colonial peoples would prefer the former. Clean latrines and operable sewers might not stir the passions on the Battlefield, but they made lives better and laid the foundations for durable democracy.

True to his word, Alan restored the democratic nature of the Belize Town Board in 1939 with six elected and three nominated members. All nine were non-European, marking the first all-local and majority-elected council in the colony's history.[101] He also added one elected member to the colonial legislature in the 1939 election, replacing a nominated member, leaving the government bloc with a slim majority of just seven to six.

In these ways, Alan was balancing his liberal instincts with his attention to administrative efficiency. "It is not logical," he would write, to tell colonial subjects that "all men are equal before the law and then to deny him the equality which he claims."[102] Democracy was clearly desirable. On the other hand, if that "right" came at the cost of death and destruction, it would be a poor trade. Like his growing interest in racial questions, his political reforms in British Honduras presaged a growing interest in the question of when and how a colony could be brought to independence. He rejected the idea that "independence should be given forthwith to those colonials who ask for it, whatever may be their competence to govern themselves, and regardless of the consequences to the mass of the population."[103] There would be nothing noble about decolonization if it caused countries to implode. "It would probably save us a lot of trouble and win us the applause of the unthinking if we surrendered at once to all the demands for self-government and rid ourselves of the burden of trusteeship," he would later comment. "But we have a duty to the people of the dependent territories and to the world at large that it would be cowardly to shirk, and we could not later escape the responsibility and the blame for the disasters that would follow if we abandoned our trust."[104]

Alan and Katie left British Honduras in June 1939 as war loomed in Europe. Their departure was called a "leave," but everyone knew it was the end. As news of the departure spread, there was a popular outpouring. An unofficial farewell committee brought children out of schools and people into the streets. They marched beside the gubernatorial car as it rolled slowly toward the jetty on a newly paved road. The "people's farewell," as the *Belize Independent* called it, "was something really out of the ordinary." "The demonstration was far ahead of any official ceremony which might have been accorded. The turnout was exceedingly large[,] and it will be something long to be remembered."[105] Several memorials were read from a small stage at the jetty, one of which listed Alan's twenty-five greatest achievements. One local notable pledged to petition London for Alan's return if it dared to purloin their popular governor. The show of gratitude was "without parallel in the history of British Honduras and one which few colonial governors" had "ever received," the *Daily Clarion* newspaper wrote.[106] Even the *Belize Independent* commented: "There have been certain things accomplished in the past five years that will cause the administration to be long remembered."[107] Alan and Katie seemed visibly touched by the sentiments. "I am going on leave with the best of impressions," Alan remarked—a clear contrast with his arrival.

Alan did return, but only briefly a few months later having been promoted to the Colonial Office. This time, despite Katie's absence, the colony put on a proper farewell. A subscription dance was held where attendees received a souvenir brochure with a large photo of Alan. "You know as well as I do that I have made many mistakes, having not yet acquired the mantle of infallibility that I shall no doubt assume when I become a member of the Colonial Office staff," he humored the gathering.[108] A prominent business leader declared that Alan had "achieved results which far exceeded expectations."[109] Nurse Seay and even Chewing Gum Turton joined in the paeans. "His Excellency showed unmistakable marks that he was greatly touched by the occasion. His voice was somewhat faint and he appeared to have been almost overcome," the *Belize Independent* observed.[110]

Alan would later joke that there were many people in the colony "with the good name Burns and I can only hope in years to come I will not be regarded as the progenitor of all those bearing the name."[111] Yet it is not too much to say that Sir Alan Burns *is* the father of modern Belize. His actions at a critical juncture in state formation and economic development in Belize are what led the country to success. When he left, it was on a pathway more like the Bahamas. Without Alan's critical interventions in the years 1934 to 1939, British Honduras might have followed the fate of other failed ex-colonies like Guyana or Sierra Leone. It slowly transitioned to independence in 1981. Today it is richer, more democratic, and more stable than Guatemala and other Central American states. Visitors to Belize today drive into town and visit Mayan ruins on highways named after colonial-era native politicians who were part of the country's smooth transition to self-government under British tutelage. Both highways were built by Alan. Someday, perhaps, one of them will be renamed the Sir Alan Burns Highway.

By 1939, European colonial rule throughout the world had laid sure foundations for human flourishing. Demands for self-government were on the rise. But this was to be expected. It was evidence of colonial success. With enough governors like Alan, those demands could be directed toward productive ends. Crude anti-colonialism remained a fringe business in most colonies. Nothing could change that unless Europe succumbed to a disaster. The disaster began for Alan in his final year as governor of the British Honduras. One day he received a phone call from old friends in Miami he had met while in the Bahamas. They were calling on behalf of the Committee of American Jews. They needed his help.

NOTES

1. Ian Graham, *Alfred Maudslay and the Maya: A Biography* (2002), p. 82; Alfred Maudslay, *A Glimpse at Guatemala and Some Notes on the Ancient Monuments of Central America* (1899).

2. Thomas Gann, "The Ancient Monuments of Northern Honduras and the Adjacent Parts of Yucatan and Guatemala," *Journal of the Anthropological Institute of Great Britain and Ireland* (1905), pp. 111, 112.

3. "Games Played by the Ancient Maya," *Belize Independent*, January 9, 1935.

4. Thomas Gann and William Francis, *Mystery Cities: Exploration and Adventure in Lubaantun* (1925).

5. Stephen Caiger, *British Honduras: Past and Present* (1951), pp. 152–53.

6. Joseph Laycock, "The Controversial History of the Crystal Skulls: A Case Study in Interpretive Drift," *Material Religion* (2015).

7. Charles Close, J. Cooper Clark, Frederic Kenyon, and Alfred Maudslay, "The Survey of the Lubaantun District in British Honduras: Discussion," *The Geographical Journal* (1928), p. 237.

8. John Eric Sidney Thompson, "Thomas Gann in the Maya Ruins," *British Medical Journal* (1975).

9. Charles Harris and Louis Sadler, *The Archaeologist Was a Spy: Sylvanus G. Morley and the Office of Naval Intelligence* (2003), pp. 162–63.

10. Thomas Gann and William Francis, *Glories of the Maya* (1938).

11. CCC, pp. 135, 138, 133.

12. Ibid., p. 151.

13. CO/123/353/19, "ACB to Beckett," June 12, 1935.

14. CO/123/353/19, "Memo by Rawson on museum in Belize," July 15, 1935.

15. John Weeks and Jane Hill, *The Carnegie Maya: The Carnegie Institution of Washington Maya Research Program, 1913–1957* (2006).

16. CO/123/353/19, "George Hill, British Museum, to Parkinson," August 6, 1935.

17. CCC, p. 150.

18. "Lord Moyne's gift to B. Honduras library and museum," *Belize Independent*, February 22, 1939.

19. Rex Niven, *Nigerian Kaleidoscope: Memoirs of a Colonial Servant* (1982), p. 4.

20. V. S. Naipaul, *A Turn in the South* (1990), p. 33.

21. CCC, p. 153.

22. Ernest Edmund Cain, *Cyclone! Being an Illustrated Official Record of the Hurricane and Tidal Wave Which Destroyed the City of Belize, British Honduras on the 10th September 1931* (1933).

23. "Relief schemes," *Belize Independent*, March 14, 1934.

24. Colonial Office, Great Britain, *British Honduras: Financial and Economic Position: Report of the Commissioner Sir Alan Pim* (1934).

25. Peter Ashdown, "Race, Class and the Unofficial Majority in British Honduras, 1890–1949," University of Sussex, Department of History, doctoral dissertation (1979), p. 68.

26. "Snakes cause police to scamper," *Belize Independent*, October 3, 1934.

27. CO/123/346/4, "Police report on disturbances in Belize Town of October 1934," November 27, 1934.

28. "New governor," *Belize Independent*, October 3, 1934.

29. CO/123/346/4, "ACB to Colonial Office," October 1, 1934.

30. CO/123/346, "ACB to Cunliffe-Lister," October 1, 1934.

31. CO/123/352/15, "Parkinson note on British Honduras," November 17, 1934.

32. CCC, pp. 151–52; CO/123/352, "ACB to Cunliffe-Lister," April 25, 1935.

33. "The fourth annual teachers' conference," *Belize Independent*, December 30, 1936.

34. CCC, pp. 151–52; CO/123/354/5, "ACB to Colonial Office memo re: Government House," September 23, 1935.

35. CCC, p. 139.

36. CO/123/352/15, "Parkinson to Bridges (Treasury) re: Burns report," April 13, 1935.

37. CO/123/352/15, "British Honduras file notes," May 15, 1935.

38. "New governor arrives," *Belize Independent*, November 7, 1934.

39. "Emancipation Day demonstration," *Belize Independent*, August 7, 1935.

40. CO/123/368, "Minute by Poynton," June 30, 1938.

41. "People of St. Creek make representation," *Belize Independent*, December 5, 1934.

42. "That address from the governor," *Belize Independent*, May 29, 1935.

43. CO/123/349/15, "British Honduras file notes," January 7, 1935.

44. CO/123/352/15, "Burns to Cunliffe-Lister," March 31, 1935 and April 11, 1935.

45. CO/123/352/15, "Parkinson to Bridges (Treasury) re: Burns report," April 13, 1935.

46. CO/123/353/5, "File notes on Stann Creek disturbances," May 22, 1935, May 23, 1935, and June 13, 1935.

47. CO/123/354, "Burns to MacDonald," November 15, 1935.

48. CO/123/354/22, "ACB to Beckett," November 15, 1935.

49. "An open letter to His Excellency the Governor," *Belize Independent*, October 23, 1935.

50. "The Animus," *Belize Independent*, June 8, 1938.

51. "Battlefield group staged comic sketch," *Belize Independent*, March 4, 1936.

52. CCC, p. 137.

53. Cedric Grant, *The Making of Modern Belize: Politics, Society & British Colonialism in Central America* (1976), pp. 131–32.

54. "A millionaire visits," *Belize Independent*, March 27, 1935.

55. CO/123/361/18, "ACB to Beckett," September 3, 1937.

56. CO/123/349/15, "Report on Development in British Honduras," November 28, 1934.

57. CO/123/352/10, "ACB to Colonial Office," February 25, 1935.

58. CCC, p. 209.

59. "His Excellency confident of the colony's future," *Belize Independent*, May 8, 1935.

60. Michael Havinden and David Meredith, *Colonialism and Development: Britain and Its Tropical Colonies, 1850–1960* (1993), pp. 161–63.

61. Ashdown, op. cit., p. 215.

62. CO/123/352, "Burns to Cunliffe-Lister," February 25, 1935.

63. CO/123/352, "Parkinson to Treasury," April 13, 1935.

64. "H.E.'s leave," *Belize Independent*, May 10, 1939.

65. CCC, pp. 149, 148.

66. Ashdown, op. cit., p. 71.

67. Anne Macpherson, "Citizens vs. Clients: Workingwomen and Colonial Reform in Puerto Rico and Belize, 1932–1945," *Journal of Latin American Studies* (2003), p. 296.

68. CO/123/373, "Treasury to Colonial Office," May 16, 1939; CO/123/373, "ACB to MacDonald," March 13, 1939.

69. "Happenings," *Belize Independent*, March 22, 1939.

70. CO/123/352/10, "ACB to Beckett," May 1, 1935; "Big free grants from imperial government for road programme," *Belize Independent*, May 1, 1935.

71. "The labour problem," *Belize Independent*, March 4, 1936.

72. "The Haulover Bridge opened; His Excellency makes pointed speech," *Belize Independent*, June 3, 1936.

73. "Intelligence needed in Education Department," *Belize Independent*, July 13, 1938.

74. "Retention of Governor Burns," *Belize Independent*, March 30, 1938.

75. CO/123/367/7, "Report on police meeting with Antonio Soberanis," June 21, 1938.

76. CO/123/356/6, "ACB memorandum on roads and bridges," April 8, 1936.

77. CO/123/354/5, "ACB on British Honduras estimates," May 12, 1936.

78. "Black Cross Nurses stage another meeting at Liberty Hall," *Belize Independent*, June 26, 1935.

79. Anne Macpherson, "Colonial Matriarchs: Garveyism, Maternalism, and Belize's Black Cross Nurses, 1920–1952," *Gender & History* (2003), pp. 522, 518, 515.

80. Grant, op. cit., p. 110.

81. CCC, p. 138.

82. CO/123/352/10, "Cunliffe-Lister to Campell," April 18, 1935.

83. "The 'prophesy' according to the professed 'Saint' Alan," *Belize Independent*, May 26, 1937.

84. "Bye-edges," *Belize Independent*, April 1, 1936.

85. "The election," *Belize Independent*, March 15, 1939.

86. "Crown colony government," *Belize Independent*, October 28, 1936.

87. "'Ayuso tops the poll in election fight' and 'R.S. Turton elected in the north,'" *Belize Independent*, February 12, 1936.

88. "A big contest," *Belize Independent*, January 15, 1936.

89. "The legislature and the estimates: A huge joke," *Belize Independent*, October 21, 1936.

90. "More about natives first," *Belize Independent*, February 26, 1936.

91. Grant, op. cit., p. 109.

92. "Britain, Mexico, or Guatemala?" *Belize Independent*, February 8, 1939.

93. Antonio Soberanis and Luke Kemp, *The Third Side of the Anglo-Guatemalan Dispute Over Belize or British Honduras* (1945).

94. "Breach of faith," *Belize Independent*, January 4, 1939.

95. "Annexation," *Belize Independent*, June 8, 1938.

96. CP, pp. 39, 11, 61, 140; IDOC, p. 20.

97. Alan Burns, "The History of Commonwealth Parliaments," in Alan Burns (ed.), *Parliament as an Export* (1966), p. 25.

98. "Insufficient," *Belize Independent*, November 11, 1936.

99. "Open letter to His Excellency the Governor," *Belize Independent*, December 9, 1936.

100. "'The new board and the new constitution' and 'The interest of taxpayers and the lower strata,'" *Belize Independent*, February 2 and January 26, 1938.

101. "Town Board," *Belize Independent*, January 11, 1939.

102. CP, p. 10.

103. CBAA, p. 299.

104. OPT, p. 8.

105. "Governor's departure," *Belize Independent*, June 21, 1939.

106. "Governor departs," *Daily Clarion*, June 15, 1939.

107. "H.E. Promoted," *Belize Independent*, November 1, 1939.

108. CCC, pp. 153–54.

109. "British Honduras advances," *Belize Independent*, October 16, 1935.

110. "Farewell for Governor Burns," *Belize Independent*, November 29, 1939.

111. CCC, p. 133.

Part II

THE SEA WE FEAR

Chapter 8

Fifty Ships That Saved the World

Stripped of its colonies after World War I and then put under international supervision by the Treaty of Versailles, Germany began to see itself as an oppressed nation. No longer part of the colonial club, it became part of the anti-colonial club. Adof Hitler considered colonialism a project of Jews, capitalists, weak-kneed Christians, and liberal cosmopolitans. The racial mixing that resulted from colonialism was as abhorrent to Hitler as it was to later anti-colonial critics, both of whom wanted to draw artificial boundaries around peoples in the name of racial purity. Nationalists in Indonesia, Palestine, India, Egypt, and Algeria, who in the 1920s had drawn support from Moscow's League Against Imperialism, were quick to see in the Nazis a powerful new international sponsor of their illiberal ambitions. They admired the fascist organizations that sprung up under Hitler and in Japan and imitated them in their own ranks.[1] The Nazi ideas of racial competition meshed perfectly with doctrines like Afrocentrism, pan-Asianism, and Arab nationalism. Battlefield radicals in British Honduras, like their counterparts in India, made contact with Japanese fascists, asking that they "liberate" the colony from European rule.[2] When Moscow and Berlin became allies in 1939, it was for anti-colonialists the most natural thing. They saw more clearly than liberals the fundamental affinity between anti-colonialism and the threat to liberal society.

The Nazi doctrine, Alan wrote, was a "catastrophic" relapse of European civilization that was "universally condemned." There was, in Alan's mind, a perfect consistency in opposing illiberal fascism and supporting liberal colonialism. "If Britain had not held the pass against Germany in 1940, the war might well have been lost with direful effects on the coloured races of the world," he would write, noting Hitler's claims in *Mein Kampf* that one might as well train "poodles" for self-government. "What chance would they have had under a triumphant Hitler?"[3]

Given their admiration for fascism, agitators in the colonies felt betrayed by Benito Mussolini's occupation of Abyssinia (Ethiopia) in 1935. It "provoked a remarkable demonstration of feeling" in British Honduras, Alan recalled. There was "rioting caused by sympathy for the Abyssinians and the belief that the European Powers were secretly supporting Mussolini." As the invasion progressed, "[Abyssinia] became a symbol of the unity of colour, and the Ethiopian emperor was regarded as a hero who was fighting the battle of the blacks against the tyranny of the white races."[4] It mattered little that Ethiopians despised black Africans or that the country was, in the words of Arnold Toynbee, writing a year before the invasion, "a byword for disorder and barbarity."[5]

In 1938, Washington intercepted a telegram from the fascist Italian envoy in Guatemala encouraging the Guatemalan government to invade British Honduras and promising equipment.[6] The envoy compared British Honduras to Italy's own "lost territory" of Abyssinia. Guatemala took the opportunity of the outbreak of hostilities in Europe to reassert its claims.[7] "If Great Britain were involved in a European war, it might well seem to the Guatemalan government that a suitable opportunity had arisen," Alan warned London.[8] Guatemala's 20,000-member army, the telegram noted, could easily overrun the small volunteer force in the British Honduras. The Foreign Office told Alan that it would be "insane" for Guatemala to act, not least because the same Italian envoy was plotting with his local German counterpart to replace the Guatemalan government with a Nazi puppet regime in the event of a border war. Alan was taking no chances. He doubled the size of the local defense force to 7 officers and 200 soldiers and requested that the "quite outrageous" claims being made by Guatemala be scotched through a friendly question in Parliament.[9]

Once the European war erupted, all manpower was diverted to Europe. British Honduras dug in to defend itself with nothing more than a dozen armed police. Guatemala prudently backed off during the war. German submarines sniffed around Belize several times but never engaged. British Honduras contributed sixty soldiers (out of thousands who volunteered) and one officer to a West Indies Regiment formed in 1944. The regiment was sent to perform garrison duties in Egypt where its only action was a bar brawl with American troops in Cairo.[10] The colony's other contribution was the dispatch of 855 lumberjacks to cut trees in Scotland when imported wood became scarce due to German submarines.

For Alan, the war would prove the enduring legitimacy of British colonial rule. "When we of the British empire stood against the Axis, with our Allies overwhelmed by the Germans, and our own armies defeated," he recalled,

"when our enemies exulted over our impending ruin, and even our friends had
abandoned hope, this was the time when our colonies stood by us—friends
indeed, and true loyal friends."[11]

World opinion had long assumed that Jews forced out of Europe by Hitler
would migrate to the British mandate in Palestine. Mounting Jewish-Arab
violence there caused diplomats and philanthropists to seek other places.
The urgent phone call to Alan in 1938 was a request for a landing permit for
a group of Jewish refugees. British Honduras loomed large in early discussions of a future Jewish homeland, and American Jewish groups approached
the Colonial Office about settlement there "on a quite extensive scale."[12]
Proponents included the editor of the *Crown Colonist* magazine, the diary of
colonial affairs, who enthused that "an invasion of Jewish energy, brains, and
capital similar to that experienced in Palestine would be a godsend." Success
might prompt other colonies to solicit Jewish groups: "There is indeed no colony which might not benefit from some influx, even though small, of Jewish
talent, thus adding to the loyal and contended citizens of the Empire."[13] A former Anglican bishop of British Honduras called it a "God-sent opportunity"
for "moral and spiritual growth."[14]

Alan expressed doubt that settlers from Europe of whatever background
could thrive in the colony, a view shared by his chief medical officer.[15] But
he saw no reason why they should not be allowed to try, especially because
the initial schemes involved private, not public, land. "Can we legally (or
morally) be justified in preventing a private land owner from developing his
land by refusing to allow him to import settlers for the purpose?" he challenged London.[16]

The Colonial Office was cautious. It worried that a landing permit might
signal "agreement to the foundation of a Jewish home in British Honduras."
Inevitably many would die, and "there would be plenty of busybodies who
would make a fuss in parliament and blame the Colonial Office." Despite
reservations, one staffer wrote, "I cannot help feeling that the proper course
is for the secretary of state to say: 'Go ahead and make the best job of it
you can.'" After all, London noted, "agriculture is Sir Alan Burns' main
enthusiasm."[17]

The scheme was on the verge of approval when the Western world failed
at the American-convened Evian Conference of July 1938 to agree on a
global plan for Jewish resettlement. Britain's delegates to the conference
were instructed to avoid any suggestion of settlement in British Honduras.[18]
A month after Alan and Katie's departure, a boatload of refugees was cruelly refused a landing permit at Belize.[19] Only the following year, as the
situation in Europe deteriorated, did the Colonial Office relent. An industrial
project was approved for five hundred settlers in the west of the colony near

Guatemala.[20] By then, most Jews had lost interest in the Caribbean and had turned their sights on Palestine. The resulting rise in anti-colonial violence by Zionist groups there closed the door on discussions of Jewish settlement in other British colonies.[21]

If Alan regretted his inability to do more for the Jews, he could take comfort from sister Essie's rescue of a young Jewish girl. Gertrude Villance had been sent to England by her parents in Vienna shortly before they disappeared into Nazi death camps. She was raised, and her Jewish identity and faith nurtured, at Essie's Catholic convent school. Gertrude was a fixture at Burns family gatherings during the war. She would remain in the family until 1948, when she emigrated to the new state of Israel.

The British Empire that Alan served was the author of that Jewish homeland. It was the British mandate in Palestine, far more than any policy pronouncements by London, that led to Jewish settlement there, and it was the British Empire that was on the spot under the desert adventurer T. E. Lawrence "of Arabia" to claim the mandate when the Ottoman Empire collapsed in 1914. British colonialism begat the mandate, and the mandate begat Israel.

Alan was sympathetic to the Jews, an admirable people who lived peaceably and productively. The "sickly sentiment of Christianity" offering love and comfort to all, Alan wrote facetiously, had been rejected by Hitler and others who preached the superiority of Protestant white races. These bigots were "extremely difficult to take seriously," not least because of their bizarre claims that Jesus was not a Jew and that Mary was a blonde.[22] At the same time, Alan was frustrated by Jewish anti-colonial violence in Palestine, a view shared by most British Jews. The frustration was personal for Alan. His friend Lord Moyne, who had sailed into Belize with gifts for the Maya museum in 1938, would be shot dead in 1944 by Zionists who thrust their pistols into his car window as he returned home one evening in Cairo.

The Jewish saga would never be far from Alan's mind. He received firsthand accounts of events in Palestine from Henry Gurney, his first chief secretary when he became governor of the Gold Coast, who in 1946 was transferred to be chief secretary of Palestine. "Nearly all British officers start here with some sympathy for the Jewish cause or at least an open mind but find it impossible to maintain," Gurney wrote to Alan from Jerusalem.[23] "Never having run a government of their own, they have no political sense whatever." The constant bombings and assassinations by Zionists showed "the state of affairs that responsible leaders of a community can create when they are always against the government."

It was a further, bitter result of Zionist anti-colonialism that Gurney would become governor of Malaya in 1948 rather than Alan, the initial choice. A China-backed communist insurgency was spreading in Malaya, and Gurney was thought suited to the job because of his experience in Palestine.[24] "You may have received some consolation in that the lot did not fall upon you when you have been surveying from afar our recent troubles in Malaya," a Colonial Office friend wrote.[25] In 1951, Gurney's car was ambushed by insurgents north of Kuala Lumpur. He fell in a hail of bullets drawing fire away from his wife and driver. "He died at the hands of a youthful fanatic who had no personal grievance against the man he killed but was stimulated to his deed by the words of others," Alan lamented.[26] That phone call from Miami in 1938 presaged for Alan the loss of two close friends and a world conflagration that would bring the British Empire to the brink of collapse.

Alan expected a plum governorship when the war broke out. Instead, he was offered a temporary position in the Colonial Office. "Of course the idea is that you move on to another governorship," a senior official assured him.[27] Alan and Katie's 22-month stay in London brought the Burns siblings together in one country for the first time since Cecil had left St. Kitts in 1895. Brother Bertie had been invalided out of the colonial service in 1929 and had bought a house at St. Leonards-on-Sea so that his two children could be close to Barbara, Dickie, and Aunt Essie. Playing on the beach one day in 1940, Bertie's daughter, aged 16, was strafed by a German fighter prowling along the English coast, miraculously avoiding harm. His son, aged 18, was sent to Canada as an RAF trainer, avoiding the high fatalities of the air war in Europe. Barbara and Dickie remained at the convent school throughout the German bombardment of the capital during the Blitz period from September 1940 to January 1941 along with other evacuated children.

In London, Alan and Katie had a few close calls. The German bomb that destroyed the Treasury Building in October 1940 and nearly killed Churchill blew out the windows of Alan's second floor office on Downing Street. He was moved to the top floor where the elevator was frequently out of action due to enemy attacks. He served on the fire brigades of both the Colonial Office Home Guard and of Kensington borough, where he and Katie rented a flat. "We were fortunate in suffering nothing worse than the breaking of our windows and the cutting off of our gas supply for many weeks, which made cooking almost impossible."[28]

The Blitz period saw Britain at its darkest hour, and Churchill summoned his advisors to forge what he called a "special relationship" with the United States. The first order of business was to rebuild the navy to counter German submarines. The British destroyer fleet had been reduced by half in the Dunkirk evacuation. A cabinet committee was created to negotiate with the United States for an exchange of fifty old destroyers. The "destroyers for bases" deal that would result has been widely cited as a turning point in the war. A popular 1965 book on the deal was entitled *Fifty Ships That Saved the*

World.[29] Yet the deal very nearly collapsed, and the world has Sir Alan Burns to thank that it did not.

The Americans had long sought access to British colonies in the Atlantic in order to protect the hemisphere from German threats, especially if Britain fell. The Nazi threat would be acute if Dutch, Danish, and French colonies in the Caribbean were converted to German airbases and Nazi movements spread to Central America. President Roosevelt's Anglophile advisor Dean Acheson, son of an English father and Canadian mother, came up with the idea of swapping old U.S. destroyers for bases in Newfoundland and the Caribbean. The trade would skirt U.S. neutrality laws and an isolationist Congress. Churchill immediately foresaw how the deal would "mix up" the two English-speaking democracies: "I do not view the process with any misgivings. I could not stop it if I wished. No one can stop it. Like the Mississippi, it just keeps rolling along. Let it roll. Let it roll on—full flood, inexorable, irresistible, benignant, to broader lands and better days."[30]

The destroyers-for-bases deal was announced in principle in September 1940. The details of the eight bases were to be decided by "common agreement." Despite the Churchillian rhapsody, the agreement was by no means clinched. Initial telegrams on the bases were exchanged through December without much progress. The Americans wanted absolute sovereignty over the bases. The British side was represented by Lord Lloyd, a bombastic secretary for colonies who would have none of it. "These people are gangsters, and there is only one way to deal with gangsters," he fumed.[31] Lloyd became "Churchill's principal problem" in the talks, according to one American historian, as "he stuck to his guns throughout the winter."[32] The foreign secretary agreed with Lloyd's grim conclusions but disagreed with his tough line, "as a result of which we can only lose more than we have lost already."[33] In January, the critical Lend-Lease bill began its journey through Congress and desperation seized the day on both sides. Roosevelt sent a three-man team to London for face-to-face talks.

Churchill needed a chief negotiator who understood the local sensitivities of British colonies in the Americas, got along well with Americans, was a master of detail, and was available for the job. There was an additional preference for a candidate who was not English, since by general agreement the English were still getting over the American Revolution.[34] With a broken gas cooker at home and long flights of stairs his biggest worries, the "Scots-West Indian" Sir Alan Burns was the obvious choice. During the three months of talks from January to March 1941, Alan—described by one historian who interviewed him about the deal as "a large jovial man with a sympathetic mind"[35]—was the chief negotiator for the United Kingdom in every meeting except for the symbolic opening and closing sessions.[36]

Despite later celebrations of the deal that saved the free world, the two sides came perilously close to failure. The British were keen to bring the

United States into the war as a bulwark, not spoiler, of the empire. That meant making sure that the terms of the bases did not amount to a de facto Japanese-style "liberation" of the colonies. Alan walked a fine line every day in the conference room—trying to be generous to keep the Americans happy but resisting demands that would challenge British sovereignty or cause an outcry among local populations. His poised stance nettled the Foreign Office, which wanted a quick deal. Asked by Lloyd for his first impressions of the American delegation, Alan replied, "They seem rather less anti-British than the Foreign Office."[37]

The Americans understood that Alan's role was to help local governments come to terms with the bases by blowing off steam in the talks. The colonial delegates, especially from Jamaica and Trinidad, "not unnaturally" objected to "the ways in which [the Americans] brushed aside any suggestions that the rights of local people should be considered," Alan noted.[38] When the talks stalled over American emergency powers near the bases, Alan brokered a compromise under which Washington agreed not to use the powers "unreasonably."[39] When the Bermudians threatened to abandon the talks, Alan convinced Churchill to meet them. Churchill handed around cigars. The Bermudians pocketed them as souvenirs and stayed. The stubborn Newfoundlanders were lectured by Churchill that if the deal fell through "it is impossible to say what would be the effect on the prosecution of the war and the whole future of the world."[40] Time and again, Alan was called upon to keep the talks going. "Try to spin it out amicably till the Lease and Lend Bill is through," Churchill instructed him. "A squabble now would be silly."[41]

A stroke of luck was Lord Lloyd's sudden death on February 4th. Alan considered his passing "a disaster to the colonies and to the Empire"[42] because he was the last great unapologetic imperialist to hold the post. But his dogged imperialism was a threat to the deal that arguably saved the British Empire. With Lloyd gone and replaced by the more cordial Lord Moyne, Alan was able to moderate the demands of the colonies, who could no longer appeal to a purblind secretary for colonies to back their demands.

On February 20th, Alan took a step back from the impasse to remind the colonial delegates of the stakes. Some of the proposed concessions to the United States, he wrote to his team, were consistent with the September agreement, but others were not. Above all, the Americans should not be left with the impression of "an attempt to chaffer or bargain" by the Brits beyond what they could force the colonies to accept.[43] By late February, only twelve of twenty-eight issues had been agreed. Alan was in danger of being hung out to dry as one of the "stupid obstinate officials" who were threatening Anglo-American cooperation, as an editorial in London's *Daily Express* charged when the deadlock became public.[44] The U.S. representative wrote ominously to Alan that it was time for the two sides to either make the deal "or to recognize the inability to do so."[45] The talks were in serious trouble and with them the fate of the West. If the talks had failed, Lend-Lease would have been at risk. Without Lend-Lease, Britain's prospects in the war against the Nazis would have been in the balance.

Alan worked day and night in the first week of March. Every telegram to the colonies was given his location by the hour—at home "from lunchtime until after tea" and back at the Colonial Office "from about 7:30 p.m." Yet the more he negotiated with the colonies, the more cavils they raised. Who would pay for new harbor lights? Which kind of cigarettes would be exempt from duties? Were wages for local hires to be the same as for Americans? Finally, in a meeting that week with Churchill and Moyne, Alan agreed that the only solution was to impose a deal on the colonies and hope they would not rebel. As Alan recalled: "The position was such that the British government had no option but to agree to practically everything the Americans asked for. We needed those destroyers, old as they were, so badly at that stage of the war that we were in a hopeless position for bargaining."[46]

On March 11th, Churchill, Alan, Moyne, and a member of the British admiralty met with the U.S. delegation to offer the grand bargain. "In less than five minutes [Churchill] had swept away as immaterial three-quarters of the objections which had been raised by his negotiators," the American ambassador, who was present, recalled.[47] Churchill wrote to Roosevelt that he had personally intervened "on turning the mountains back into molehills," using language that Roosevelt had put into a draft letter to Churchill shown to the U.K. ambassador, and invited Roosevelt to "lend a hand with the shovel" if he could.[48] Churchill was at his diplomatic best in suggesting that he had brought his naughty officials to heel for the sake of Washington. The deal was ratified by both sides the next day.

"I wrote the other day that Palestine work was the most exacting not to say exacerbating work which falls to the staff of the C.O. But I am very doubtful whether Bases do not have a prior claim to that distinction," Moyne wrote to Alan the following day, their last correspondence before Moyne's fateful assignment to Cairo. "It seems to me wonderful how you have stood up to it all and you must certainly have a holiday as soon as you get this famous (infamous?) document signed."[49]

The "infamous document" was signed by Churchill at Downing Street on March 27th, with Alan standing behind him (see figure 8.1). The ceremony was, according to a British historian, "deliberately engineered as a high-profile, up-beat affair in an attempt to silence murmuring contention over the merits of the agreement."[50] Souvenir pens, a new American idea to replace cigars, were handed out to the signatories. Background briefings informed the press that Churchill viewed the deal as important to "the future of Western civilization."[51] After affixing his name, Churchill stood up and turned to Alan.

Figure 8.1   Churchill Signs Bases Agreement in London, Alan Standing, 1941. *Source:* Private Collection of Alan Dixon.

"Thank you," he said, "for bringing my ship safely to port."[52] Before leaving England, the American delegates sent Alan a brief telegram: "Just to have the last word. Best of luck."

The deal was "one of the most celebrated pieces of diplomacy of the war and a milestone in the wartime Anglo-American relationship," wrote a British historian.[53] The military value was questionable. The destroyers arrived late, only nine were operational, and the rest needed repairs. Their four-inch guns had a tendency to fire themselves when loaded. Four of the ships collided because of their rusty steering, and one ran aground in New Brunswick.[54] By May 1941, only thirty were in service because of a lack of crews and the need for lengthy refits for antisubmarine work. The bases, on the other hand, were wildly popular among local populations because of the inflow of American money and goodwill. For places like Jamaica and Trinidad, the only thing worse than being colonized by the Americans, it seemed, was not being colonized by the Americans. For the Americans, they were too costly to run and were abandoned after the war.

The destroyers were "an earnest of American intent," noted one historian, which is what mattered.[55] The United States was brought into the war—and indeed into the postwar order that it would steward—as a partner rather than as a spoiler of the British Empire. The editor of the *Crown Colonist* wrote that the Americans, who thought of colonialism only "in the old and bad sense," had come to understand through the talks "not only that the structure of the British Commonwealth is democratic, but that in this democratic system there is a place provided for the colonial peoples."[56] The American ambassador agreed, noting that the British war effort "rested on the firm foundation of the loyalty and goodwill of the colonial people themselves." The talks provided an education for the Americans, whose knowledge of British colonialism seemed about 150 years out of date. "At a time when colonial empires everywhere are under constant fire of criticism," the U.S. ambassador wrote, "it is well that these relationships should be remembered and recorded."[57]

The conclusion of the bases deal freed Alan for the promised governorship. With Moyne as secretary for colonies and Churchill in his debt, he had friends to vouchsafe the promise. In July 1941, he was made governor of the Gold Coast (today's Ghana). It was the most important governorship in Britain's African colonies during the war and the apogee of Alan's long ascent in the colonial civil service.

There was little time for pomp. German fighters and submarines pursued the 50-ship convoy in which Alan, Katie, and Barbara travelled to the Gold Coast in October 1941, reflecting the closing menace of German submarines along the West African coast. A month earlier, a German submarine torpedoed and sunk a steam ship at Accra, and the following year another submarine opened fire on helpless Ghanaian fishermen.[58] Hitler seemed very close to the Gold Coast in those days. When France fell to Germany, its colonies mostly aligned with the collaborationist Vichy regime. All the colonies surrounding the Gold Coast aligned with Vichy, while only the territory on the eastern side of Nigeria aligned with the Free French.

On arrival, Alan was added to the West Africa War Council (see figure 8.2). As a decorated war veteran, he had a credibility that other governors lacked. The head of West African forces called him "easily the most efficient and effective" of the four governors on the council.[59] The council was headed by a new super-governor or "resident minister" sent from London. He was a sort of advance cabinet member in case things got really bad on the home front, just as the Free French had plans to remove to Brazzaville in the French Congo if London fell. Having spent the early war years working with Newfoundland as one possible refuge for the British government, Alan found himself on arrival in Accra preparing another.

Figure 8.2 At West Africa War Council Meeting, 1942. *Source*: Private Collection of Alan Dixon.

The resident minister sat at the center of a council that included the four West African governors, British (and later American) military officers for the region, an influx of bureaucrats from Britain overseeing logistical imperatives like shipping and commodities, and—a new development—throngs of spies engaged in intelligence gathering, misinformation, sabotage, and covert operations. Like Casablanca in war time, Accra seethed with suspicious characters using false names, "hush-hush types" as Alan called them. Much of the intrigues revolved around the evening gatherings at the American Officers Club that made Rick's Café look like a Temperance Society tea hall.

The use of code-names was an annoyance to Alan, whose strict administrative discipline required accountability by name. He might find himself playing bridge one evening with a person named "B237." A secret transmission for an agent of that description arrived in his safe box one day, and a minor bureaucratic stand-off ensued: "One of the many heads of the secret gang was asked [by my staff] to let me know who B237 was, but replied that he did not feel justified in telling me," Alan recalled. "So the letter remained in my safe until B237 came and confessed his identity."[60]

The saboteurs—mostly under Britain's Special Operations Executive, formed in 1940—were charged with disrupting shipping in and out of Vichy territories and making sure that Hitler's submarines did not get a foothold in West Africa. The military commander for the Gold Coast called the spies "a menace to the safety of the colony," according to an internal memo, and insisted that "either they must be entirely disbanded or put completely under his command." A cabinet order told the spies, "Your activities conform with wishes of local authorities, military and civil."[61] The spies in turn complained that the top brass had gone soft in the tropics, living in a "Nirvana" where the war was a distant distraction. The official "ban on bangs"—prohibiting sabotage operations in Vichy territory—was naïve, they believed. To prove the point, they carried out the greatest coup of the war in West Africa.

In early 1941, British informants learned that an Italian freighter and a German tugboat were anchored at an offshore island port in the nominally neutral but pro-Nazi Spanish colony of Spanish Guinea on the West African coast. The ships could be used to resupply submarines, allowing them to menace the West African shore. A naval commander working in the embryonic secret services in Britain named Ian Fleming devised a scheme to steal them. It was approved in secret cabinet in November 1941.[62] Since it involved the governors of Nigeria and the Gold Coast, as well as the War Council, Alan was briefed on the plan after it was given the final green light on Christmas Day, 1941. The core group of commandos sent from Britain re-provisioned in the Gold Coast on their way to Nigeria, where more commandos were recruited in early January 1942. Alan was at that time preparing to step in for five months as acting governor of Nigeria—"to realise my ambition, if only for a few months"[63]—whose incumbent was closely involved in supporting the operation. Alan recalled cryptically that while acting as governor of Nigeria, one of the spies told a member of his staff to keep him in the dark about some top-secret issue. "*That* was soon dealt with," he wrote.[64]

The operation, code-named Postmaster, began with the British vice consul in Spanish Guinea taking photographs of the Spanish governor in a hot tub with his black mistress. "From a post of vantage, he beheld not only an unchaste Susannah in her bath, but also the Governor, clad in his natal suit, emptying watering cans over the head of his inamorata," an SOE memo described.[65] The photos were used to blackmail the governor so that the British could survey the harbor and approaches without complaint from the Spanish police. On the moonless night of January 14th, 1942, forty-one British commandos in two tugboats entered the harbor. The twenty-five German and Italian officers and mates on the ships, as well as most of the top Spanish officials in the colony, were being entertained at a fortuitously planned banquet at the Casino Terrace Restaurant complete with free passes to the local brothel hosted by a local Spaniard in the pay of the British. The all-clear signal was given from the window of the Anglican minister's parsonage. A diamond ring for the wife of the harbor engineer paid for the flood lights to be turned off early. Using explosives to crack the anchor chains, the commandos stole not only the Italian freighter and German tugboat but a German diesel-powered barge for good measure. The boats were towed into international waters where they were "captured" by a waiting British warship. The Germans were furious. The British professed innocence. The Spanish kept silent, not least because their embarrassed officials did not want to explain where they had been that evening or, as one historian notes, "with whom."[66] Commander Fleming, inspired by the adventure, put pen to paper in a 1953 novel called *Casino Royale* with a new hero named James Bond.

The Nigerian government performed two final roles in Operation Postmaster during Alan's tenure as acting governor. The twenty-eight hapless Italian sailors who had been left on board the freighter while their officers went whoring were sequestered in a jungle prison camp in Nigeria for the duration of the war to keep them silent. The British informant in the port was then brought to safety. Denied an exit visa, he stole a canoe and paddled forty miles to Nigeria with a broken thumb after leveling a Spanish policeman trying to arrest his flight. His arrival in Nigeria set off a major cover-up by Alan's government, because London continued to insist that it had no role in the theft. He was finally shipped home on March 5th aboard the SS *Mary Slessor*, named after that "good and simple lady whom it was a privilege to know" as Alan recalled of his first stint in Nigeria. She was an emblem of the justice of liberal colonialism and the ship a fitting conveyance for a key actor in this brilliant strike against Hitler in West Africa.

Operation Postmaster coincided with the United States' entry into war and Hitler's increased attention to Russia and North Africa. The German threat to West Africa receded, but there was still the possibility of an invasion from Vichy territories. Alan was at the center of war planning because of his experiences in the last war.[67] The key lesson he brought to the table was that no matter how convinced you are of the justness of your cause and the eagerness of natives to be part of the British Empire, those natives were likely to rally strongly around their European rulers. Alan's war plans against Vichy West Africa called for significant sabotage and propaganda work before any invasion, a "softening up" designed to prevent any recurrence of the massacres at Duala and Jabassi in which he was involved thirty years earlier.

The softening-up made use of the broadcasting system in the Gold Coast that Alan's predecessor had created in order to douse subversive chatter among educated natives.[68] A nightly half-hour French program was broadcast into Vichy territories that otherwise heard only pro-Vichy radio from Dakar. There were also broadcasts to Togolese in both the British and the French Togoland mandates. One of the most popular members of the African broadcast team was Mabel Dove Danquah, wife of the prominent Gold Coast lawyer and politician Joseph Danquah. Her radio talks urged solidarity with the British and a yeoman's patience with war-time deprivations. By contrast, the English artsy types who were sent to oversee the operations were a plague.

One BBC team sent to the Gold Coast against Alan's "strongest recommendation," he recalled, "began to quarrel among themselves almost as soon as
they arrived and very soon . . . were all recalled."[69]

Softening-up also involved the recruitment of native women to cross into
Vichy territory and "suborn" the enemy.[70] One of the hush-hush types sent
to West Africa at the time to hatch sexual schemes was the young novelist
Graham Greene, aged thirty-eight in 1942. Posing as a trade inspector and
then as a police investigator, Greene's job was to hang around the docks
seeking information on Vichy French and Nazi German activities in West
Africa. His big idea was to establish a brothel in Portuguese Bissau where
Vichy French officials on holiday might disclose information. The plan was
nixed by London, which Greene's biographer considers a mistake since it
might have revealed key information about a French battleship in dock for
repairs there.[71]

The novel that would result from Greene's war-time posting, *The Heart
of the Matter*, painted colonial officialdom in awful strokes. A photo of a
beach party features "the Director of Education holding up what looked like
a dead fish, the Colonial Treasurer's wife." The spouse of Scobie, the novel's
protagonist, is stuck in the colony by war: "The danger of submarines had
made her as much a fixture as the handcuffs on the nail." The stately colonial courthouse is "the grandiloquent boast of weak men."[72] Greene, who
had experienced the Blitz, hoped for a bombing of British colonies in West
Africa "with their huge drinking parties and their complete unconsciousness
of what war is like." The only redeeming thing about Accra, Greene wrote,
was Christiansborg Castle, "the superbly beautiful old Danish fort in which
the governor lives—like a stage set of Elsinore in dazzling white with the surf
beating below on two sides."[73] Greene did decoding work for a few months
in Lagos in February and March 1942 while Alan was acting governor. It
is irresistible to imagine the two devout Catholics attending mass together
at Lagos Cathedral, Greene lamenting the moral corruption of colonial rule
while Alan prayed for its endurance.

Like Greene, Alan advocated "fraternization" with Vichy officials, which
became official policy in West Africa in August 1942. The idea was to
convince Vichy officials that Britain had no designs on French colonies
and wanted only the Restoration of French independence. This also meant
keeping a distance from the Gaullist Free French, whom the Americans in
particular viewed with suspicion. The policy "had the justification of history on its side,"[74] according to one historian, because once the Allies began
their counteroffensive in North Africa in November 1942, the governor of
Vichy West Africa quickly declared for the Allies. A year-and-a-half later,
Alan and Katie were in Lomé, where they were treated like long-standing

friends (see figure 8.3). Greene returned to England convinced that the empire was at an end.

A month after Alan arrived as governor of the Gold Coast, railway and port workers at the harbor of Takoradi staged a one-day strike for better pay. Alan sent police to arrest the ringleaders, the strike being illegal during war time. Once the grievances were resolved, he released all but two. For the third time in his career, he paid tribute to the professionalism and bravery of

Figure 8.3 Alan and Katie Fraternizing with Vichy Officials, Lomé, 1944. *Source:* Private Collection of Alan Dixon.

local police. When a similar strike was threatened during his five months as acting governor of Nigeria, he took to the airwaves to warn against "acts of disloyalty" and gave a nanny-like scolding that was translated into several languages, including pidgin English: "Are you going now to help Hitler by stopping work? . . . Are you going to give Hitler the satisfaction of knowing that the people of Lagos are doing what they can to prevent the Allies from winning the war? I shall be very disappointed if you do."[75]

As with everyday protest in World War I, the Takoradi and Lagos unrest has been interpreted as "anti-colonial resistance" by later historians. If regime-change was the goal, it would have been easy. The police force of the entire Gold Coast colony was reduced to just a few dozen, fewer than normally attached to a single bush camp and air strip.[76] As Alan would recall: "Had the people of the Gold Coast wished to push us into the sea there was little to prevent them."[77] Colonial peoples by and large understood that the fight for liberal colonialism was a fight against illiberal alternatives—fascism, communism, and socialism—that would render their lives miserable. Large donations came into funds to pay for Spitfire fighters and Mosquito bombers, so much that squadrons of both were named after the Gold Coast and their exploits followed closely in the local press. A total of 350,000 natives from British east and west Africa fought for the Allies as soldiers and workers—69,000 soldiers from the Gold Coast alone.[78] Alan was never forced to use conscription because traditional chiefs told their men to join when recruiting parties arrived.[79] "We felt we were British, that we were safe under British administration," explained the son of a minor chief who was the first to volunteer when a recruiting party came to his village. "If they had trouble elsewhere, we went."[80]

The natives also supported war-time limits and exactions—special metering on taxis, black-outs, extra taxes, rationing, community service requirements. Kofi Busia, a prominent Gold Coast intellectual who later became the prime minister of independent Ghana wrote: "There is not much doubt as to what would happen to the African under a German regime. Did Hitler himself not write of the Negro that 'It is an act of criminal insanity to train a being who was only born a semi-ape?' Hitler himself has thus raised the racial question which has contributed to the loyal support that the colonies have to Britain. It has made the war a racial war which is Africa's as well as Britain's."[81] As in the last war, Alan found the response a bracing reminder of the legitimacy of colonial rule: "This was the time when the people came forward in their thousands, not with empty protestations of loyalty but with men to serve in the army . . . and with liberal gifts to war funds and war charities," he recalled. "This was curious conduct for people tired of British rule."[82]

The doughty participation of the Africans made Alan apoplectic about British conscientious objectors in the colony. These included nine academic staff at Achimota College, which had been founded in 1927 to be the Gold Coast's equivalent of Eton and Oxbridge combined. "It is always a good thing to have a crank or two in a community . . . but crankiness should be well-diluted," Alan insisted.[83] In his memoirs, he carried on the point: "A few people with unusual ideas do no great harm . . . but it is unfair to African youth to expose it to the teaching of so many of this type at one time."[84] A Colonial Office memo noted that Alan's "reaction was a desire to sack the lot" and "bordered on the violent." In the end, the college carried on with its pacifist professors and about half the normal student body, while the British military occupied most of the campus. Fortunately, as one African alumnus reported, "the standard of tennis at the college remained high."[85]

With Hitler's defeat at Stalingrad and the opening of the Allies' North Africa campaign in late 1942, the Gold Coast shifted from defense to offense. Takoradi harbor became the staging point for a remarkable feat of logistics known as the "Takoradi Ferry." About 200 bombers and fighters per month were shipped from Britain via an evasive sea route to Takoradi. There, they were reassembled and flown across the Sahara to bases in Egypt. The 3,000-mile, 7-day, 13-stop route crossed through Nigeria and the Sudan. It may have turned the tide of war in North Africa more than the better-known "tanks of the desert."[86] The sprawling operation at Takoradi also included expanded shipping facilities for transport to India and Australia, as well as a rail line operated by the Americans to bring bauxite, manganese, and timber from the interior. The large concentration of British and American servicemen in one place transformed Takoradi into a boom town, with all the appurtenances. Women from Nigeria streamed into the area to offer their services. The spike in venereal diseases was so worrying that Alan and his cabinet passed an emergency law in 1942 to deport the ladies and prohibit their commerce. Along with weekly reports of manganese exports, Alan carefully tracked the decline in sexual license, complete with forecasts and charts.[87]

Like a replay of the bases talks, Alan found himself balancing the rights of a colony with the war-time needs of the Americans. The behavior of the American soldiers was "deplorable" at first, he commented. One drunk soldier fired his revolver at a taxi driver, killing a hapless African clerk. Another ploughed his truck through a platoon, killing one British soldier and eleven African soldiers. Both men were court-martialed. When Alan complained about the incidents to the local American diplomat in Accra, the complaint was sent to the American ambassador in London who took it up with Churchill. "I am the King's representative in the Gold Coast and I must stand up for my people," Alan wrote to the prime minister defending his actions. Churchill told him to stand down.[88] It was the first crack in Alan's relationship with Churchill.

Despite the tensions, Alan and Katie were gracious hosts to American officers during frequent garden parties at Christiansborg Castle. If he nursed any
resentment, Alan certainly did not show it. They mixed easily on the lawn
with American officers who seem amused to be in the presence of a "colonial
oppressor." Alan left the castle open to visiting American soldiers, two of
whom mistook him for a tour guide: "Had I been quicker on the uptake, I
might have earned a tip."[89] Fortunately, small talk with Americans came
easily to both Alan and Katie. It was an opportunity—which Churchill
had encouraged all colonial officials to seek—to educate American top
brass in the realities of colonial rule. "I can remember the surprise of an
American general when he heard that I was going on tour in the interior
of the Gold Coast in 1943 with no escort and only a single orderly," Alan
recalled, noting that American governors in Puerto Rico travelled under
armed guard. "There certainly was much friendship between British officials
and the peoples of dependent territories, a friendship which astonished many
critics of colonialism."[90]

The timing of the war could not have been worse for Barbara and Dickie,
already somewhat abandoned by their father's career. Dickie had left British
Honduras to study medieval history at Oxford in 1937. When the war came,
she had to abandon her studies, aged twenty-one. Rather than follow her parents to the Gold Coast, she stayed behind and worked for British intelligence
at Blenheim Palace. Barbara, aged only eighteen in 1941, was forced to follow her parents to the Gold Coast just a few months short of her high school
exams. Katie felt that it was more important for her to find a suitable husband
than to complete her studies.
    Barbara's prospects as the governor's daughter were unbeatable. There
were RAF pilots, American officers, Free French attachés, British spies, and
budding novelists, to name a few. Yet Barbara hated the role. She and Dickie
had not been raised in colonial society and did not share their father's enthusiasm for the mission. Alan recalled a "blissful" three-month family vacation
with Katie and Barbara to South Africa in 1943 where the trio "observed anti-
erosion work," "saw some excellent housing schemes," and "held a meeting
with the Bunga."[91] There was "much tennis and bridge but a serious shortage
of whisky."[92] Their homebound plane nearly crashed, which for Alan only
enhanced the derring-do. Barbara, by contrast, was miserable, and carries a
pained expression in every photo from these years.
    The final straw for Barbara came when she was pressed into service as part
of the "fraternization" with Vichy French on a 1944 trip to Lomé. She was
surrounded by ghoulish-looking French *douanes* in dark glasses at every turn.
Back in Accra, Barbara declared that she was returning to Britain to join the
war effort, *sans mari*. Uncle Bertie, who had used his premature retirement

from the colonial service to author with sister Essie a series of practical grade-school textbooks on Latin and French, promised to tutor Barbara to continue her studies. She would be forever grateful to Uncle Bertie for rescuing her from colonial society.[93]

Given her pedigree and her felicity with numbers, Barbara was a welcome recruit. She joined the Women's Royal Naval Service, the legendary Wrens, in September 1944, just as the service reached its peak of seventy-five thousand women. Sent to the HMS *Caledonia* base in Scotland, she had the job of recording and translating signals from North Atlantic ships. Even at this late stage in the war, German submarines remained active, and Barbara's signals corps had the distressing job of listening to the final signals of merchant vessels as they sunk.

Both Dickie and Barbara completed their studies after the war and joined the workforce. Dickie became a probation officer, Barbara a department store clerk. Their abandonment of the colonial mission was emblematic of a larger shift in middle-class attitudes. Alan and Katie were still full of imperial zeal, saluting native recruits and holding meetings with the Bunga. But the next generation saw the devastation of the war on the home front. It wanted a warm flat and a cooker that worked. Churchill was thrown from office in 1945 by a new Labour Government that declared, "British 'imperialism' is dead." By 1945, Europe was exhausted, and its appetite to provide global public goods to alien peoples began to fade.

The views on colonialism of the British Labour Party and its official partner, the Communist Party of Great Britain (CPGB), had changed with time. At first, they did not push an anti-colonial agenda because, as one leading labor activist noted, "the average workers would consider this treason."[94] Indeed, many on the Left shared Marx's view that colonialism was a positive force for people living in feudal conditions. By the 1930s, however, it was the diktat of Stalin, not the theories of Marx, that mattered. Alan's brother Emile played a leading role in turning the British Left toward anti-colonialism in his role as chief propagandist for Britain's communist movement.

The initial impression of Emile by spy chasers was that he was "one of the leading members" of the movement, though "seldom in the limelight."[95] They called him "one of the few good brains in the CPGB." Despite his difficult relations with "the more plebeian comrades," it concluded, "he is most definitely one of the principal people in the conspiratorial circle, and there can be very little that goes on in the communist movement of England about which Burns does not know." The counterespionage file on Emile would eventually grow to be the third largest on British communists.[96]

On the crucial question of Emile's relationship with the Soviet Union, London pointed to his role in Moscow's Control Commission for disbursing

financial aid from the Soviet Union and his equally legal but suspicious former role as a director in the Soviet Union's trading company, All-Russian
Cooperative Society (Arcos), which Moscow's official historians later admitted, was the center of its "extensive network of spies" in Britain.[97] As one
surveillance report noted: "He is, of course, undoubtedly trusted by one or
other of the leading cliques in Moscow."

The war brought Emile luster within the communist movement. In 1935,
he rushed into print a denunciation of the Italian invasion of Abyssinia,
arguing that opponents of colonialism should rally behind the leadership of
the Soviet Union which "alone has unmixed motives." The United States,
he added, was in "late capitalist" decline, a fact so obvious that it was "not
necessary to prove it statistically."[98] The future lay with a Soviet-led world
order scrubbed clean of both capitalism and colonialism. At the outbreak of
European hostilities in 1939, Emile produced another handy pamphlet, *What
Is Marxism?*, that urged the people of Britain and its colonies to resist service:
"The working class only helps to fasten new shackles on itself if it supports
its ruling class in such wars."[99] Good Marxists instead should "make com-
mon cause with the colonial peoples against their common enemy," namely
British officials and their business backers. Alan, on this theory, was a tool of
American manganese interests.

With Stalin and Hitler at first professing to be allies, Emile was aware of
the dangers of his work to Alan. In 1940, he telephoned to say he was cutting
off contact to protect Alan's career. "Nonsense, you are my brother!" Alan
retorted.[100] With Hitler's invasion of Russia, the British communists unified
around a pro-war position, making Emile's position less awkward for Alan.
At the same time, it was becoming clear that the Soviet Union would emerge
from the war as the West's principal rival, especially on colonial matters.
The hypocrisy of the Soviet Union, which had put Central Asia, the Baltic
States, and Eastern Europe under its colonial rule while insisting on freedom
and democracy which were "so dear to communist authorities" as Alan put it,
would never cease to enrage him.[101]

Was Emile a Soviet spy? There is no doubt that he was aware of Soviet
spies in the ranks of Britain's communist movement. He was present at
CPGB headquarters in 1941 when an avowed Moscow spy told the party to
sack the journalist and future Labour MP Tom Driberg, an MI5 mole inside
the CPGB, after one of Moscow's own spies inside MI5 had intercepted a
report Driberg had filed on the workings of the CPGB.[102] Emile was also
present at a meeting at headquarters in 1945 when his fellow party member
and paid spy for Moscow, James Klugmann, told the group that he had been
asked by Moscow to engage in espionage while working on a UN mission
in Yugoslavia. During the meeting, Klugmann recalled having carried out an
earlier assignment for Moscow in 1937 to recruit one of Emile's Cambridge

classmates from the Foreign Office to work for the KGB. In the intercepted transcripts of the 1945 meeting, Emile warmed to the news that Klugmann was again in the pay of Moscow and expressed the hope that he would use the entrée to expand his contacts with Eastern European communist leaders then being prepared to take over these countries under Soviet rule.[103]

Experts on communist espionage do not believe that Emile was ever in the direct pay of Moscow. "Emile Burns was seen in Moscow as a very useful pro-Soviet propagandist, but I don't know of any solid evidence that he was a Soviet spy," attested the Harvard historian Mark Kramer. "Burns and other British Communists willingly put themselves at the service of Moscow, but only a smaller number went on to take up government jobs (or other sensitive posts) to smuggle secret information to Soviet spymasters."[104] Emile was a moral traitor to the United Kingdom, if not a legal one.

The first reference to Alan in an MI5 file appeared in 1942. Transit from Britain to Cairo invariably took notables through Accra, where the guests would stay with Alan and Katie at Christiansborg Castle. "He has to entertain distinguished travelers, such as [cabinet member Sir Richard Stafford] Cripps and the King of Greece, and may even have entertained Mr. Churchill on his journey to Cairo this week," one report noted.[105] A 1944 memo from a phone call at CPGB headquarters reported: "[Emile] Burns said that his brother (Sir Alan Burns) had returned for talks with the Colonial Office and that these talks were 'confidential.'"[106] This was getting very close to crossing the line for Alan.

One can only speculate about whether Emile was encouraged to recruit Alan, who would have been a high-value asset for Moscow. If so, Emile probably knew Alan too well to suppose that the attempt would succeed, unless Alan intended to become a double-agent, not exactly his cup of tea given his dislike of *all* "hush-hush types." If anything, Alan would have viewed Emile as an intelligence asset for the British, but there is no evidence that Alan tried to recruit Emile. So many of Emile's Cambridge colleagues were Soviet spies in the Foreign Office that such a move would have been discovered. More practically, it seems that many Soviet officials did not realize until many years later that the two were related. "We have a friend in your country also surnamed Burns. But you probably do not have any dealings with him," a Soviet official would tell Alan at the United Nations. "Actually, I know him quite well," Alan replied. "He is my brother."[107]

Emile's direct impact on Alan was the training of anti-colonial agitators from the Gold Coast. Emile was a member of the British Communist Party's 8-member "colonial group," and he was described by one member as a "guru to colonial students" studying in Britain.[108] There were 4,000 African students studying in London during the war, and the restless and lonely men made easy prey for party hacks offering Utopian hatred. Emile held classes on

Marxism for over 40 of them. One, named Kwame Nkrumah, arrived in May 1945 and found special favor with Emile. In his autobiography, Nkrumah referred to Emile as a "close friend," and it is clear the relationship was both long-lasting and of political significance. Emile provided Nkrumah with a clutch of membership cards in the CPGB, which were illegal in the Gold Coast since it was a foreign political party.[109]

Emile's anti-colonial group came into ascendancy during the war under the British Communist Party's acknowledged anti-colonial henchman, Rajani Palme Dutt, the progeny of a Bengali father and a Swedish-Finnish mother who, along with Emile, had imposed a rigid Stalinization on British communism.[110] For the most part, the party's anti-colonial activities were more comical than threatening. Moscow's files show a penny-poor organization holding late-night debates on "establishing contact" with worker groups in the colonies which either did not exist or were not interested in "solidarity" with strange British men.[111] Emile's "secret" dealings with communists in India, according to MI5 notes, revolved around "matters of intellectual theory."[112]

Alan was likely apprised of his brother's activities since the MI5 files on Emile were shared with the agency's West Africa station. While always cordial with his brother, Alan was scathing in his description of the British Left's coffee-house radicals intent on laying waste to an empire whose absence they would never have to experience themselves. "Self-righteous people, who are often completely ignorant of conditions outside their own narrow circle, are only too ready to criticise those of their own race who are facing the realities of life and doing their best under very difficult circumstances," he would write. "Imperialism is denounced by people who have never left the security of their own home town."[113]

Alan celebrated victory at the V-E parade in Accra in 1945 by donning his feathered and medaled gubernatorial costume made of heavy wool, "designed by the Colonial Office to kill off governors in the tropics," as he joked. What did the future of colonialism look like to Sir Alan Burns as he paraded in his lethal finery? As with the last war, nothing would ever be the same. "The lunacy of European wars, in which the white races have nearly succeeded in destroying their own civilization, has lost them, possibly forever, their scarcely questioned position of authority over the coloured world," Alan would write.[114] In addition to the carnage, the frequent appeals to liberty, democracy, and human rights by the Allies again redounded at home once the last shots were fired.[115] The Anglo-American Atlantic Charter of 1941 insisted on "the right of all peoples to choose the form of government under which they will live." It was inevitable that large numbers of young men put into a liberal organization for an extended period would return home inspired by this promise of change. "The war has generated new ideas and created a new sense of values throughout the world, and West Africa too has caught the spirit of the age," one Ghanaian soldier wrote. Another who served in India, where independence talks were proceeding, recalled: "We saw no reason why India should be granted independence and not our African colonies, because we didn't see much difference between India and Ghana."[116]

As ever, colonialism begat nationalism which begat decolonization. It was a self-liquidating enterprise, and for those who took the long view, this had been the plan all along. One could not as a liberal country engage another area without that same liberalism seeping through. As Alan would write: "Many people believe that the clamour in British colonies for independence is proof of the failure of colonialism. . . . We believe it to be, on the contrary, an indication of the success of our policy, which was designed to make these people fit to govern themselves."[117]

The international politics of colonialism had also shifted. The United States was willing to accede to the necessity of continued colonialism in the short-term if colonial powers promised political independence in the long term. The United States itself became a "colonial" power after the war with a mandate (now called a trusteeship) in the Pacific islands from the new United Nations. The rise of the Soviet Union as a Cold War rival also motivated Washington to support the colonial status quo. Yet this new international politics—UN involvement and a superpower rivalry—also posed problems for colonialism. If middle-class support for the colonial endeavor evaporated on the home front, then UN agitators would push for an acceleration of plans for independence while the United States, fearful of being outbid by Moscow, would throw its weight behind rapid decolonization. As Alan marched in full regalia across the parade ground in Accra that day in 1945—"the grandiloquent boast of weak men"—his own doubts were on the rise. The new Labour Government, he noted, had "a tendency to allow events to take their own course without the exercise of that control which, in my opinion, is the duty of a trustee."[118] In a moment of despair, Alan told brother Bertie: "In ten years, there will be no empire."[119]

NOTES

1. Romain Hayes, *Subhas Chandra Bose in Nazi Germany: Politics, Intelligence, and Propaganda 1941–43* (2011); Yannick Lengkeek, "Staged Glory: The Impact of Fascism on 'Cooperative' Nationalist Circles in Late Colonial Indonesia, 1935–1942," *Fascism* (2018).
2. "Japan," *Belize Independent*, August 27, 1941.
3. CBAA, pp. 82, 97.
4. CP, p. 40.

5. Arnold Toynbee, *A Study of History* (1934), vol. 2, p. 365.

6. CO/123/365/2, "Foreign Office to Robinson re: Italian encouragement to Guatemala," April 12, 1938.

7. Guatemala, Secretary of External Relations, *White Book. Controversy between Guatemala and Great Britain Relative to the Convention of 1859 on Territorial Matters. Belize Question* (1938).

8. CO/123/365/2, "ACB to Colonial Office re: Guatemala dispute," May 29, 1938.

9. CO/123/375/3, "ACB to Colonial Office re: British Honduras Defense Force," April 4, 1939; CO/123/365/2, "ACB to Beckett," May 29, 1938, and "File notes," July 12, 1938.

10. Michael Healy, "Colour, Climate, and Combat: The Caribbean Regiment in the Second World War," *International History Review* (2000).

11. CCC, p. 318.

12. CO/123/370/2, "Jewish refugees file notes," May 10, 1938.

13. William Edward Simnett, "Land for refugees," *The Times*, November 22, 1938; "Honduras for the Jews," *Times*, April 4, 1939.

14. CO/123/370/2, "Jewish refugees to British Honduras, Letter from the Rector of Dorset," December 13, 1938.

15. CO/123/370/2, "Jewish refugees to British Honduras, file notes," May 27, 1938, July 5, 1938, and June 10, 1938.

16. CO/123/375/14, "ACB to Secretary for Colonies," April 15, 1939; CO/123/370/2, "ACB to C.O.," April 4, 1938, July 5, 1938, June 2, 1938.

17. CO/123/370/2, "Jewish refugees to British Honduras, file notes," May 23, 1938, May 23, 1938, and August 17, 1938.

18. Ari Joshua Sherman, *Island Refuge: Britain and Refugees from the Third Reich, 1933–39* (1973), p. 109; also see Joanna Newman, *Nearly the New World: The British West Indies and the Flight from Nazism, 1933–1945* (2019).

19. "The Jews!" *Belize Independent*, February 8, 1939.

20. "British Honduras gives terms for refugee settlement," *Jewish Telegraphic Agency*, April 26, 1940; "British Honduras refugee project awaits arrival of 80 families," *Jewish Telegraphic Agency*, September 29, 1940.

21. Anne Hugon, "Les Colonies, Un Refuge Pour les Juifs? Le Cas de la Gold Coast (1938–1945)," *Vingtième Siècle: Revue d'histoire* (2004).

22. CP, pp. 75, 77.

23. "Henry Gurney (chief secretary of British mandate in Palestine) to ACB," personal letter, February 15, 1947, private collection.

24. CO/850/206/1, "Appointment of ACB to governor general of Malaya Union," September 3, 1945.

25. "C.O. to ACB," personal letter, June 15, 1946, private collection.

26. FBCE-G, p. 9.

27. "A.C.C. Parkinson to ACB," personal letter, October 27, 1939, private collection.

28. CCC, p. 256.

29. Philip Goodhart, *Fifty Ships That Saved the World: The Foundation of the Anglo-American Alliance* (1965).

30. House of Lords, *Debates: 5th Series, 1938–1941*, vol. 117, pp. 304–6.

31. FO/371/24263/A5125/5125/45, "Lloyd to Scott," December 11, 1940.

32. David Reynolds, *The Creation of the Anglo-American Alliance, 1937–41* (1982), p. 169.

33. FO/371/24262 A5203/3742/45, "Eden minute," December 29, 1940.

34. Rhodri Jeffreys-Jones, "The Inestimable Advantage of Not Being English: Lord Lothian's American Ambassadorship, 1939–1940," *Scottish Historical Review* (1984), p. 108.

35. Goodhart, op. cit., p. 220.

36. IDOC, p. 316.

37. Goodhart, op. cit., p. 221.

38. CCC, p. 171.

39. Richard Strauss, "The Diplomatic Negotiations Leading to the Establishment of American Bases in Newfoundland, June 1940–April 1941," Memorial University of Newfoundland, Department of History, master's thesis (1972), p. 101.

40. Goodhart, op. cit., p. 223.

41. CO/971/15/3, "Berir to Garner," February 17, 1941.

42. CCC, p. 170.

43. CO/971/15/3, "Bases memo by ACB," February 20, 1941.

44. "Bases talks," *Daily Express*, February 25, 1941.

45. CO/971/15/3, "Fahy to ACB," March 8, 1941.

46. CCC, p. 172.

47. John Winant, *A Letter from Grosvenor Square: An Account of a Stewardship* (1947), p. 25.

48. Francis Lowenheim et al., eds., *Roosevelt and Churchill: Their Secret Wartime Correspondence* (1975), p. 132.

49. "Moyne to ACB," personal letter, March 18, 1941, private collection.

50. Charlie Whitham, "On Dealing With Gangsters: The Limits of British 'Generosity' in the Leasing of Bases to the United States, 1940–41," *Diplomacy and Statecraft* (1996), p. 619.

51. PREM (Prime Minister's Office) 3/461/2, "Confidential note for use with editors and the BBC," March 24, 1941.

52. CCC, p. 172.

53. Charlie Whitham, "The Thin End of the Wedge: The British Foreign Office, the West Indies, and Avoiding the Destroyers-Bases Deal, 1938–1940," *Journal of Transatlantic Studies* (2013), p. 234.

54. Robert Shogan, *Hard Bargain: How FDR Twisted Churchill's Arm, Evaded the Law, and Changed the Role of the American Presidency* (1995), pp. 248–49.

55. Jeffreys-Jones, op. cit., p. 108.

56. William Edward Simnett, "Britain's Colonies in the War," *Foreign Affairs* (1941).

57. "Winant says war knit empire ties," *New York Times*, September 16, 1947.

58. CCC, p. 186.

59. Stephen Kojo Addae, *The Gold Coast and Achimota in the Second World War* (2004), p. 84.

60. CCC, p. 259.

61. HS/3/80 (Special Operations Executive, Africa and Middle East), "West Africa," March 23, 1942; HS/3/79, "Telegram 1405 to Lagos," January 5, 1942.

62. Brian Lett, *Ian Fleming and SOE's Operation Postmaster: The Untold Top Secret Story* (2012).

63. CO/967/115, "ACB to Parkinson," January 24, 1942.

64. CCC, p. 259.

65. Lett, op. cit., ch. 14.

66. Nancy Lawler, *Soldiers, Airmen, Spies, and Whisperers: The Gold Coast in World War II* (2002), p. 125.

67. Lawler, op. cit., pp. 233–34.

68. Sydney Head, "British Colonial Broadcasting Policies: The Case of the Gold Coast," *African Studies Review* (1979), p. 43.

69. CCC, p. 259.

70. Lawler, op. cit., p. 113.

71. Norman Sherry, *The Life of Graham Greene. Volume 2, 1939–1955* (1994), p. 121.

72. Graham Greene, *The Heart of the Matter* (1948), pp. 18, 15, 15.

73. Sherry, op. cit., pp. 154, 113.

74. Lawler, op. cit., p. 159.

75. CCC, pp. 315–16.

76. Addae, op. cit., p. 22.

77. CCC, p. 318.

78. David Killingray, "Military and Labour Recruitment in the Gold Coast During the Second World War," *Journal of African History* (1982).

79. Wendell Holbrook, "British Propaganda and the Mobilization of the Gold Coast War Effort, 1939–1945," *Journal of African History* (1985).

80. Christoper Somerville, *Our War: How the British Commonwealth Fought the Second World War* (1998), pp. 4, 35.

81. Kofi Busia, *West Africans and the Issues of War* (1942), p. 11.

82. CCC, p. 318.

83. Addae, op. cit., pp. 124, 126.

84. CCC, p. 199.

85. Addae, op. cit., p. 121.

86. Deborah Wing Ray, "The Takoradi Route: Roosevelt's Prewar Venture Beyond the Western Hemisphere," *Journal of American History* (1975).

87. Carina Ray, "The Sex Trade in Colonial West Africa," *New African* (2007).

88. Author's interview with Sarah Pavey, June 14, 2016, Epsom, UK.

89. CCC, p. 182.

90. CBAA, p. 147.

91. CCC, p. 194; CP, p. 58.

92. CO/967/115, "ACB to Thornley," November 21, 1943.

93. Author's interview with Christine Barrett, June 16, 2016, Macroom, Ireland.

94. Marika Sherwood, "The Comintern, the CPGB, Colonies, and Black Britons, 1920–1938," *Science & Society* (1996), p. 143.

95. KV/21760/86A-PF/38458/DS/10, "Note on Emile Burns," July 27, 1934.

96. Helen Lindsay, "Jack Lindsay and MI5: More than Surveillance," *Australian Literary Studies* (2015).

97. Fredrik Petersson, *Willi Munzenberg, the League Against Imperialism, and the Comintern, 1925–1933* (2013), p. 325.

98. Emile Burns, *Abyssinia and Italy* (1935), pp. 9, 221, 74.

99. Emile Burns, *What is Marxism?* (1939), p. 101.

100. Author's interview with Sarah Pavey, June 14, 2016, Epsom, UK.

101. IDOC, p. 13.

102. Francis Beckett, *Enemy Within: The Rise and Fall of the British Communist Party* (1995), p. 88; Andrew Lownie, *Stalin's Englishman: The Lives of Guy Burgess* (2016).

103. Geoff Andrews, *The Shadow Man: At the Heart of the Cambridge Spy Circle* (2015); KV/2788/95/AB, "Burns suggests Klugman for the *World News* job," July 11, 1945.

104. Mark Kramer, personal email communication to author, April 6, 2016.

105. KV/21762, "Burns' brother is . . .," August 14, 1942.

106. KV/21762, "Burns said that his brother. . .," March 21, 1944.

107. Author's interview with Alan Dixon, Chelmsford, June 17, 2016.

108. Sherwood, op. cit., p. 145.

109. KV/21762/237B, "Extract from B.L.A. source report re: the West African Students' Union," February 16, 1948.

110. John Callaghan, *Rajani Palme Dutt: A Study in British Stalinism* (1993).

111. Ben Bradley, *Colonies, Mandates and Peace* (1938).

112. KV/21762/232H, "Emile Burns," December 15, 1947.

113. CPCW-G, p. 6.

114. CP, p. 39.

115. Bonny Ibhawoh, "Second World War Propaganda, Imperial Idealism, and Anti-Colonial Nationalism in British West Africa," *Nordic Journal of African Studies* (2007).

116. Adrienne Israel, "Measuring the War Experience: Ghanaian Soldiers in World War II," *Journal of Modern African Studies* (1987), pp. 160, 167.

117. CCT-G, p. 5.

118. RCD-G, p. 1.

119. Author's interview with Sarah Pavey, June 14, 2016, Epsom, UK.

Chapter 9

The *Ju-Ju* Murder

In 1943, a Scottish army doctor in the British Gold Coast stopped for the night at a military cantonment while on his way to the capital Accra. A British administrator and his wife invited him to stay at their bungalow a mile away. When the doctor explained the change of lodgings to his African servant, the young man took fright. "The Queen Mother go die today. They go kill me if I come tonight. No strangers go out tonight," he explained.[1]

In the culture of the Akan peoples, who surrounded the military cantonment, it was common to kill a few people when a tribal leader died. Their blood would be used to prepare for a successor by "washing the stool" representing tribal authority. This is according to a work on the subject written by a young Akan lawyer named Joseph Danquah in a 1928 book *Akan Law and Customs*. "Human sacrifice was an inseparable part of the funeral ceremonies of kings," Danquah wrote. The victims would include "slaves, servants, wives, and even court officials."[2]

The following week in Accra, the doctor was recruited to play for a local British soccer team in a friendly match against another Akan kingdom. Its paramount chief or king, Chief Nama Ofori Atta I, presented a commemorative cup to the winning British side. The British modestly returned the cup, explaining "we are only passing through your country." The native fans hooted in appreciation.[3] Three weeks after presenting the cup, Chief Atta I died of a heart attack, ending thirty-one years in power. The hunt for blood to wash his stool began. The doctor and his servant prudently detoured around Atta I's kingdom on their homeward journey.

The British ruled many of their African colonies indirectly through traditional chiefs like Atta I, believing this was more effective and legitimate. With rapid economic and social change under colonialism, the system was coming under strain. The ability of the chiefs to sell land and mineral rights raised the stakes of gaining even a minor position in a kingdom. Between 1904 and 1944, there were thirty-five "destoolments" or local coups against minor chiefs in Atta I's kingdom alone.[4] "Fishing in the muddy waters of stool intrigues," as Alan called it, had become a full-time occupation for many ambitious young men.[5] Rare was the succession of a major chief like Atta I that did not involve blood-letting.

Following Akan tradition, there were two funerals for Atta I. The first took place at the royal palace, where his body was buried so that it could decompose. Six months later, the various factions had settled on a successor. The second funeral was arranged where the bones would be disinterred to be placed in the kingdom's royal mausoleum alongside the stool of authority. The stool would be smeared by a trio of priest-like lesser chiefs with a mixture of eggs, soot, and blood.

On the day of the second funeral, there was a frenzy in the air. "Some of the [officials] and the executioners ran helter-skelter, dancing passionately with ferocious grimaces. Some, with fearsome gestures, brandished their guns and clashed their knives together," one tribal member recalled.[6] Early in the morning, one of the three priests arrived at the palace for his duties. He settled under a tree in an inner courtyard to await his colleagues. He had been a favorite of Atta I, perhaps an illegitimate son. Suddenly eight men — all descendants of former chiefs — rushed into the courtyard and seized him. They thrust a ceremonial dagger through his cheeks and cut off his tongue to prevent him from uttering an oath that would dispel the magical power of his blood. As his mouth flooded red, a bowl was thrust under his chin to catch the precious liquid. "For hours on end the murderers' cold dagger gagged him alive while his innocent blood gushed profusely on that wretched stool," recalled his relatives later.[7] At the end of the agony, he was beheaded, and more blood was gathered.

Several stools, including that of the departed king, were smeared with the blood. "Eight insecure, grief-stricken men combined in an act which they felt to be appropriate to this staggering recent loss," one historian concluded. "By that act they would protect themselves from the late king's ancestral wrath at being ill-served in death."[8] In his official summing up, the judge would be more blunt: "This was a premeditated murder committed in cold blood." The luckless priest's body was buried at a nearby riverbank.

The next day, the freshly washed stool appeared in the stool house, signifying that a new reign had begun. The new king, styling himself Atta II, claimed that the funeral rites, from which police had been told to stay away, had been followed to perfection. Except that a minor priest was missing.

The priest's murder was part of a long and complex tradition of witchcraft in West Africa known variously as *ju-ju*, or the related practice of *obeah*, sometimes just "fetish." It was nothing new to Alan, who had spent his career surrounded by West African cultures. In St. Kitts, he recalled, a black legislator once refused to take his seat because a *ju-ju* charm had been stuck in the desk opposite him. During his second stint in Nigeria, Alan had supported the research of a junior British administrator into the practice, later published as *Ju-Ju and Justice in Nigeria.*[9] While governor of the British Honduras, he arrived at work one day to find his office chair decorated with feathers, broken sticks, and dirt, a classic *ju-ju* curse. A police orderly told him they were placed there by a female cook he was planning to sack. The orderly gasped as Alan brusquely swept the debris into a rubbish bin. "She was apparently as incompetent at *obeah* as she was at cooking," Alan remarked.[10]

To Alan, *ju-ju* was "a terrible affliction and handicap" that was one of the "grossest forms of superstition and savagery" in Africa.[11] "Everywhere in [British] territories men suffered from the cruelty and rapacity of indigenous rulers, and were liable at the whim of a chief, or through the instigation of a fetish priest, to torture and brutal punishment," he recalled. Along with "slavery, cannibalism, human sacrifice, the burning of widows, child marriage, and tyrannies of the worst sort," these practices had been "suppressed, or at least significantly reduced, during British rule."[12] The universal human rights promised by colonial rule, Alan believed, should not brook such customs, especially because they were "viewed with horror by the vast majority of the people" and "African public opinion" strongly supported their elimination.[13] There was no hypocrisy in Britain's own sordid history of slavery, floggings, and debtors' prison. Those practices had been corrected in Britain and should be corrected in the British Empire as well. "Two or more wrongs do not make a right."[14]

Alan held fast to the universalism of colonial rule, refusing to succumb to the cultural relativism starting to afflict others in the colonial service. The "conspiracy of silence" among anti-colonialists in the West about barbaric practices in the non-Western world, as one scholar noted later, was not shared by those in Africa who loudly complained about them.[15] The 2001 African Charter of Human Rights and People's Rights would refer to *ju-ju* as an "obnoxious cultural practice" and urge countries to stamp it out.[16]

In 1944, however, something odd was happening. What should have been a straightforward case of premeditated murder suddenly was looked upon as a matter of cultural preference. Hadn't medieval Christians in Britain engaged in similar occult killings? Who gave the Brits the right to dispense justice in the first place? And what on earth were Englishmen doing in darkest Africa trying to sort out stool disputes? These questions would not have been asked a decade earlier. Now, they came to center stage in the response to a *ju-ju* murder on Alan's watch.

Alan was unprepared for the change. His attempts to enforce justice on *ju-ju* would be thwarted over the next three years, leaving him bitter and stunned. The micropolitics of this ritual murder reflected a calamitous change in the macropolitics of colonialism.

The *ju-ju* murder would become the most astonishing event in Alan's storied career. It would take him on a roller-coaster ride of politics and intrigue, fundamentally define his career, and remain the most powerful emotional memory of his life. The only time brother Bertie saw him cry was when he was recalling the case.[17] It extended over two-thirds of his time as governor and overshadowed everything he did.

Many years later, a young British doctoral student interested in colonial constitutions named Richard Rathbone interviewed Alan at his London club.[18] By then, most people had forgotten the ordeal. But not Alan. He kept steering the conversation back to the *ju-ju* murder. "And then it all came out," Rathbone recalled. "He had acted, he said, throughout the wretched affair in accordance with the law and always supported by the evidence. He was undermined by shifty, lying lawyers both in Ghana and especially in London. He had, in effect, been publicly made to look not just a fool but also an inhuman man. His indignation was considerable as the events crowded back. He became rather red in the face and what had been a calm exchange became an irate lecture."[19]

In his personal items, Alan left behind a large collection of newspaper clippings, correspondence, and evidence about the murder. It takes up twenty pages in his memoirs, including excerpts from a lengthy memo he wrote to his superiors after the case ended.[20] This memo was the only item that Alan chose to share with a colonial records project at Oxford University. "The murder case, and his vast sense of the unjust treatment he had received in the course of it from successive secretaries of state [for the colonies], never left him," Rathbone observed. Alan would continue this "obsessional concern with self-vindication" for the rest of his life.[21] Any mention of the affair was sure to raise Alan "to a pitch of righteous indignation."[22]

In Rathbone's view, the murder "marked him for life, alienated him from the Colonial Office, and haunted him until his death." Yet, as we will see, the affair also raised Alan's profile as a stout defender of colonialism and, no less importantly, stirred his passion to defend colonialism on the public stage. It raised rather than lowered his status and pushed him into a high-profile decade as Britain's most eloquent diplomatic defender of the colonial mission. If the *ju-ju* murder had not happened, Alan would never have been thrust into the spotlight of global politics. Despite the anguish, the murder was the event that defined his career.

The day after the priest went missing, search parties were formed. Chief Atta II declared that the missing man had probably gone for a long walk. Rumors quickly spread of a murder. The surviving priests appealed to the local British constabulary to intervene. The police chief wrote diffidently to Atta II seeking an explanation. Atta II brushed away concerns but allowed missing person notices to be posted. The police did not want to press the matter. The last thing they wanted was another stool intrigue in an otherwise loyal kingdom.

Alan did not take the news well. This was the third time since becoming governor that *ju-ju* had jostled his affairs. A year earlier, he had instructed the Gold Coast broadcasting service to air a message dispelling a widespread rumor that the coincident illnesses of Churchill and Roosevelt were caused by a *ju-ju* curse from Gandhi, then fasting for independence.[23] The same year, he swiftly sent to the gallows a *ju-ju* priest who had killed a five-year-old girl for her bones. Alan sent word to Atta II that the priest's disappearance was a stain on the good name of the kingdom.

Weeks dragged by. By April 1944, newspapers in Accra were wondering whether Alan had lost his nerve. "We trust that the Government has not let the matter drop," said one.[24] A breakthrough came in early May when another *ju-ju* priest wrote to police to tell them that one of the eight men had tearfully confessed to taking part in the murder. Police interviews with the priest, mainly done by African officers, built up a picture of the crime. An African corporal from the local police station, H. A. Nuamah, was put in charge of the investigation. He convinced one of the stool carriers who was in the courtyard during the murder to talk.[25] The carrier led police to the riverbank where they recovered the remains of the body. The same night, Nuamah ordered the arrest of eight men for murder. They were a "who's who" of the kingdom, including a son of the deceased Atta I, the prime minister, the chief of native police, the state drummer, and the keeper of the stool house. All had a stake in the patronage of the new king.

Atta II wrote a frantic letter to Alan. Native autonomy had been violated, he complained. Those arrested were all good men, pillars of the community. Alan replied that "no personal feelings or other considerations" would stand in the way of the investigation: "Real responsibility," he wrote, "rests, not with the authorities but with those whose criminal activities made it necessary for such steps to be taken." The eight men would stand trial in Accra in October.

The dragnet was closing, and Atta II needed a legal team. The man he chose to lead it was Joseph Danquah, who belonged to this Akan tribe. Danquah had been sent to Britain on the tribal payroll in 1921, aged twenty-six, to obtain his legal qualifications.[26] He was a brilliant student and was offered an appointment in philosophy at University College London, where he could easily have remained. But he was intent on leading the Gold Coast to independence and returned to found his own political movement in the 1930s. It was during a trip to London in 1934 to discuss moves to self-government that Danquah discovered research done by French and Swiss archaeologists on an ancient black empire of the Middle Ages known as Ghana. Even though it did not extend as far south as the Gold Coast, Danquah liked the idea of naming the new country after this symbol of black imperialism. Imperialism was, after all, what powerful civilizations did.

Alan was one of Danquah's strongest supporters and friends. He underwrote Danquah's efforts to establish a University of Ghana, and he provided funds to support Danquah's writing of a mini-constitution for his Akan kingdom. Danquah dedicated one of his books on Akan culture to Alan.[27] Yet Danquah was also dependent on the patronage of his kingdom and politically ambitious. He constantly demanded money from the kingdom's coffers, in part due to his failing law practice in Accra.[28] A treasury official in the kingdom published a pamphlet arguing that Danquah ordered the murder because the priest was privy to Danquah's extortion and misuse of kingdom funds.[29]

Whatever the truth, when the *ju-ju* scandal erupted, Danquah saw his long-awaited opportunity. He explained to fellow Gold Coast firebrand Kwame Nkrumah, then studying communist subversion with Alan's brother Emile in London, that he took up the case for "mainly political" reasons: "Enemies of the country were anxious to hang around the neck of the Gold Coast people, who wanted self-government, the guilt of ritual murder in the twentieth century!" he wrote. Defending the accused was necessary "to save our Gold Coast name."[30] Perhaps with some clever lawyering, he could remove this embarrassing stain and emerge a national hero. Many of Alan's staff hoped he would succeed. As historian Rathbone noted, "the colonial authorities had no motive for destabilizing an African [kingdom] and besmirching a ruling family who had been by-words for cooperation."[31] In private, Danquah told Atta II that the evidence against the eight men was "very strong."[32]

Alan and Danquah were playing a high-stakes game for the future of the Gold Coast. For Danquah, that meant pressuring colonial authorities to hand over power to his movement. For Alan, it meant building up government capacity and training a new generation of responsible leaders who would protect human lives. Neither man was really in control of events. War-time staff shortages had forced colonial governments everywhere to accelerate the localization of top posts in the civil service. Alan approved the promotion of Africans to serve as district commissioners in the Gold Coast, two of whom were promoted in 1942. Sanders of the River could now be Kwame of the River. Alan's widely quoted minute to his staff explaining the change was a stirring call to progress and empathy as colonialism reached its most important phase.[33] "Africanization is the settled policy," he wrote. "There will be little room for officials who do not regard the having of African staff as their primary responsibility" and department heads "will not tolerate colour prejudice."[34]

The real prize, however, was not the bureaucracy but the legislature and executive. Alan warned London that those power centers needed to be opened up faster to meet rising demands for political inclusion: "I assure you that I am not an alarmist, but each day I get fresh evidence of the increasing feeling of Africans against Europeans, and against the government which Europeans represent."[35] As he recalled: "Too often in our colonial history we have waited too long in making these concessions, waiting in fact until they were practically forced from us, and given with a reluctance which robbed them of any political value." The greater danger, he believed, lay in "excessive caution" which would create "the mistake of being too late."[36]

Alan wanted to bring Africans from outside of government into his executive council (cabinet). His fellow governors in West Africa worried about stoking "extravagant political demands" but deferred to his judgement.[37] In 1942, feeling emboldened, Alan wrote to London: "If we do nothing now we will probably be forced later by popular clamor to go further than is wise." The mandarins put on the old silence, and Alan cabled with new vigor. "The negro peoples, both in the West Indies and in West Africa, are learning that the colonial administrations take no notice of popular feeling until this feeling is manifested in disturbances. This is one of the principle reasons why the people of these colonies choose as their leaders, not the moderate and reasonable men, but those irresponsible agitators who stimulate racial feeling against the whites and political movements against the government." While he begged pardon for pressing his demand, he felt the stakes were high: "I should be lacking in my duty if I did not express the views I so strongly hold."

The Colonial Office worried about a contagion of cabinet localization spreading to other colonies where suitable candidates might not be found. Even in the Gold Coast, it worried, Alan was creating future problems: "We must ask whether Sir A. Burns is not making a bid for a popular and harmonious term of office at the risk of leaving his successor with a *damnosa hereditas* [an inheritance that is a liability]." The secretary for colonies politely thanked Alan for his "forcibly urged" proposal. Alan was not to be denied: "I am afraid that I may be boring you with this argument, but all fanatics are rather boring and I confess to being a fanatic in the matter of giving the colonial peoples what they would like up to a reasonable point and not just 'governing' them."

In the end, London relented. The appointment of two nongovernment Africans to Alan's cabinet was spun as a natural progression since governors had the right to appoint outsiders. Nigeria's governor also placed two nongovernment Africans in his cabinet. "I am confident that this decision will have very good results," Alan promised. It became the template for the localization of cabinets throughout the empire and boosted Alan's popularity in the Gold Coast, where he became known as the "Sunshine Governor."[38] "He is respected by both white and coloured populations of the Gold Coast and is regarded as an eminently fair man," one African journalist wrote. "He is approachable, has a powerful handshake for all, and is nearly always smiling."[39]

The trial of the eight men accused of the *ju-ju* murder opened in Accra on November 3rd, 1944. "This promises to be a *cause célèbre* which will throw other controversies in the shade for a time," London warned.[40] Alan chose a Turkish Cypriot to be the judge. The prosecution was led by a black African who had risen up the ranks from police officer to assistant attorney general. The seven-man jury was composed of six Africans and one European. All of the key witnesses were Africans. For Alan, the battle for colonialism could be won only by those whose fates lay in the balance.

The trial lasted a month. The prosecution was meticulous and overwhelming, including two eye-witnesses to the murder as well as the *ju-ju* priest who had written to police. As the judge later noted, the eight accused men seemed puzzled that their participation in this cultural practice was something that they should have concealed. "No precautions were taken by the prisoners to conceal this crime."[41] Rathbone concluded that the case was "undeniably a strong one."[42] Attempts by Danquah's defense team to discredit the witnesses or to cast doubts on Akan funeral customs failed. Danquah himself was briefly charged with instigating a witness not to testify. The judge called his alibi "a complete fabrication" but thought better of making him a martyr.[43] After a brief deliberation, the jury passed a guilty verdict on all eight men on December 3rd. The judge sentenced them all to death.

Alan braced for a negative reaction. While the man in the street hated ritual murder, the educated classes seemed more obsessed with "persecution by the Europeans" and thus saw many of those convicted in court as "martyrs rather than a criminals," he noted.[44] "There is the feeling, particularly among the educated classes [of Africans] that the failings of their brethren should be concealed. The punishment is always considered excessive, although the guilt may be manifest."[45]

A few months before the *ju-ju* verdicts, for instance, one of the colony's most colorful black legislators had been convicted of seeking a bribe from an association of British trading interests.[46] During the trial, the legislator did not deny the facts. Instead, he claimed that he was trying to entrap the business association into offering a bribe.[47] As Alan recounted: "The local press reported everything connected with the trial at such length that other events had to go unrecorded; a reader of the local papers at this time might have been excused for thinking that there was no war raging in Europe—or in

Burma where Gold Coast troops were fighting."[48] When he was found guilty
and sentenced to one day in prison, the black legislator immediately "became
a martyr and a popular hero," Alan recalled. "I believe that the vast majority
of the people of Accra knew in their hearts that he was guilty, although their
misguided sense of racial loyalty (or their lack of moral courage) made them
pretend otherwise."[49]

Alan worried about a similar response to the *ju-ju* verdicts. Instead, "there
was rejoicing among the African population."[50] He wrote to London, "Popular
sentiment is violently averse to this deplorable practice and determined that it
should now come to light and be stamped out."[51] If Danquah had hoped that
the man in the street would rally around the *ju-ju* murderers, he was mistaken.
Now he needed other tactics.

It was normal for death sentences to be sent to the West African Court of
Appeal. Danquah filed the expected motion in January 1945. It claimed that
the prosecution's main witnesses were too young to know anything, whereas
the defense had called kingdom elders who were more credible. The three-
member bench turned the argument on its head in denying the appeal. It was
precisely the elders, the judges wrote, who might be more interested "in
averting the stigma" that a conviction would attach to the kingdom.[52]

Before Alan had a chance to sign the death warrants, he received word
from London that Danquah had hired a lawyer, named A. L. Bryden, who
was certified to make appeals to the Privy Council, Britain's highest court of
appeal. Alan was told to delay action pending such an appeal.

While there was no reason to think the facts would change when examined
in London, the shift of venue was disastrous. A war-weary nation with a
new anti-colonial Labour government was being asked to sanction the killing of loyal Africans. The new culturally relative Left and the old culturally
disdainful Right would unite against the cultural universalists like Alan and
declare that Britain had no business carrying out justice against *ju-ju*. Bryden
knew that if the case were to be won, it would be won in the court of public
opinion in Britain. "Now began that series of fruitless appeals which held
up the executions and brought the law into disrepute in the colony," Alan
would write.[53]

To allow steam to build, Bryden delayed the filing of his Privy Council
appeal for nine months. At first, he explained that he was moving house. Then
he pleaded that some files had been misplaced. Not until October 1945, when
the Colonial Office threatened to nullify the appeal, were the papers filed. It
took just two weeks for the Privy Council to deny. By this time, it had been
sixteen months since the arrests. Alan exercised mercy over the two young-
est of the accused, commuting their sentences to twenty years. "Public vengeance for the crime committed will be satisfied and . . . sufficient deterrent
will be produced if a lesser number [are] executed," he explained.[54]

Bryden was not done. He told Danquah to file another appeal with the West African court on the grounds that the body dug up by the river was not that of the priest. This was a red herring, since the judge had explicitly excluded that evidence in his advice to the jury. The appeal was rejected and the remaining six men were transferred to a prison in Accra where executions were carried out. "There must be no surrendering of the principles of justice to powers of money and influence," Alan insisted.[55]

A day before the executions, Danquah and Bryden gave notice of another Privy Council appeal. As one British journalist observed at the time: "No one had seriously doubted the guilt of the accused and no one had realized, until Dr. Danquah and his colleagues found them, that so many loopholes existed in British law."[56] The Colonial Office should have advised Alan to proceed. But it was nervous. Bryden sniffed their fear and lobbied them incessantly. In December 1945, the Colonial Office told Alan to delay again.[57] Alan complained about the "gross abuses of the judicial system" that were "unnecessarily cruel to the condemned men."[58] But he was duty-bound to obey. This was in Alan's view, "the first real delay . . . against my advice which caused all the later trouble."[59]

Danquah's legal tenacity reflected the failure of his political ambitions. At Alan's invitation in 1943, Danquah had drafted a reform plan that called for a fully elected legislature and an executive cabinet drawn from it. "No people can become fit for responsibility until they have exercised it," Alan explained.[60] Under Danquah's plan, expatriates would be relegated to bureaucratic roles and the governor would lose his veto. Danquah fancied the powerful home minister position for himself.[61]

Alan rejected Danquah's plan as too ambitious. His alternative proposal called for eighteen of the thirty seats in the legislature to be elected—four directly and another fourteen indirectly through tribal councils. Of the remaining twelve seats, six would be government officials and the other six would be nonofficials chosen by the governor. The proposal, known as the "Burns Constitution," was the most far-reaching step on the road to self-government in any British colony in Africa. London warned that the "gesture" would have unstoppable consequences, and the resident minister in West Africa took Alan aside to express alarm.[62] Alan was able to work his famous charms. He invited the minister to inspect an honor guard and to present medals to returned veterans. "Afterward, we sat together while the band played and I told him about the constitutional proposals," Alan explained.[63] Alan then invited him for a drink at the police mess and they "parted the best of friends." The next day, the resident minister declared that Alan was the best governor he had ever known and approved the plan.[64]

The first election under the Burns Constitution was held in 1945, followed by a gala opening of the new legislature in 1946 (see figure 9.1). It marked the first place in Africa where elected members, which included the now sidelined Danquah, held a majority. When the appointed African members were included, blacks held twenty-one of the thirty seats. The opening was a day of national celebration, and Alan bathed in the glory of being a progressive governor. Alan urged the legislature to seek a constructive relationship with the executive "refraining from the cheap tactics of demagogues." Power used abusively or oppressively, he noted, "does not last long," and the success of the legislature would determine the Gold Coast's "fitness for further political advance."

Privately, he told his staff to be patient. As he had experienced in the Bahamas and British Honduras, things moved slowly when a legislature had a say: "The electors are going to make mistakes in electing the wrong kind of people . . . and the members . . . are going to make mistakes in the exercise of their authority. But they will learn from these mistakes[,] and unless we are prepared to take the risk of having mistakes made we will never succeed in our avowed intention of leading the Gold Coast Africans along the road of complete self-government."[65]

For Danquah, the dashing of his plans and the success of Alan's alternative marked the zenith of his "celebrity as the Sieyès of the Gold Coast," noted

Figure 9.1 First Legislature under the Burns Constitution, 1946. *Source*: Private Collection of Alan Dixon.

one historian, referring to the architect of the French Revolution.[66] Rejected as Sieyès, he began to act more like Robespierre.

On Danquah's advice, Bryden delayed his second appeal to the Privy Council. "These are Fabian tactics with a vengeance," *The Economist* noted, indicating a growing interest in the case in the British press.[67] Alan was dismayed and compared the delays to the speedy move to justice in another *ju-ju* murder case whose five perpetrators had killed a ten-year-old girl to make medicine. They all went to the gallows in early 1946 despite similar attempts at procedural delay by Bryden on their behalf.[68]

As expected, the Privy Council swiftly rejected the second appeal. Danquah had readied several more procedural ploys, including a direct appeal to King George VI and a complaint of malice because Alan had not invited him to a garden party at the castle the previous year. As Rathbone noted: "The defense were cleverly creating such a tangle of legal process that further delay was unavoidable whilst legal experts sought their way through the thicket."[69]

The Colonial Office agreed with Alan that this was mere obfuscation, but it would not approve executions while any matters were pending. There was simply no appetite, especially as many of the new cabinet members in the Labour government were opposed to capital punishment. "The wretched people of the Gold Coast—if they live in lonely places—[will] continue to go in fear . . . whenever a chief dies," one frustrated mandarin opined.[70]

All along, it seems, Danquah's plan had been to take the issue out of the courts and into the realm of British politics. Bryden even wrote a small pamphlet entitled *A Gold Coast Mystery* that simultaneously appealed to Conservative MPs in opposition with charges about the incompetence of the government and to Labour MPs with attacks on the idea of colonialism. The lengthy delay of the executions, it charged, was evidence of the cruelty of the colonial system. After the pamphlet was circulated, MPs began to write outraged letters to the secretary for colonies. Suddenly, the whole murder was being re-litigated among British politicians. Danquah added to the literary efforts with a fawning memorial to the speaker of the British Parliament—"none in whom the intangible reality called British conscience is better embodied"[71]—urging him to allow a parliamentary debate on the matter. As one Colonial Office mandarin observed: "The expected campaign has begun."[72]

Here was the new optics of colonialism. High-minded progressives in the West would take it upon themselves to expose the "crimes" of colonialism, never noticing, in the words of a later scholar, that the "victims" they defended were often "victimizers," and the colonial oppressors the protectors.[73] The mourning members of the murdered priest's clan wrote to the

Colonial Office in disgust: "Oh, that we were as wealthy to work subtle propaganda in high British circles as these rich murderers."[74]

The governor's residence at Christiansborg Castle—"a stage set of Elsinore in dazzling white with the surf beating below on two sides," as Graham Greene called it—was built by the Danish in 1661 and then sold to the British in 1850. It was "probably the most interesting Government House in the colonial empire," Alan proposed. It was used by the Danish as a slave depot and then by the British as a lunatic asylum. "Now, as the governor's residence it has probably reached its nadir."[75]

The castle was damp, drafty, and ill-fitted for its emergent role in the 1940s as an exhibition of the British Empire. Along with American officers during the war, pretty much every visiting journalist, scholar, writer, Vichy attaché, London bureaucrat, novelist, and adventurer treated the castle as a sort of welcome center where they could take part in the great universalizing project of colonialism. According to the castle guestbook, Alan and Katie hosted 432 overnight guests during their 5-and-1/2 years of residency— roughly two guests per week. "It is unique, combining the romance of the past, the comforts of the present, and the embodied hopes of the future," wrote one guest.[76] The burdens of playing host were immense, and recriminations among those who had to put up with lesser billets were bitter. It was socially awkward for the hosts to play hotelier to visitors "whom they have never met and with whom they have nothing in common," Alan complained. This was worse during the war years when booze was rationed: "The arrival of a thirsty visitor was a serious menace to his host's quota," he recalled. The sense of entitlement to stay at the castle seemed greatest among those with the least claim. High-ranking visitors "were the most diffident in accepting it."[77]

Katie's practical concern was a lack of bathrooms. She had several internal walls demolished in order to add more.[78] Then she refurbished the main floor to accommodate larger receptions and dinners. "We like our castle, and some of the worst drawbacks of a medieval fortress are being overcome," Alan wrote to a colleague.[79] The previous governor's staff were "quite good aside from their rooted aversion to work," Alan noted.[80] Katie had them clean out rooms that had not seen a broom in years. Opening an old shed, they discovered the governor's car. "It is the same one that Noah used when he emerged from the Ark," Alan reported to London. "The car caught fire at Tamale but the fire was unfortunately put out by an over-zealous staff."

Alan converted an upper room into an aviary where he could commune with his growing collection of West African birds. Along with orioles and Barbets, he had several Giant Crested Plantain Eaters that "were tame enough to follow me about the garden" and a group of magnificent Touracos "which, when I opened the door of the aviary, would fly to me and perch on my hand."[81] The legendary British ornithologist David Bannerman visited the castle several times while working on his eight-volume illustrated series on the birds of West Africa. Alan begged for a concise single-volume edition. Bannerman obliged. Alan wrote the foreword and claimed to be its "godfather."[82]

The castle served another important function for Alan: in a small writing room near the aviary, he wrote his memoirs (see figure 9.2). Alan would turn sixty in 1947, and he believed that retirement was not far off. The *ju-ju* case was a drain, and Katie's health was deteriorating. "I am very fed up and anxious to escape to the haven of retirement," he wrote to a friend.[83] The castle thus became both an *hôtel de ville* of the British Empire as well as the place where Sir Alan Burns made sense of that empire.

Writing his memoirs to the sonata of aviary sounds while the *ju-ju* murder case rose to its crescendo seems to have inspired Alan. As Rathbone argued, "There is little doubt that anger haunted the drafting of his memoirs." The result was "an unusually forthright, boisterous and angry memoir for those more conservative and deferential days."[84] The book is no tired recounting of colonial derring-do, but a historical, empirical, and theoretical defense of his career and the purpose that it served. *Ju-ju* infuriated Alan, but it also propelled his intellect in a way that no other event could have. Alan practically wrote himself into existence.

The case for colonialism that Alan brought to life in the castle room—and would expand upon in subsequent writings and speeches—begins with the origins of European imperialism in general and the British Empire in particular. European expansion began in the fifteenth century, when conquest and expansion was what all powers did. Europe was no different, only more powerful. And it was Europe where norms to control expansion and set standards emerged during the high tide of colonialism from the early 1800s to the mid-1900s. In the wars that were fought, the Europeans were usually fighting alongside local groups against their rivals. Some colonies—Hong Kong, Sierra Leone, the Bahamas—were settled with virtually no indigenous populations. Most, like India, Malaya, and those in Africa, resulted from a mixture of treaties, wars, and invitations. What conflict there was paled in comparison to what had come before. "It is probable that fewer of the indigenous people were killed in all the colonial territories during the establishment of the British regime than were killed in a single year in tribal warfare and slave raids in the preceding period."[85]

No less important, the most likely alternative to British rule in most places was rule by another European power or by a non-European imperialist, whether Arab, Turk, or indigenous, all of which were far less liberal and developed. These "worse evils" were what justified European rule: "Impartial

Figure 9.2   At Castle Writing Desk, 1945. *Source*: Private Collection of Alan Dixon.

government has shielded the people from all that was worst in their past history, from slavery and human sacrifice, from corrupt judges and tyrannical chiefs, from famine and disease. It is the fashion today to decry colonialism, but it has saved millions of people from worse evils."[86]

Criticisms of the "artificial" borders drawn by European imperialists were absurd, since natural borders were obscure at best, and what was needed for human progress was not ethnic cleansing but a shared *civic* culture and institutions. "The 'tyranny' of European rule has replaced tyrannies less bearable."[87]

In the event, being a colony brought immense benefits to the lives of the peoples, as shown by surging populations, expanded life expectancy, and protection from crime, war, and slavery. It created systems of education, the rule of law, public health, and professional ethics, alongside the better-known provision of infrastructure and undreamt-of economic opportunities in the forms of transportation and communications, provision of wage employment, and cheap foreign finance. Cultures and ecologies had been protected against ravages that would have befallen these places. "It has sometimes been argued that they were poor because they were colonies, but in fact they were colonies because they were poor, and unable without help to improve their condition."[88]

Failures there were: land seizures were sanctioned in some places that left farmers worse off; education was a low priority from the start, as were preparations for self-government. London was too stingy with financial support because of Victorian principles of self-reliance. But the overall record was something to be proud of: "In the past we have made many mistakes in our colonial administration and we will probably make more in the future, but against our mistakes we can set a record of achievement which has not been excelled by any nation in the world, and on balance we have nothing to be ashamed of."[89]

Most important, local people agreed. Colonialism was legitimate because the colonized understood reality far better than later generations of anti-colonial critics. Army garrisons and police presences were thin on the ground. Most colonialism was done by natives. "I doubt whether at any time British rule could have been maintained in the larger colonial territories against the will of the majority of the local inhabitants."[90] Alan was fond of quoting the testimony of natives who had reached similar conclusions, such as one Sudanese commenting on British rule there: "The realities here are that the Government released slaves and suppressed slavery; they increased prosperity, gave education, protected the weak and the outraged, defended and taught strength and courage to those who were the predestined victims of chiefs and priests; fought disease and postponed death."[91] Thus when Alan insisted that "British colonial rule was generally right when it was imposed and right for a long time afterwards,"[92] he was using the word "right" (or "rightful") in its fullest sense, both from the objective point of view of ethical analysis as well as the subjective point of view of those concerned. Colonial authorities had the right to rule in most places; they were legitimate. That is why Alan found it hard to believe circa 1946 that the push for immediate independence in some colonies would find much support: "Even if good government is not a real substitute for self-government, there are not many of the subject peoples who would willingly change their present government for the uncertainties of independence."[93]

The Gold Coast itself was a perfect miniature of these arguments. The most powerful Akan kingdom, the Ashanti, was on the war path when the British stepped in to save the Fanti and other Akan tribes. The British treaty with the nine Fanti Chiefs of the Gold Coast in 1844 created the crown colony of sixty-three separate tribal states and "had protected the people of the colony from otherwise certain annexation by the Ashantis."[94] The British expedition of 1874 against the Ashanti was precipitated by Ashanti resentment of the growing prosperity of the British ports along the coast. The Ashanti had menaced the British, beheading twenty-five soldiers in one foray in 1873. The British sent an expedition to chasten the Ashanti with a mutual pledge of cooperation and to pre-empt a French invasion. The British and their native allies fought for twelve hours an uninspired Ashanti force that then fled into the jungle along with the entire royal family. The British entered the palace, took some booty to show their victory, and left. The Ashanti king then signed a treaty of friendship, promising trade and peace under the British crown's protection, and was packed off to exile in Sierra Leone. The newly incorporated Ashanti kingdom thrived, and the Gold Coast boomed. Had the British not taken the Ashanti under their protection, the French would certainly have done so, pressing in from the north where they had defeated a slave-trading warlord.

Alan's book was written in a postwar period when many in Britain were starting to doubt the colonial enterprise. By contrast, his own thinking had veered sharply in the direction of a defense of the British Empire. As a Colonial Office functionary wrote of the book: "It is refreshing to find that he takes, upon the whole, a favourable view both of our past colonial record and of our future prospects."[95] The book's angry tone resulted from his realization that those carefully laid foundations could easily succumb to the irresponsible politics of lawless natives and their Western admirers. "It is our business to show them the *constitutional* way to political and economic independence."[96]

Bryden and Danquah were engaged in a full-press publicity effort in London. A group of eighty-seven parliamentarians wrote to Alan warning that "the weight of public opinion" in Britain was against the *ju-ju* sentences. Alan indignantly fired back, "the real weight of public opinion is in *this* colony . . . manifesting itself in growing indignation and impatience at the manner in which condemned prisoners have been allowed to obstruct the course of justice in this brutal murder."[97] Alan warned London of "disorder and even bloodshed" if the sentences were not carried out.[98]

Alan returned to Britain on leave in September 1946 (now made immeasurably faster thanks to the British Overseas Airways Corporation) and agreed to meet five of the politicians face-to-face. The exchange was testy. They called him "obdurate" and "a deaf adder."[99] The two Colonial Office mandarins who attended took Alan's side. Any further intervention in the case by the secretary for colonies would be interpreted in the Gold Coast as evidence of "favouritism, impotence, or cowardice by HMG," they cautioned.[100] True enough, when he returned, Alan received a letter from a chief in the powerful Ashanti kingdom warning that a festive *durbar* scheduled for later in the year was "a trap" where his life might be in danger for failing to carry out the sentences.[101]

Events took a turn for the worse when a new secretary for colonies, Arthur Creech Jones, was appointed. In Rathbone's words, Creech Jones "was more interested in protecting his back than his civil servants."[102] A conscientious objector during World War I, he became a Fabian socialist and authored works denouncing colonialism.[103] At first, Creech Jones wanted simply to overrule Alan. His advisors warned that it would be unprecedented and would likely force Alan to resign.[104] Creech Jones then secretly wrote to the MPs asking them to make a direct appeal to the King for commutation. This would allow Creech Jones to "advise" the king to agree. Two days before Christmas 1946, Creech Jones told Alan to stay his hand yet again.

The Conservatives were making hay out of Creech Jones' indecision and seeming loss of control over the *ju-ju* case. Radical Labour MPs were pressing even harder. The Colonial Office mandarins finally rebelled against Creech Jones in early 1947, forcing him to behave. This was a *British* Colony, they noted snidely, where courts had the final say, not a French colony where bureaucrats did. Alan's opposition to clemency for the five remaining prisoners (one had since died of natural causes in hospital) needed to be respected: "All the evidence available here supports his view."[105] Clamped down, Creech Jones wrote to Alan: "The decision rests with you."[106] Alan scheduled the executions for 11:30 p.m. on February 4th.

The five men were taken on February 3rd to the prison where hangings were carried out, their fourth trip to the prison since the defense filibuster began. On the evening of February 4th, the protesting MPs sent a letter to the king seeking a delay. Creech Jones, who had ignored a plea from the MPs earlier in the day, sent a "most immediate" telegram to Alan at 11:00 p.m. ordering him to stay the executions pending the king's response. Seven minutes before the first man was to swing, the hangman stood down.

Alan went to bed disgusted. In the morning, he telegrammed London to warn of "serious consequences" in the colony.[107] The matter now went all the way to the prime minister. He scolded the Labour backbenchers for their violation of party discipline and told Creech Jones that he should have found a legal loophole to overrule Alan. By this time, the five men had been sent back to the original prison, and Alan did not want them moved again until he was sure justice would be done. Creech Jones sent a spineless telegram on February 20th telling Alan he did not plan to advise the king to hold up the executions despite his "personal views." Six days later, Alan received another green light. He set March 3rd to move the men to the gallows prison for execution the following day.

The politics in London were out of control however. Rather than being chastened by the prime minister's scolding, the Labour backbenchers were enlivened. Seeing the government in disarray fired up the Conservatives as well. A regular question time was scheduled for Parliament on the afternoon of March 3rd, shortly before the condemned were to be transported to the gallows prison. Every MP imagined himself a great humanitarian, calling out misrule in the colonies in the grand tradition of Edmund Burke. The member most eager to speak was Winston Churchill.

The House session of March 3rd, 1947, opened at 2:30 p.m. Around supper-time, a Labour MP rose to set off the debate on *ju-ju* using a procedural tactic. The speaker ruled the discussion out of order. It carried on nonetheless for a full forty minutes. Rising with a growl and waving his paper to attract the speaker's attention, Churchill was given the floor.

Churchill was a liberal imperialist like Alan. He had won his second term in Parliament in 1906, aged thirty-one, by drawing attention to Boer brutalities against imported Chinese workers in the Transvaal. In the words of one author, Churchill felt that "cruelty had gone unpunished, justice had been denied, and the Empire had been tarnished in the eyes of its humblest subjects."[108] He was rewarded with a cabinet post as junior minister for the colonies. Forty years later, with his political career ending and the indignities of old age pressing in, Churchill may have seen in the *ju-ju* case an echo of his earlier self. Perhaps a shot of colonial vigor in the late English winter could buck up the seventy-two-year-old gaffer. He went quickly to the offensive:

Is this not an affront to every decent tradition of British administration?

[MPs] "Yes! Shame!"

"Must we go quietly away and learn that these men, after being four or five or six times brought to the threshold of death, have at last been executed? And is this not a matter of great urgency affecting the life and the honour and the decent administration of British government not only in this country?"

[MPs] "Yes! It is! Shame!"

"Let us make sure that these men are not executed without Parliament [*sic*] having an opportunity to consider the matter. Will the Right Honorable Gentleman the Secretary of State for the Colonies make it perfectly clear that he will not approve the execution of these men, pending further consideration by this House? Can we rest in uncertainty upon a matter of life and death?"

[MPs] "Promise! Promise!"

"This is a matter of life and death. Will the Colonial Secretary not get off, and send his telegram now?"

[Creech Jones] "I will immediately communicate with the Governor of the Gold Coast. I will ask him."

[MPs] "No! Tell Him! Tell Him!"

[Creech Jones] "There are limitations on my own power in this matter. I will ask the Governor of the Gold Coast if he will most seriously consider the postponement."

[MPs] "No! Not enough!"

[Creech Jones] "I think the House may take it that if I make this suggestion the respite will probably take place."

[MPs] "Go! Go now!"[109]

Creech Jones skittered from the House like a cockroach. "In the mood which the House then showed, any show of obstinacy on my part would not have availed," he pleaded to Alan.[110] *The Economist* called the scene "a classic case of parliamentary solicitude for the welfare of colonial peoples at its most belated, ill-informed, and mis-directed" and "a startling illustration of the degree of ignorance in high quarters of colonial affairs."[111] The House had been "swept off its feet emotionally by Winston," an MP wrote to Alan.[112]

Six years earlier, Alan had been burning the midnight oil on Churchill's behalf. Now he was burning the midnight oil on Churchill's repeal. Late in the evening, Creech Jones sent the fateful telegram, which began tapping out in Accra shortly before midnight:

Secret and Most Immediate. Parliament informed by Private Member today of the execution tomorrow of men condemned for the murder. Speaker ruled question out of order but discussion pursued in great excitement and efforts in all quarters of the House to compel my intervention to overrule your decision that the men should be executed. Whole House deeply moved and demonstrated hostility to your decision. Attack was led by Winston Churchill . . . House in uproar for forty minutes demanding that death sentence should be stayed.[113]

Alan did not blame the House. It was *supposed to* act foolishly and represent popular opinion. "I have too great a respect for the Mother of Parliaments to criticise the proceedings themselves (even though the old lady is liable at times, as on this occasion, to become hysterical)," Alan insisted.[114] Rather, it was the responsibility of Creech Jones to ignore the vox populi, and in this he had failed. Alan felt he had no choice but to stay the executions. "Churchill Saves Lives of Five *Ju-Ju* Slayers," proclaimed the *Los Angeles Times*.[115]

Again, Alan warned London, "Local feeling here will be strong," saying also, "There will probably be bloodshed."[116] A group of minor chiefs wrote, cautioning, "If British justice fails to atone for the innocent blood of [the priest], surely we can avenge this death."[117]

The time had come for high drama. "There seemed to be only one course open to me" given that the government "had failed and were unwilling to support me in this matter." The people of the Gold Coast would feel that "one in whom they had trusted had betrayed them."[118] He sent a telegram to Creech Jones on March 4th tendering his resignation: "I cannot conscientiously make myself a party to what I consider to be a gross miscarriage of justice."[119] The gauntlet was thrown.

Sir Alan Burns was by all accounts a likeable man, as popular with the ladies as Katie was with the gentlemen. He was generous, funny, and sociable. Throughout his career, his friendships extended in many directions. He counted white, brown, and black alike among his chums, as well as male and female. Scattered throughout his papers and letters are occasional funny notes and inside jokes with lady friends, of whom there appear to have been at least a dozen during his career. In the Gold Coast, he told one lady friend that he was considering a milk-only diet. "Please don't go on a milk diet. You are just nice now. Horrible to have a thin Governor—most unmajestic," she replied.[120] A copy of his memoirs contains a personal inscription to another lady friend: "In happy memory of television."

There is no reason to suppose that any of these friendships was illicit or sexual. Rather, Alan found support in the attentions of like-minded women who rallied around him when the going got tough. Katie was a steadfast partner but not particularly interested in the intrigues of life at the top of the colonial service. Like Barbara, she found colonial politics a bore. For these moments, Alan always seemed to have a *confidante* at hand.

Among Alan's lady friends in the Gold Coast was Lady Dinah Quist (see figure 9.3). She was a handsome West African woman with an immediately disarming smile and a ready interest in local politics. Her husband had been in the legislature since 1925. Unlike Danquah, his law practice in Accra was a success, and unlike Danquah, he was invited to garden parties at the castle. He was the first African speaker of the colonial legislature under Alan's reforms. Lady Quist was no wallflower. She served in several responsible positions during the late colonial period—town councils, lay magistracies,

Figure 9.3 Katie and Lady Quist, 1946. *Source*: Private Collection of Alan Dixon.

and commissions of inquiry. Throughout the ugly business of the *ju-ju* murders, she kept in close correspondence with Alan.

When Alan's offer of his resignation became public, it seized the colony. The *Ashanti Pioneer* newspaper pledged its support against the "Parliamentary wolves." The entire legislature, except for Danquah, passed a motion of support for Alan's governorship. Lady Quist sent a hurried note to the castle:

> The news of your alleged resignation reached us with extreme regret yesterday. It gave us a great shock and I have not yet got over it. My husband and I regret the circumstances that have compelled you to take such a step, and we trust that H.M. the King may not accept your resignation, in which case we hope that you may reconsider your decision and stay with us a little longer. After all you have not done anything wrong and why should you go away in this manner?[121]

Lady Quist was not alone in sending letters of support to Alan. But hers is the letter he kept, along with her photo. As the *ju-ju* murder moved toward its climax, there was a sense that Alan's time in the Gold Coast was ending. The "wrench" of his leaving, as his Nigerian friend had called it a decade' earlier, would be particularly hard for Lady Quist. Things suddenly did not feel so certain. "Stay with us a little longer." Do not crumble before the coming tide of anti-colonialism. The words, written tenderly to Alan, had a larger meaning.

Alan was playing a game of bluff. Stop your moralizing and posturing, he was warning Creech Jones, or I will unleash chaos. Alan dropped word of his threat to all quarters. "Burns [has] huffily threatened to resign over this kibitzing by the House," *Time* magazine reported as the case drew global attention.[122]

The threat seemed to work. Telegrams poured in from sixty-two of the sixty-three tribal chiefs (except Atta II) begging him to remain and deploring the contemptible tactics of Danquah's defense team. His resignation would be "inimical to the economic, educational, political, and social development of this country," the chiefs warned.[123] The Gold Coast press was inundated with letters and published streams of them alongside leading articles: "For the loss of such a governor, the survival of a few guilty lives is no compensation," the *Gold Coast Observer* fumed.[124] The *Ashanti Pioneer* in a leading article titled "Our Sir Alan Burns" spoke of his "vast prestige among Africans" and ended with the assurance, "The whole Gold Coast public is solidly behind your actions."[125]

Not for the first time, Western progressives who claimed to speak on behalf of the "oppressed" people of the Third World were contradicted by actually existing Third World people. To be a "nationalist" on the ritual murder case was to be pro-colonial. "We hope the people of this country will not be forced to wage a major counter-offensive against the organized might of the British House of Parliament and the equally emotional British public," one local newspaper averred.[126]

Creech Jones wrote to the prime minister warning of the "unfortunate effects in the Gold Coast and possible repercussions in the Colonies and the Colonial Service," if Alan resigned.[127] The prime minister ordered him to grovel and get Alan back. In an obsequious note to Alan, he fretted that "deplorable consequences may and almost certainly will follow [and] may well spread beyond the Gold Coast."

It is unimaginable that Alan, who had devoted his life to colonial peoples, planned to walk off the job at such a critical moment. "Unless I have read the life of Sir Alan to no purpose, I have never known him to be a quitter," a prominent Ghanaian economist and civil servant wrote to Katie in one heart-felt letter begging her to intervene. "Not even the debate of parliamentarians or the boisterous waves of the Christiansborg sea can tone down the wishes that we NEED Sir Alan."[128] Alan was too much a fighter and too intellectually engaged with the future of colonialism to end it all in a huff. Superannuation in Putney would seem wholly unattractive.

Creech Jones implored Alan to await his statement to the House on March 5th. Alan agreed. Even if Creech Jones knew that Alan was putting on a show, he probably felt that the time had come to tame the wolves.

The mood in the House on March 5th was like the day after a drunken binge. The unprovoked attack on Alan might cost Britain "one of the very best men the colonial service has ever known," one member noted ruefully. Reading the Hansard, it is hard to believe that it was the same group. "Many members began to wonder whether in fact the House had not made a fool of itself," one London daily noted.[129] Each mention of Alan by Creech Jones was greeted with cheers. There had been "popular demonstrations of public indignation" in the Gold Coast at the delays, he scolded, and "the administration of British justice in the Colony has already been discredited." Who but Alan was in a position to dispense mercy in light of the local situation? Was it not a travesty to force this governor "who has contributed so much and with such distinction to African development" into retirement?

Churchill ambled into the chamber half-way through Creech Jones's speech. He pricked up his ears at the topic, waved his papers, and was given the floor. He had no idea that sentiments had swung. "I did not hear the open-ing discussion. I presume that it is understood on all sides that these men will *not* be executed until there has been a further debate in this House?" He had misread the tone. Sit down, old fool, a colleague insisted. Your actions "undermine British judicial authority in Africa." Six years earlier, Alan had brought Churchill's ship into port. This time, he torpedoed it.

Again, Creech Jones scurried from the House to send a telegram to Accra. "The atmosphere was very much changed," he wrote. Every mention of Alan was greeted with "appreciative cheers from all sides."[130] In a personal letter, he repeated the news of a "generous echo" in the House. He had been on Alan's side all along, but needed to allow the MPs their say: "I fear it had to be. Such is Parliament."[131]

Alan "had won the propaganda battle" and "was back in the saddle, the horse subdued," Rathbone wrote.[132] On March 19th, after a final procedural delay in Parliament failed, Creech Jones sent what would be his last telegram on the matter: "No, repeat no, reason why you should delay your decision."[133] Alan convened his executive council which set the date of execution for March 24th.

Governor Sir Alan Burns finally laid justice on *ju-ju* at James Fort Prison, Accra on Monday, March 24th, 1947. The first man swung at 2:00 p.m., the second and third shortly after. The fourth and fifth were being marched to the scaffold when Bryden indicated he planned to file yet another appeal to the Privy Council in London. Alan delayed the execution of the final pair, perhaps because Bryden had threatened Alan with prosecution for murder if he ignored another Privy Council appeal.[134] At 7:30 p.m., Alan informed Creech Jones that the two men had been sent back to their original prison so that he could mull the matter.

Alan's thoughts were turning to the future. He did not flinch from his duty. Nor did he delight in the task, for as he would tell the legislature, "I am myself no enthusiast for capital punishment." While he found Bryden's threat "impudent," he did not want the case following him back to England.[135] A little tender mercy at this point might go a long way.

On Friday morning, Alan announced that the sentences of the two remaining men would be commuted to life in prison. As he explained to the legislature that afternoon, the two men "knew that three of their accomplices had actually paid the supreme penalty and that the tactics of the defence had failed. In such circumstances, they must have anticipated a similar fate for themselves and suffered mentally in anticipation." He urged the people of the Gold Coast to take heart that all of the accused had been punished: "Do not think that because of what has happened that law and justice have failed. . . . Justice will always prevail in the end however it may be abused."

Alan's final act was a master class in politics and governance. The calibration of force and of mercy offered succor to both sides. There were no reprisals against Chief Atta II and his kingdom. "Sir Alan's attitude has been exemplary, and he has gone through a very trying period with restraint, impartiality, and dignity," a Gold Coast newspaper concluded.[136] The act also played well back home. "Sir Alan Burns's conception of his responsibility, first in withholding and finally in exercising his prerogative of mercy, should be generally approved," the *Times* wrote.[137]

Within the Colonial Office, a relieved staff celebrated Alan's deft conclusion of an alarming affair. "Here was truth speaking at last," the Colonial Office's legal advisor wrote to Alan of his address to the Gold Coast legislature.[138] Downing Street had a team of secretaries to send copies of the address to everyone in Britain who had written "abusive and/or intercessory letters" on the matter.[139] Creech Jones added a heartfelt letter: "The reaction has been all your way."

It is tempting to glorify Alan and pillory Creech Jones in the *ju-ju* murder case. Time and a broader perspective offer more nuanced judgments. Alan was probably too eager to bring off the executions in the early stages of the appeals. His disgust with Danquah and Bryden was unfair, given that they were simply pursuing every avenue as legal counsel should. He also probably blustered to excess about the dangers of delay. As eminent British historian of African law Gordon Woodman commented: "His conviction that the executions were essential to good government and social progress seems to have become obsessive." Alan was "unfairly traduced" by his opponents to be sure, Woodman allowed. "However, he himself did not always keep a wise distance from the arena."[140] The fact that Alan would continue to squabble with Bryden in the letters pages of the *Times Literary Supplement* years later suggested a lack of equipoise.

By contrast, Creech Jones was in an altogether different role. Rathbone's "scathing criticism" of him "would be justified if the highest duty of the [secretary for colonies] had been to support a colonial governor," Woodman wrote. However, his duty was to consider multiple issues, only one of which was keeping Alan happy. "Creech-Jones saw his position as more complex than this" and "he followed a consistent, if not simple, policy." Not only were his moral concerns valid, but his constitutional role was at first uncertain, and he was correct to err on the side of the defense. "The dilemma, of personal moral conviction against constitutional duty, is familiar in public affairs, but that does not reduce its intensity in any particular case." Creech Jones might have been better prepared for Churchill's outburst in the House. He might have been better briefed on the constitutional issues. "But it is difficult to agree that he performed less creditably than Burns performed in his different, politically simpler role," Woodman concluded.

In his heart, Alan seems to have known this. He did not malign Creech Jones in his memoirs, admitting that "he was in a difficult position." Creech Jones's statement to the House on March 5th contained "all the facts" and made "kindly reference to my services."[141] Even as the two men locked horns over *ju-ju*, Creech Jones' wife was helping Katie to find a new flat in London in anticipation of the Burns' return to Britain. "I fear it will be a sharp contrast with the lovely place you have vacated in the Gold Coast," Creech Jones wrote personably after describing peeling wallpaper in one unit.[142] This was not the stuff of bitterness but of two men who understood each other better than later historians. Alan and Creech Jones would remain fast friends in the years ahead.

At the height of the *ju-ju* murder case, Alan complained, he was portrayed as "a bloodthirsty tyrant."[143] He told historian Richard Rathbone that "the exercising of his gubernatorial powers was made to look oppressive." As Rathbone wrote, "The opinion in some sections of the House was that Burns was some form of latter-day Governor Eyre, a cold-hearted and even sadistic brute."[144]

Governor Edward Eyre of Jamaica had suppressed a general uprising during a chaotic five days in 1865, leaving 250 dead and another 350 executed summarily for treason. It was "one of the most depressing stories in West Indian history," Alan would write. Eyre was insufficiently sympathetic to the poverty of blacks on the island, and he had not exercised supervision over the militia after his declaration of martial law. "His excuse that he was not aware of these things can hardly be accepted, as it was his business as Governor to ascertain what was going on."[145]

In Eyre's defense, Alan noted, such riots were always times of chaos and fear in the Caribbean that made normal lines of command break down and governors err on the side of caution. The actions of soldiers may have been disproportionate, but the declaration of martial law itself was appropriate. "He undoubtedly saved Jamaica from the disaster of a racial war. If the insurgents had met with more than a momentary success, the state of excitement prevailing in other parts of the island was such that the revolt must have spread and involved a more fearful loss of lives and property."[146]

To put it bluntly, Alan agreed with Eyre's view that 600 dead was preferable to tens of thousands left dead by civil war and economic decline on the island of 440,000 people (80 percent of them black). It is hard not to read in Alan's coda for Eyre a defense of himself in the *ju-ju* murder case: "Throughout his long retirement, Eyre maintained a dignified silence and made no attempt to defend himself against his enemies or to justify his actions in Jamaica."

In fact, Eyre would continue the defense long into his retirement and was eventually vindicated in the English courts. It was a clarifying moment in colonial history when the Colonial Office stared down populist politicians fishing in the muddy waters of colonial affairs while claiming to be, as the government put it, "the exclusive champion of the oppressed."[147]

From that perspective, maybe Alan *was* "some form of latter-day Governor Eyre." If anyone was actually calling Alan a "cold-hearted and sadistic brute" because of his insistence on proceeding with the *ju-ju* executions, Alan probably would not have flinched. It was his responsibility to make difficult decisions to save lives, even at the cost of his reputation and the cavils of busy-bodies on the home front. If British administration unraveled in the Gold Coast, what would happen after independence?

Alan's imposition of justice on *ju-ju*, as with Eyre's imposition of martial law in Jamaica, was a critical saving grace in one colony's history. To be sure, Alan's humiliation of Danquah moved the would-be liberator and his kin in a more radical direction. Among educated elites in the Gold Coast, "a hidden agenda of anti-colonialism emerged in the protracted course of this case," Rathbone concluded.[148] One biographer believes that Danquah's subsequent radicalism was an attempt to regain popular support having failed in his effort to protect elite privileges.[149] A later colonial report would agree: "The [*ju-ju*] affair changed the pattern of Gold Coast politics. . . . The bitterness over the trial and conviction resulted in [Danquah's and his followers'] instituting an uncompromising political campaign against the Governor and the Government."[150] The independent country's first president, Kwame Nkrumah, wrote that most nationalists "were affected in one way and another" by the case and that "this was what influenced them to join" the movement.[151]

Does this mean that Alan was wrong to uphold due process and insist that even the rich and well-connected should obey the law? Aside from the principles, it is hardly plausible to assume that if Alan had given way and vacated the convictions, Danquah and Nkrumah would have lost their political ambitions or that worse unrest would not have followed. Having held the pass against Danquah's radical constitutional reforms, Alan in *ju-ju* defended the rule of law against Danquah's destructive legal tactics. If Alan had given way, it might have precipitated worse consequences by signaling at a critical moment that the British had lost their nerve and would cave into any political demand—the same risk that motivated Eyre in Jamaica. By holding fast to colonial authority, Alan sent a signal to aspirant power-grabbers that their ambition would be contained as long as the British were in charge. As Rathbone perceived, the case was a clarifying moment in Ghana's history, because it presented educated Africans and tribal leaders with a stark choice: good governance under the British or racial destructiveness under the nationalists.[152]

In other words, rather than seeing Alan's firm leadership as having stoked radicalism, it is better seeing it as having moderated that radicalism and kept social peace in the meantime. Alan's principled handling of the *ju-ju* murder gave hope to millions of Ghanaians, including the moderate, educated elites in

Accra like the Quists, who held fast to the promise of the British inheritance (see figure 9.4). They would eventually reclaim this promise after the coming tumult of Ghanaian "liberation" under Nkrumah (which would kill Danquah, among others). If Alan had invalidated the convictions, it would have suggested that the rule of law was crumbling in the face of nationalist protest. By laying justice on *ju-ju* at a critical moment, Alan created a small but essential ten-year window in which the depredations of decolonization could be lessened and the foundations for recovery laid. As the colony's tribal chiefs noted in their memorial to Alan at his departure: "Your Excellency fulfilled your commission by doing justice to all and sundry without fear or favour; and we trust that your inspiring example will have a lasting impression on the Administration as a whole."[153]

Alan and Katie left the Gold Coast on August 4th, 1947. Alan wore a simple linen suit and pith hat, dispensing with the pomp of his formal uniform. The

Figure 9.4 With Church Friends, Accra, 1946. *Source*: Private Collection of Alan Dixon.

staff at the castle arranged themselves in a cluster so that Katie, who had been ill for a week, could bid each of them farewell from one spot. The birds in the castle aviary had been sent to the London Zoo. As in the Bahamas and British Honduras, Alan's departure was the occasion for spontaneous demonstrations of goodwill from commoners and chiefs alike. Never one to waste an opportunity, Danquah joined in the adulation, proposing that a memorial be built in Alan's honor.[154] "Keep your trust in the impartiality of the law and your faith in the principles of justice," Alan urged. As he and Katie were rowed through the surf to a mammy chair to hoist them on board their homebound ship, it suddenly seemed easier said than done.

In the five months since the *ju-ju* executions, Danquah had worked feverishly to set up a new political party demanding independence "as soon as possible." Alan's popularity was too great to launch the party while he remained governor. Instead, Danquah waited until the day after the departure. With Alan gone, he saw a new dawn unfolding. Alan's constitution, Danquah now declared, was "window-dressing" intended to keep power in the hands of London.[155] Alan's warnings about an ungovernable country if independence was rushed were "utter rubbish," Danquah charged.[156] Alan was not progressive but "oppressive." Why accept a political system that "depends upon the whims and caprices of a man from anywhere who may be sent to us as Governor?" India and Burma were about to become independent, so why not Ghana? "Our duty is clear. We must fight against the new domination. And we must fight with the weapons of today, constitutional, determined, persistent, unflinching, unceasing, until the goal of freedom is attained."[157] As a later colonial secretary for the Gold Coast wrote of the Burns Constitution: "What was intended to be, and indeed was, an important step towards self-government did in practice put a clapper on a head of steam emanating from the post-war nationalist fervor among the semi-educated youth."[158]

Danquah's new party won mixed reactions. Instead, it was the more radical Convention People's Party of Kwame Nkrumah that captured the popular imagination by demanding "immediate independence." Alan "was defeated by circumstances too strong for him," Nkrumah commented, feigning innocence.[159] A later colonial official was more blunt: "Nkrumah was quite capable of plunging the country into disorder. There was no alternative government to the CPP, none of whom had any training or experience in public affairs. We had to build anew with what was then a crowd of agitators as our material."[160]

It did not take long for the agitators to act. The CPP rioted on the road leading to the governor's castle in Accra in early 1948, leaving twenty-nine dead. Danquah declared, "[T]he hour of liberation has struck," hoping to ride to power Gandhi-like. Fortunately, the colonial government still had the capacity and nerve to prevail, sending both Danquah and Nkrumah to their brief detentions in the north furnished with bungalows, sitting rooms, type-writers, and fine dining.

Later that year, Danquah was a Gold Coast delegate to a conference in London. By his own account, he was met at Euston station by Alan, who headed the welcome party. Danquah's recollection bristles with self-importance.[161]

"Hello, Sir Alan," I ventured, extending my hand.

Then the most astonishing thing happened. Sir Alan Burns at first stretched forth his hand to take mine, then he made as if to withdraw.

"I don't know whether I should shake hands with you at all, you Danquah, who has ruined me so," said Burns.

I was, to say the least, quite flabbergasted and, of course, delighted. But I said: "Why, Sir, how have I ruined you? Come on shake hands."

"Oh, I don't know," he said, "all the things that you have said against me."

Another member of the Gold Coast delegation appeared: "Oh, Sir Alan, shake hands with the doctor. It is all over now."

And before I knew where I was and before Sir Alan knew where he was, I had shaken hands with him, and had passed him over, leaving him standing there on the Euston Station platform, and gazing after me, disconsolately. Apparently, there was something I had done that had hurt Sir Alan deeply. Quite obviously these things have had their effect in the proper quarters. They have gone deep home to Sir Alan Burns.

Obsessed with his humiliation by Alan, Danquah did not notice that he had lost control of the nationalist movement in the Gold Coast to the self-professed Man of Destiny, Kwame Nkrumah. One of Danquah's comrades warned of the "rot to come."[162]

NOTES

1. William Reid, *Bush Proper 1941–43: The War-Time Experience of an Army Surgeon in the Gold Coast* (1997), p. 116.

2. Joseph Danquah, *Akan Laws and Customs and the Akim Abuakwa Constitution* (1928), p. 238.

3. Reid, op. cit., p. 118.

4. MCGC, pp. 446–47.

5. CCC, p. 204.

6. Kwame Frimpong, "The Final Obsequies of the Late Nana Sir Ofori Atta, K.B.E. Abuakwahene," *Africa: Journal of the International African Institute* (1945), p. 84.

7. MPCG, p. 180.

8. Ibid., p. 168.

9. Frank Hives, *Ju-Ju and Justice in Nigeria* (1930).

10. CCC, p. 140.

11. Ibid., pp. 140, 179.

12. CBAA, p. 81; CPCW-G, p. 7.

13. CCC, p. 234.

14. CBAA, p. 71.

15. Robin Law, "Human Sacrifice in Pre-Colonial West Africa," *African Affairs* (1985).

16. Kofi Akosah-Sarpong, "Battling ju-ju marabou mediums," *Modern Ghana News*, May 20, 2008.

17. Author's interview with Sarah Pavey, June 14, 2016, Epsom, UK.

18. Richard Rathbone, "The Transfer of Power in Ghana, 1945–57," University of London, Department of History, doctoral dissertation (1968).

19. Richard Rathbone, personal communication to author, May 31, 2016.

20. CO/96/802/6, "ACB memorandum on Apedwa case," June 12, 1947.

21. MPCG, pp. 189, 190.

22. Ibid., p. 132.

23. Archibald Trojan Steele, "*Globe* writer finds on trip sun never sets on U.S. Army," *Boston Globe*, March 19, 1943.

24. "Disappearance," *Daily Echo*, April 15, 1944.

25. Henry (H.A.) Nuamah, *Murder in the Palace at Kibi: An Account of the Kibi Ritual Murder Case* (1985), p. 31.

26. Lawrence Henry Yaw Ofosu-Appiah, *The Life and Times of Dr. J. B. Danquah* (1974), p. 37.

27. Joseph Danquah, *The Akan Doctrine of God: A Fragment of Gold Coast Ethics and Religion* (1944).

28. MPCG, pp. 156–58.

29. David Ofori, *Kibi 'Ritual Murder': An Inside Story of a Sensational So-Called 'Ritual Murder' Case* (1947).

30. Joseph Danquah and Henry Kwasi Akyeampong, *Journey to Independence and After (J. B. Danquah's Letters) 1947–1965* (1970), vol. 3, pp. 115, 116.

31. DPWA, p. 47.

32. MPCG, p. 80.

33. "Lord Swinton to ACB," personal letter, September 24, 1942, private collection.

34. CO/8501/13/710, "ACB memo," February 21, 1940.

35. CO/554/131/4/33702, "ACB to Cranborne," July 8, 1942.

36. CCC, p. 195.

37. Following from CO/554/1314, "Governor, Sierra Leone, to ACB," January 2, 1942; CO/554/1314, "ACB to Moyne," January 29, 1942; CO/967/115, "Cranbourne to ACB," June 24, 1942; CO/554/1314, "ACB to Cranbourne," July 8, 1942; CO/554/1315, "Appointment of non-official Africans," August 6, 1943; CO/554/1314, "ACB to Secretary for Colonies," September 10, 1942; CO/554/1314, "Appointment of Africans to executive councils in Nigeria and Gold Coast," various 1942–43.

38. CO/967/115, "Thornley to ACB," January 28, 1944.

39. Benjamin Wuta-Ofei, "Sir Alan Burns," *Daily Express*, March 29, 1947.

40. CO/96/783/1, "Williams file notes on Apedwa case," October 16, 1944.

41. CO/2/323/1, "Bench notes Justice Mohammed Fuad," November 20, 1945.

42. MPCG, p. 98.

43. CCC, p. 238.

44. Ibid., p. 65.

45. CP, pp. 94, 93.

46. "Saviour," *The African Morning Post*, September 17, 1935.

47. Gold Coast Colony, *Report by a Select Committee of the Legislative Council Appointed to Investigate an Allegation made by the Honourable R. Borrow against the Honourable A. W. Kojo Thompson* (1944).

48. CP, p. 93.

49. CCC, p. 282.

50. Ibid., p. 221.

51. "ACB to Stanley (Colonial Office)," secret telegram, December 28, 1944, private collection.

52. CO/96/783/2, "West Africa Court of Appeal, transcript of appeal in Apedwa case," February 15, 1945.

53. CCC, p. 221.

54. Ibid.

55. CO/96/783/3, "ACB to Hall," November 20, 1945.

56. Elspath Joscelin Grant Huxley, *Four Guineas: A Journey through West Africa* (1957), p. 92.

57. CO/96/783/1, "Williams to ACB," December 3, 1945.

58. CO/96/783/1, "ACB to Secretary for Colonies," December 4, 1945.

59. CO/96/802/6, "ACB memo on Apedwa case," June 14, 1947.

60. CCC, p. 195.

61. Martin Wight, *The Gold Coast Legislative Council* (1947), p. 201.

62. Robert Pearce, *The Turning Point in Africa: British Colonial Policy 1938–48* (1982), p. 88.

63. CO/967/115, "ACB to Secretary for Colonies," July 2, 1944.

64. Swinton Papers (Churchill College, Cambridge), "Letter to Lady Swinton," October 9, 1942.

65. CCC, p. 206.

66. Wight, op. cit., p. 201.
67. "Ritual murder?" *The Economist*, April 20, 1946.
68. Roger Gocking, "A Chieftaincy Dispute and Ritual Murder in Elmina, Ghana, 1945–6," *Journal of African History* (2000).
69. MPCG, p. 115.
70. CO/96/783/3, "Minute by Williams," May 1, 1946.
71. CO/96/783/5, "Danquah to Clifton Brown," July 4, 1946.
72. CO/96/783/4, "Minute," June 27, 1946.
73. Victor Igreja, "Frelimo's Political Ruling through Violence and Memory in Postcolonial Mozambique," *Journal of Southern African Studies* (2010).
74. Nuamah, op. cit., p. 54.
75. CCC, pp. 181, 182.
76. Hugh Roach, "Christiansborg," *African Affairs* (1945), p. 133.
77. CCC, pp. 62–63.
78. "A castle in Africa was their home," *Daily Mirror*, June 19, 1959.
79. CO/967/115, "ACB to Parkinson," January 24, 1942.
80. CO/967/115, "ACB to Parkinson," November 29, 1941.
81. CCC, p. 219.
82. Sir Alan Burns, "Forward" in David Armitage Bannerman, *The Birds of West and Equatorial Africa* (1953).
83. CO/537/2099, "ACB to Thompson," March 17, 1947.
84. MPCG, p. 189.
85. IDOC, p. 42.
86. OPT, p. 9.
87. CP, p. 48.
88. CBAB, p. 82.
89. CCC, pp. 311–12.
90. FBCE-G, p. 8.
91. John Almeric de Courcy Hamilton, *The Anglo-Egyptian Sudan from Within* (1935), p. 340.
92. CBAA, p. 17.
93. CP, p. 48.
94. CCC, p. 200.
95. John Evelyn Shuckburgh, "Review of Colonial Civil Servant," *International Affairs* (1950), p. 256.
96. CCC, p. 311, italics added.
97. CCC, p. 227.
98. CO/96/783/5, "ACB to Creech Jones," December 24, 1946.
99. CO/96/783/5, "Minute by Williams" and "Memo Bryden to Dove," September 12, 1946.
100. MPCG, p. 128; CO/76/783/5, "Minute by Dale," October 19, 1946.
101. "Chief Commissioner Kumasi to ACB," personal letter, December 11, 1946, private collection.
102. MPCG, p. 124.

103. Arthur Creech Jones and Rita Hinden, *Colonies and International Conscience: Report To the Fabian Colonial Bureau* (1945).

104. CO/96/783/3, "Kibi murder file notes," September 19, 1946.

105. CO/96/783/5, "Minute," January 4, 1947.

106. CO/96/802/5, "Creech Jones to ACB," January 27, 1947.

107. CO/96/802/5, "ACB to Creech Jones," February 5, 1947.

108. Lawrence James, *Churchill and Empire: A Portrait of an Imperialist* (2014), p. 45.

109. "Death Sentences, Gold Coast (Respites)," *House of Commons Debates Hansard*, March 3, 1947, sections 37–51.

110. "Creech Jones to ACB," personal letter, March 5, 1947, private collection.

111. "Ritual murder," *Economist*, March 8, 1947.

112. "Keeling to ACB," personal letter, March 7, 1947, private collection.

113. CO/96/783/5, "Creech Jones to ACB, confidential," March 3, 1947.

114. CCC, p. 229.

115. "Churchill saves lives of five juju slayers," *Los Angeles Times*, March 5, 1947.

116. CO/96/802/5, "ACB to Creech Jones," March 4, 1947; CO/96/802/5, "ACB to Lloyd," March 5, 1947.

117. CO/96/802/5, "Amantoommiensa Council Akin Abuaka to Creech Jones," March 8, 1947; CO/96/783/5, "Kwadjo Asante to Creech Jones," March 8, 1947.

118. CCC, p. 230.

119. "ACB to Creech Jones," secret and personal telegram, March 4, 1947, cited in MPCG, p. 144.

120. "Alison to ACB," personal letter, undated (mid-1940s), private collection.

121. "Dinah Quist to ACB," personal letter, March 5, 1947, private collection.

122. "One should not peel an orange," *Time Magazine*, March 17, 1947.

123. Gold Coast Western Provincial Council, "Resolution on Proposed Resignation of Sir Alan Burns," March 15, 1947, private collection.

124. "Burns threatens to resign," *Gold Coast Observer*, March 21, 1947; "ACB to Secretary for Colonies," personal telegram, March 25, 1947, private collection.

125. "Our Sir Alan Burns," *Ashanti Pioneer*, March 10, 1947.

126. "Pity Parliament and the British public," *Ashanti Pioneer*, March 14, 1947; "ACB to Secretary for Colonies," personal telegram, March 14, 1947, private collection.

127. CO/537/ 209/9, "Creech Jones to Atlee," March 5, 1947.

128. "E. V. Mamphey to Katie Burns," personal letter, undated 1947, private collection.

129. "The House," *Daily Tribune*, March 7, 1947.

130. CO/96/802/5, "Creech Jones to ACB," March 5, 1947.

131. "Creech Jones to ACB," personal letter, March 6, 1947, private collection.

132. MPCG, pp. 147, 146.

133. CO/96/802/6, "Creech Jones to ACB," March 19, 1947.

134. CCC, p. 236.

135. Ibid., pp. 233, 236.

136. "Leader," *Daily Echo*, March 31, 1947; "ACB to Secretary for Colonies," personal telegram, March 31, 1947, private collection.

137. "Crime and punishment," *The Times*, March 31, 1947.

138. "W. L. Dale to ACB," personal letter, April 10, 1947, private collection.

139. "J. K. Thompson to ACB," personal letter, April 8, 1947, private collection.

140. Gordon Woodman, "Review of Murder and Politics in Colonial Ghana," *Journal of African Law* (1995), p. 113.

141. CCC, pp. 229–30.

142. CO/967/115, "Creech Jones to ACB," September 22, 1947.

143. CCC, p. 230.

144. Richard Rathbone, personal correspondence to author, June 1, 2016; MPCG, p. 142.

145. HBWI, p. 676.

146. Ibid., pp. 672–76.

147. Brian Knox, "The British Government and the Governor Eyre Controversy, 1865–1875," *Historical Journal* (1976), p. 890.

148. MCGC, p. 456.

149. Ofosu-Appiah, op. cit., pp. 44–45.

150. CO/537/5812/1, "Draft report on disturbances in the Gold Coast," October 12, 1950.

151. Kwame Nkrumah, *Ghana: The Autobiography of Kwame Nkrumah* (1957), pp. 86, 57.

152. MPCG, p. 133.

153. Joint Provincial Council, Gold Coast Colony, *Address Presented to His Excellency Sir Alan Cuthbert Maxwell Burns at Cape Coast*, June 24, 1947, private collection.

154. Nee-Abossey Kotey, "Good-Bye, Sir Alan and Lady Burns," *African Morning Post*, June 30, 1947.

155. Ofosu-Appiah, op. cit., p. 50.

156. Joseph Danquah, "Were the Cromwellians educated?" *Gold Coast Spectator*, December 20, 1947.

157. Ofosu-Appiah, op. cit., pp. 57, 51–52.

158. Reginald Saloway, "The New Gold Coast," *International Affairs* (1955), p. 469.

159. Kwame Nkrumah, "On Freedom's Stage," *Africa Today* (1957), p. 8.

160. Saloway, op. cit., p. 471.

161. Danquah and Akyeampong, op. cit., vol. 1, pp. 92–94.

162. Dennis Austin, "The Working Committee of the United Gold Coast Convention," *Journal of African History* (1961), p. 292.

Chapter 10

Lake Success

During the war, the United States proposed a specialized agency of the new United Nations to assume responsibility for all colonies. Churchill reacted violently to the idea. Britain, he said, would never "consent to the fumbling fingers of forty or fifty nations prying into the life's existence of the British Empire."[1] The result was a papering over. The UN charter required colonial powers "to develop self-government, to take due account of the political aspirations of the peoples, and to assist them in the progressive development of their free political institutions." The only concrete requirement was for colonial powers to provide regular reports on economic, social, and educational conditions in their colonies to what came to be known as the Fourth Committee of the UN General Assembly. The British had been sending copies of their voluminous annual reports on each colony to the League of Nations for years, so this was little more than a continuation of that practice. Other major colonial powers—France, Belgium, Portugal, the Netherlands—were less used to sharing information.

A separate agency, the Trusteeship Council, was created to inherit the League of Nations mandate territories in Africa controlled by Britain, France, and Belgium and new ones under Italy resulting from the war in Somaliland and in the Pacific under Australia, New Zealand, and the United States. The council was split evenly between administering countries and other UN members. Its mandate extended *only* to these eleven trust territories, accounting for about fourteen million people, or 10 percent of the global colonial population after India became independent. An Indian resolution of 1947 called for all colonies to be forcibly put under the council. It passed the Fourth Committee but ended in a tie vote in the General Assembly.

Unlike the League of Nations mandates, the UN trust territories were not sanctioned with the language of "tutelage" by the administering countries.

The role of the administering countries was simply to carry out the will of the UN, which consisted of little more than making them independent. One commentator called it "a kind of international slum clearance project."[2] South Africa refused to put its mandate of Southwest Africa (later Namibia) under the council for that reason.

The whole UN set-up was a recipe for failure. It dangled before UN members the illusion of determining the fate of European colonies while denying them the means. It was like telling a group of children, "Look; don't touch!" A seasoned Australian diplomat warned that colonial issues at the UN would be "a battleground for ideological and political conflict."[3] The job of representing Britain—which accounted for forty-six of the eighty-seven colonies and trust territories enumerated by the UN at its founding—would be formidable.

As the *ju-ju* murder came to an end, the secretary for colonies, Arthur Creech Jones, was rooting around in the civil service for someone to fill the post. Despite his anti-colonial youth, Creech Jones was in maturity more cautious.[4] In Alan's pert phrase, he was "a poacher who has become a gamekeeper."[5] Creech Jones needed help to guard the paddock. Who better than Alan, an experienced colonial governor who had proven to be a stout advocate of the colonial mission while under fire? The new UN system for colonies, Creech Jones wrote to Alan, had "little new except its defects."[6] "I do not doubt that its work will sometimes be diverted by political influences." Alan would have to deal with "many tricky matters."[7] The important thing was to parry the criticism.[8]

Alan downplayed his suitability for the post. He was too plain-spoken, and better suited to "rough and ready work in the colonies." Still, if London wanted an unashamed defender of colonialism, he was their man. "I would be glad to serve in a post which would interest me and in which my colonial experience may make me useful."[9]

Over the next ten years, Alan would become the de facto spokesman of the British Empire, "the official interpreter on the world stage of British aims and achievements," according to the *Times*.[10] He would lead British delegations at both the Trusteeship Council and the Fourth Committee, sometimes in New York, other times in Paris or Geneva. In that decade, he crossed the Atlantic by ship roughly once every six weeks—sometimes with Katie and sometimes without. When in England, claiming, as he told one reporter, to be doing something he was "very good at—nothing,"[11] he was feverishly consulting on diplomatic strategy.

His job, in the words of one commentator, was to spend "a good deal of time slapping severely these prying fingers" that Churchill had warned of.[12] The debates at the UN would signal to political opportunists in the colonies whether they should make a dash for power. France and the Netherlands were fighting postwar insurgencies in their Asian colonies while Britain was trying to regain the upper hand in Malaya, Sudan, Cyprus, and Palestine. A bad showing at the UN would suggest that the national will was flagging. There was as yet little talk of a *general* rush to independence. India's plan for nationhood had been a thirty-year process. Other countries that became independent as a result of the war—Lebanon, the Philippines, Jordan—or which were being prepared for independence—Burma, Sri Lanka, Palestine—were seen as special cases. Most colonies were seen as far behind these places. The attitudes of the British would be closely watched.

Later historians have debated whether the UN hastened the demise of colonialism, extended its life, or had little effect. The truth is that it depended on each colony. India became independent separate from any UN influence. Somalia's independence, by contrast, was mechanically determined by a UN timetable. In most cases, the UN worked both to slow and to accelerate decolonization, strengthening colonial rulers while also stoking their oppositions. No account of the end of colonialism is complete without paying attention to the various influences exerted by the UN system as well as its interplay with the Cold War, changing politics in European capitals, and events on the ground.

The more important question is whether the UN adequately *prepared* colonies for independence. On this issue, scholars have been silent for an obvious reason: the failure of the UN to direct its attention to the post-colonial future was an inexcusable mistake, arguably a crime against humanity that the body continues to celebrate. Under the growing influence of anti-colonial voices, the UN became what one scholar called a "decolonization machine,"[13] more concerned with ending colonialism than with the lives left behind. It was a mistake that Sir Alan Burns would try to avert.

Alan had one aim when he accepted the position in 1947: to urge on the international community a duty of care to ensure that decolonization did not bring mass human suffering. As he prepared for his new role, the "hideous massacres" of India's independence, as he called them, were unfolding in a way that should have brought pause to heady plans for change: "It is distressing to think of those once happy and comparatively prosperous communities which today are torn with racial hatreds and oppressed by the fear of violence," he lamented.[14] The task, as he saw it in 1947, was to bring to the fore British "empirical" arguments that emphasized different facts on the ground in each colony. The UN needed to present a united front to would-be power-grabbers in the colonies, many of them European-educated intellectuals who neither understood nor represented the nations they demanded to steer. "Some form of international organization is essential, if peace is to be preserved, and the standard of civilization in the world is to be raised," Alan noted.[15] To achieve that, the UN needed to direct its efforts not to moral posturing and tearing down colonial foundations but to building up the empirical conditions for post-colonial governance. "The damage that could be done by mischievous or 'fumbling' fingers in those colonial areas that are approaching self-government is considerable," he warned.[16] "If colonial territories are given self-government before they are fit to govern themselves, the result must be inefficiency, anarchy, and chaos."[17]

In a speech at Oxford University shortly before leaving for New York in September 1947, Alan lamented the "orgy of self-depreciation" in some quarters that had "provided a handle for our enemies which they can use to attack our so-called Imperialism."[18] The suggestion that "our Empire is coming to its end" was untrue because the average person in the colonies wanted steady improvements, not revolutionary change. Colonialism, he promised, would be around "for many years to come." The haven of retirement beckoned. But the British Empire was not yet done with Sir Alan Burns.

Alan's first appearance was in November 1947 at Lake Success on Long Island, where Trusteeship Council meetings were held while the new UN headquarters was raised in Manhattan (see figure 10.1). It seemed fitting that the first petitioner was Sylvanus Olympio, nephew of the man who had written to the commander of a young "A.C. Burns, Lt. W. Afr. Rf." in 1914 asking if the British would be so kind as to take over Togoland from the retreating Germans. Stranded on the French side of the Togoland mandate after World War I, the Olympio family had become a constant irritant to French authorities. In his testimony, Sylvanus demanded a redrawing of colonial borders to unite all ethnic Ewe areas so they could "collaborate in the same way toward self-government which, after all, is the avowed object of the trusteeship system."[19]

Olympio's highly publicized appearance in 1947 set the template for aspiring nationalist leaders in the colonies. An appearance at the UN became the favored way to bolster one's political position back home. His speech went on for so long that Alan and his colleague had to wait until the next day to respond. Uniting all the Ewe areas, Alan's French counterpart warned, would reignite endemic tribal rivalries, "a return to the fragmentation which the European colonizers found when they first came to Africa, and which is totally opposed to the general welfare of Africa."[20] As Alan could attest from his own experiences, large tribes in Africa often fell prey to internecine disputes which would be disastrous if played out in a country's politics: "Before we plunge into making any violent changes, we must be sure that we do not make greater mistakes," he warned the council.[21] Alan and his French counterpart convinced the council that their alternative plan to ease trade barriers, accelerate local self-government, and hold a referendum on the future

Figure 10.1 First Appearance at the UN Trusteeship Council, 1947. *Source*: Private Collection of Alan Dixon.

of the Ewe areas was more prudent. Olympio declared the plans "hopelessly inadequate."

A second petitioner was an Italian adventurer named Marius Fortie who had served in various minor government positions in German and later British Tanganyika.[22] His charge sheet against the British in Tanganyika repeated many criticisms he had made in a 300-page autobiography published in 1938 entitled *Black and Beautiful: A Life in Safari Land*.[23] Alan had the wits to send a member of his staff down to the local library in New York to borrow a copy. He then read excerpts at the council meeting. Among the anecdotes were Fortie's reminiscences of buying a fifteen-year-old girl as a slave, siring many children by her whom he abandoned, having sex with dozens of "simple and willing village belles" while on safari, and meting out "the customary twenty-five lashes" with a Hippo leather whip to a native who spilled a container of milk. "This is a curious mentality for a man who poses as a champion of the natives against their British oppressors," Alan commented. The council went into an uproar. The Soviet and Philippines delegates accused Alan of citing the book out of context. Fortie's petition was quietly dropped.[24]

Alan was discomposed by what he witnessed at this first session. The hearings had demonstrated that fumbling fingers would indeed be prying into the lives of the British and other European empires. Petition writing, he warned, would become "the national sport in tropical Africa (and perhaps elsewhere)," if every petitioner were "taken seriously and flattered by the representatives of the 'anti-colonial' bloc." Rather than solving problems, the UN would become "merely a political forum in which ideologies can be aired and propaganda broadcast." Important debates about the future of each place would be shifted to the UN, to the detriment of local autonomy. "There could be no hope of proper constitutional development if the political arguments that should take place in the territory itself were to be transferred to New York."[25]

When he accepted the UN errand, Alan imagined himself following in Lord Lugard's footsteps at the League of Nations, offering sage advice in a collegial setting. Instead, he found himself blindsided by a barrage of propaganda in which, as an Australian diplomat noted, the British were "the arch-villains."[26] Most unsettling was the attitude of the Americans, who seemed to view every native petitioner as another George Washington. The "disgruntled colonial politicians" who appeared at the UN or who spoke to "itinerant journalists and writers of travel books" were treated by the American delegation as authentic representatives of the common good mainly based on their skin color, while the colonial powers were not.[27] Before returning to England in December 1947, Alan told a gathering in New York that Americans "must learn to go the slow way and not make bad matters worse." "There is no need to rush to Africa to change the current of events unless we first find out what most of the people of that continent want."[28] The current of events was changing faster than anyone expected.

The powerful emotions on display in this early jousting over colonialism were explained by one thing, in Alan's view: racial animosity. At a time when ideological divisions were attracting more attention, Alan foresaw a cultural divide between the West and the Rest that would be more enduring. While serving in Nigeria in the 1930s, Alan and his black friend Henry Carr had planned to write a book on race relations. Re-assignment to British Honduras caused Alan to write the book alone with Carr's comments. It sat untouched for a decade. In 1947, with *ju-ju* fresh in his memory, Alan dusted off the manuscript. If the world community was to rally around the urgent needs of protecting the lives of people in European colonies, he believed, it would need quickly to rid itself of racial animus on both sides. Europeans would need to accept the peoples of the newly independent states as equals in world society, abandoning any notions of innate superiority. The formerly colonized peoples would need to rid themselves of a belief that all their ills resulted from white racism and accept some of the blame for centuries of slow progress.

Africans in particular had been too eager to accept the mythical role assigned to them by Greco-Roman and later biblical fantasies of "blameless Ethiopians," as Homer called them, a race set apart from the greed of humanity and visited by the gods when they left Olympus. "There is no such thing as a blameless Ethiopian," Alan said in his New York speech. Rather than quelling the racial animus generated by this ancient fantasy, the UN system had, in Alan's view, made it worse.

Alan's 1948 book *Colour Prejudice: With Particular Reference to the Relationship Between Whites and Negroes* was the work of a "liberal realist" according to one reviewer.[29] As the book explained, humans had always protected themselves by developing animosities toward other groups. When those animosities were validated by one group's greater wealth, power, or cultural sway, racism became ingrained. It was difficult for Europeans to avoid the assumption that their developed societies did not reflect innate racial superiority, and the fashionable Darwinian theories of human development taking hold in Europe had only reinforced that notion.[30] The idea was absurd: "The brilliant achievements of coloured individuals, academically and otherwise, make it obvious that race has little to do with the comparative underdevelopment of the coloured races as a whole."[31]

White racism had caused an equal and opposite reaction among non-European peoples. National identities emerged based on nothing more than anti-European sentiment: "The resentment of white domination, whether political or economic, is being made by unscrupulous persons to whip up hatred for the whites and this hatred is certainly growing. It is encouraged by ambitious politicians under the guise of nationalism and those who refuse to be stamped into a hate campaign are denounced as traitors to their country."[32] The result was that practical colonial issues were being overshadowed by emotive race ones. "In many cases 'anti-colonialism' is merely a cover for intense racial feeling," he observed. "Most of the agitation for constitutional reform is, in its essence, racial rather than political."[33]

Both sides, Alan insisted, had a responsibility to fix the problem. Whites had to develop an empathy for colonized peoples who had been scorched by the encounter with a powerful Europe. Fortunately, he saw progress on this front, noting that if a European newspaper were to publish an offensive account of non-Europeans "there would be an outburst of indignation throughout the coloured world, but, here is the difference, white people also would join in the protests."[34] Indeed, Alan worried that some Europeans were falling into an equal and opposite form of racism with their torrid attempts to praise and promote native cultures. The anthropologists who treated native cultures like precious objects forgot that they were composed of the universal ingredients of imperfect human beings: "I have often wondered why the African does not retaliate by sending a commission to study and report on the peculiarities of Englishmen and Americans."[35] What colonial subjects needed, in Alan's view, was to be treated as equals, not to be praised merely for being nonwhite: "This may give some immediate satisfaction but in the long run I cannot believe that it helps indigenous peoples."[36]

Among native peoples, there was a need for "intellectual honesty . . . which will make them realise that all the handicaps under which their race labours are not due to the machinations of others" but to historical and geographical issues beyond anyone's control. Alan remained optimistic: "There is no reason why, in the future, if they are given a fair chance economically and socially, they should not advance in civilization and culture, and contribute their undoubted qualities to a world which has not yet reached perfection under white domination."[37]

Colour Prejudice was a small book on a big subject. Several reviewers were surprised, in light of the grand theoretical projects of Alan's brothers Emile and Cecil, that the book avoided sweeping proposals, offering instead little sermons about the need for people to be decent to one another. "It is of course inherent that so wise a man as Sir Alan distrusts loose ideologies, with their large mesh," wrote one reviewer.[38] By abjuring grand solutions, Alan was in effect endorsing the time-tested approach of the Old Coasters and the French to racial harmony: racism would be overcome not with grand theories but with everyday intercourse of every sort. It was fitting that the French colonial administrator who translated the book into French was the author of *La Vie Sexuelle en Afrique Noire*.[39]

Alan's book appeared the same month as Kwame Nkrumah's riots in Accra, and he was pressed into service at the London conference where Danquah disparaged him at Euston train station. Alan convened a group of five Nigerian and five Ghanaian delegates to formulate recommendations on race relations in the colonies. It was indicative of Alan's practical approach that the three grand ideas that emerged from his working group were a pamphlet on travel decorum, the promotion of mixed race dining clubs, and a royal visit.[40]

The Colonial Office worried that any pamphlet written by Alan in his characteristically blunt style that "goes so straight to the point and speaks directly" might make matters worse.[41] Alan allayed the concerns with a promise to cowrite the pamphlet with Robert Kweku Atta Gardiner, a black economist from the Gold Coast. The writing went quickly. But the draft ran into opposition from the government in Accra, still reeling from the riots. Alan protested, noting Gardiner's hard work: "I am not going to let him down, or further embitter race relations by making him suspicious of our motives."[42] After a year's delay, the Gold Coast governor finally gave the green light.[43]

Today, the pamphlet *Other People, Other Ways: Some Suggestions to Africans and Europeans Visiting One Another's Countries* reads as endearingly innocent. "If the young European could join with the African in playing cricket, football, and tennis, he could do a great deal towards inter-racial sympathy," Alan wrote encouragingly in his section. Gardiner advised Africans to make a careful budget before visiting England. It would take the combined efforts of both sides "to free their minds from dread and from the suspicion that they are going to be badly treated or insulted."[44] That was a tall order for a slim book, much less a wispy travel brochure. Alan would leave the grand theories to others.

Alan's second session at the UN in 1948 yielded stranger things than the first. A year earlier, a Chicago nun working for a London missionary society in British Cameroons had written an article in her order's newspaper railing against a remote chief, the Fon of Bikom. He had too many wives, who she said numbered six hundred. Many African kingdoms were organized as "family states" in which authority was exercised through the forced marriage of females with the chief or his subordinates. The French had banned the practice in 1939 in response to complaints from Catholic nuns in French West Africa.[45] Similar efforts by nuns in British West Africa met with less success. British officials had little interest in upsetting the customs of loyal chiefs and preferred development, not laws, as the solution to polygamy.

The creation of the United Nations with a human rights charter prompted the nuns to renew their campaign. The London society filed a petition with the Trusteeship Council demanding an investigation.[46] At first, the petition attracted only guffaws. British officials reported that the nun was "sex-starved" and "hysterical." Alan dismissed her as "an English busybody" and called the petition an abuse of process.[47] The Iraqi delegate on the council suggested that the Fon of Bikom was more to be pitied than censured, noting that he himself was a contented bachelor. The matter lay outside the council, added the delegate from China, because the practice was not introduced by the British. Alan asked the governor of British Cameroons to send his local district officer for a parlay with the Fon. The district officer then flew to Lake Success, where he reported the gratifying news that the Fon had only 110 wives, 44 of whom he had inherited.[48]

The delegates from the Catholic Philippines and Mexico insisted on an investigation. So in late 1949, a cavalcade of two hundred people—including the governor of British Cameroons, the district officer, Trusteeship Council delegates from the United States, Iraq, Belgium, and Mexico, and a herd of UN staff carrying typewriters and portable tents—traveled into the remote jungle and scaled a twelve-mile footpath to the Fon's mountaintop redoubt. There, they held a five-hour parlay about his better sides. "Probably at no time in Africa's history was there a more confused and startling scene as the day when the United Nations' representatives, the Fon, his wives and his friends met to decide what should be done about polygamy," wrote the American men's magazine *Esquire* in an amused piece.[49] A group of thirty-nine wives signed an affidavit saying they were perfectly happy. The Fon threatened a libel suit against his detractors. Would the UN reimburse him for the dowry he paid for any wives who ran away? He also accused the UN of elder abuse, since he reckoned he was one hundred.

Back at Lake Success, the 121-page report on the expedition was greeted with "much ribald laughter," Alan recalled, as the finer points of keeping so many wives were debated.[50] "The chief was, in fact, required by tribal tradition to keep this large establishment, and many of the so-called wives were actually pensioners he had inherited from his predecessor," Alan explained.[51] One delegate commented that "any man who can cope with so much feminine charm deserves, not the censure of the world, but its unstinted admiration."[52] More seriously, the report argued that polygamy among the Kom people was a form of social security and a practice not easily ended until development gave women other options. While women should not be forced into the Fon's harem, his polygamous arrangement should not be banned. As a former British district officer in the area wrote: "The British administration attempts to see native cultures as entities, *sui generis*, and to be studied as such and not from the ego-centric viewpoint of the rightness of our own culture."[53]

For Alan, these conclusions jibed with more general aversion to rapid UN-driven changes. There was a "unanimous" feeling among experienced British officials that "the present movement towards the objective is too hurried and that those responsible are not taking sufficiently into account the true interests of the colonial peoples or even the obvious fact that the inhabitants of the various territories are at different stages of cultural development," he would write.[54] In his talk at Oxford he had noted: "I am no believer in rapid change" for "the rapid changes that some people would like to make, good in themselves as they may be, present sometimes a real difficulty to the social organization of a primitive community."[55]

So the matter of the hundred wives of the Fon of Bikom was dropped. "Rome again at Lake Success," huffed an American journalist, Rebecca Reyher, comparing Britain to its ancient colonizer. Reyher decided she would investigate the matter for herself.[56] She flew to Nigeria and made overland for the Fon's lair with the help of British officials: "I felt it imperative to examine well the conclusions of those who accepted polygamy as satisfactory for *other* women," she wrote in her account of the adventure. The Fon received her warmly, especially for the case of gin she brought. By the time she arrived, fifty-four wives had already fled, leaving rows of empty houses. Many more asked her secretly if she could help them to escape. Her book about the one-week visit, *The Fon and his Hundred Wives*—which in the French translation was given the Tintin-like title *Chez le Roi Aux Cent Femmes*—concluded that behind the Fon's "good-humored raillery" was a cruel system. "How long must African women wait before their cries are heard and who will help them?"[57] British efforts were inadequate, she insisted, noting that meaningful consent was hardly possible when the social costs of fleeing were immense.[58]

Reyher's high liberal criticisms were misplaced in Alan's view. What bothered him more was censure from officially patriarchal countries like Pakistan, Iraq, and Ethiopia. In Mexico, which had led the charge against the Fon, women were at that time not allowed to vote in national elections, while in Iraq and Honduras, which sat on the council, women could not vote at all, he noted. The criticisms were richer in the Fourth Committee coming from officially sexist Islamic states like Egypt, Lebanon, Saudi Arabia, Syria, and Yemen, Alan noted. They preferred "seeing the beam in his colonialist neighbor's eye while missing the mote in his own."[59] The comedy of the Fon of Bikom raised serious issues. In the debate on colonialism, British empiricism was slowly being overwhelmed by politics, theory, and emotion.

Alan found two early opportunities to escape from the bureaucratic world of the UN back to "rough and ready work" in the colonies. In late 1949, he joined a mission to the trust territories of East Africa—later Tanzania, Rwanda, and Burundi. These were the largest trusts in terms of population, and it was no surprise that UN ambitions for "global governance" loomed largest here. The UN's trusteeship system, Alan noted, was seen by noncolonial powers "as a means of rescuing backward peoples from the clutches of the imperialists."[60]

At the start of the East Africa mission, a quarrel erupted over whether the UN flag should fly alongside that of the administering power. The issue came to a head when the delegation discovered a pamphlet that had been produced for East Africa by the UN's public information department called *The Story of Aman and the United Nations*.[61] The booklet featured a fictional East African boy in a trust territory. In every illustration, colonial officials were replaced by UN personnel shown inoculating cattle and administering schools. The pamphlet suggested that it was the UN, not the colonial power, that was in charge. "Improvements have been occurring for a long time, before the United Nations or even the League of Nations came into existence," the Belgian representative to the council, Pierre Ryckmans, complained when the pamphlet was discovered. When pastoral farmers were shown copies of the pamphlet, Alan noted, they thought it meant that the UN had agreed to look after their cattle. The clumsy *pidgin* English, meanwhile, was "an insult to their intelligence."[62] After a brief discussion, it was agreed to send all fifteen thousand copies of the pamphlet to the dump: "I suggest that the matter—and indeed *Aman* himself—might now be decently buried," Alan concluded.[63]

The East Africa trip also afforded Alan his first glimpse of the British colonies of Kenya and Uganda. When Alan arrived in Kenya in November 1949, the colony was suffering from the initial assaults of the so-called Mau Mau insurgency. It was led by a faction of the Kikuyu tribe that claimed its traditional lands had been stolen by white farmers. The movement "flared up with a suddenness which took the Kenya government by surprise," Alan noted. It might have been averted if more district commissioners knew the Kikuyu language rather than only Swahili.[64] Most Kikuyu, who had found ready employment and access to modern medicine and education as a result of white farms, rejected the insurgency and were loyal to the British. The Kikuyu provided the bulk of counterinsurgency forces and the special prison wardens. The rebel movement would eventually cause about fifty thousand deaths—about twenty-five thousand children from malnutrition caused by the economic disruption, another fifteen thousand at the hands of the Mau Mau, and a further ten thousand from the sharp and unforgiving British counterinsurgency campaign.[65]

The Mau Mau represented several things to Alan. Attempts by violent minorities to seize power were emerging as a common template for "freedom fighters" in Africa. Those "who regard Mau Mau bestialities in Kenya as armed resistance to British 'oppression'" or "whose indignation is aroused when British aircraft bomb Mau Mau murderers," he wrote, should recall that the vast majority of black Kenyans, including the majority of Kikuyu, supported the British colonial response.[66] Mau Mau was also a stark reminder of the pernicious effects of international communism and UN-fired anti-colonialism. The main sponsor of the Mau Mau, Jomo Kenyatta, had, like Nkrumah, been trained by brother Emile under the Communist Party of Great Britain. The Mau Mau leaders, meanwhile, were fired by pan-Africanism in the United States and at the UN. On the other hand, Mau Mau was also evidence to Alan that when the British took a strong stand, they could defeat those who would bring down colonialism in a sudden heap of violence and tyranny. After his visit to Kenya, Alan began referring to critics of colonial rule at the UN as "the Mau Mau bloc."

Less than five months after East Africa, Alan was on safari again, this time to the Pacific trust territories of the United States, Australia, and New Zealand. His detailed letters to Katie from this trip offer insights into his dimming view of the UN. The group left New York in April 1950 and returned in July, making thirty-nine stops and travelling in everything from primitive Samoan boats to a U.S. navy supply ship. His clothes were constantly unwashed, torrential rains washed out and delayed road travels, and meetings were often delayed by elaborate native ceremonies. The UN staff assigned to the delegation could not keep up with Alan's torrid pace and rebelled, forcing him to send them ahead for rest. In several places, accommodations were simply bare rooms. "I have never been so uncomfortable in all my life," he wrote after one night sleeping on a floor.[67] Given his career, this was saying something.

The Pacific Islands mission reinvigorated Alan's love of the practical and the everyday. Even as the other delegates begged off meetings and complained about their lodgings—"being as difficult as they can be, grousing all the time, and not a bit interested in anything"[68]—Alan relished a return to the business of colonial rule. At leper colonies in Papua New Guinea and the Mariana Islands, the other delegates "kept as far as possible" from the patients while Alan interviewed them. He learned about phosphate mines and talked to local chiefs about hurricane survival. In Nauru, he brokered a compromise over how many children imported Chinese phosphate miners could bring to live with them (two).

Everywhere he went, Alan's empirical "colonial" eye saw more than the ideological anti-colonial eye ever could. In New Guinea, he found a place with too few roads, much like British Honduras had been on his arrival. He made sure that road-building was a priority. On another island, there were 75 American naval service officers in charge of a mere 1,500 people. "In the Gold Coast one junior District Commissioner would have done the whole thing and done it better, if indeed it had been possible to spare a man for such a small community," Alan wrote to Katie. "I believe that the naval people must tuck them up in bed at night."[69] Of the three powers, "the Americans are most inefficient, and haven't the foggiest idea how to run things." The American officers he met were "most kind, very hospitable, astonishingly friendly, and quite uncivilized."[70] The Americans should be invited to enroll in colonial training courses in Britain, he suggested to London half-jokingly.

Even on days off, Alan was not idle. In a rainstorm in Samoa, he used a free morning to climb a tortuous 700-foot path to the grave of Robert Louis Stevenson, stopping only once to catch his breath as the local staff urged him back. "I suppose they think the poor old man can't do these things but I swear I can do more than some of these young wasters."[71]

The three-and-a-half months of island-hopping in the Pacific changed Alan's views on global government for good. The UN staffers "realise that I am the only one who is ready to do anything. So far I have gone everywhere and attended every meeting, while others are often 'too tired' to go somewhere," he wrote to Katie.[72] Alan was dismayed by the arrogance that seemed to infuse everyone and everything associated with the UN. He spent most evenings writing thank you cards. "I don't believe any of my colleagues has ever written a letter to the people who put them up. [They] take it all for granted."[73]

The arrogance of the UN was embodied in the person of Victorio Carpio, the Philippines delegate who was already at loggerheads with Alan before the trip (see figure 10.2).[74] Carpio was the "most objectionable" of the anti-colonial delegates at the UN, Alan wrote to London. He saw himself as "an inquisitor prosecuting the crimes of colonialism,"[75] and his colleague described the Philippines as representing "the force of history."[76] He was "the most utter damned fool I have ever met," Alan complained, and "the most stupid of my colleagues" at the UN.[77] At a meeting with Samoan chiefs, "Carpio told them that they should have the ballot box instead of their own system of choosing representatives and they bit him rather hard."[78] Following the rebuke, Carpio declared the Samoans unfit for self-government, on which Alan commented: "It is a strange position when Carpio is more reactionary than Burns."[79] After locals in the American trust territory told the delegation that they hoped the United States would annex their islands, Carpio demanded the petition be censored lest it cause other peoples in trust territories to likewise ask their colonial rulers to annex them.[80]

Carpio was bored by irksome details but loved high politics. In Wellington, he "delivered a long harangue to the P.M., although he was

Figure 10.2 Pacific Islands Mission in Hawaii with Victorio Carpio of the Philippines (center right) and Delegates from France (far left) and Taiwan (far right), 1950. *Source:* Private Collection of Alan Dixon.

told this was merely a social call," Alan bewailed.[81] Alan had to put a
press gag on the delegation while visiting the Australian trust territory
since the Indonesian government, which had come to power in 1949 over
an exhausted Dutch administration, laid claim to part of it: "Carpio is such
a fool that he would easily fall into any trap."[82] On another occasion, to
prevent Carpio from delivering a lecture on democracy to natives, Alan
told him that head-hunting persisted in the village they were about to visit.
Most inexcusably, Carpio told Alan that he wanted to extend the mission
as long as possible in order to draw the maximum allowance from the
UN.[83] He was "a nuisance and an embarrassment" throughout the trip, Alan
complained.[84]

Alan had approached the Pacific Islands mission as he had approached any
bush travel while in the colonial service: as a chance to identify and solve
practical problems. Carpio better understood that the "work" of the mission
began when it returned to New York: to use the mission report to shame the
colonial powers and continue building international solidarity against the
West. At Lake Success, Carpio came to life, lambasting Alan's handling of
the mission at a meeting of the Fourth Committee, complaining that Alan's
insistence on detached observation had dissuaded the people from making
"known their grievances."[85] Alan came to understand that such missions operated under a false pretense; the pledge to carry out the sacred trust was in fact
a chance to shame the trustee. "Never again will I take on an international
mission," he pledged to Katie.[86] To London, he requested "a special medal for
my gallantry in dealing with Carpio."[87]

There was at least one practical payoff. Returning to Britain, Alan convinced the Royal Mail to make it cheaper and faster to get periodicals from
Britain to Australia and New Zealand. It "depressed him greatly," the *Times*
wrote, that American magazines arrived in the region within days while
British ones could take weeks or months. "Not only did we appear to be
lacking in enterprise, but American ideas thus gained greater ascendancy,
with serious long-term implications for British commonwealth ideals and
inter-Empire trade," it noted of Alan's petition.[88] Alan believed that articles
on inter-empire trade would outsell celebrity gossip from Hollywood if only
they arrived with greater dispatch. In that respect, the mission highlighted the
colonial world that Alan had left behind and the new world that was dawning.
Whatever practical contributions he made, it was clear that his efforts were
being overtaken by forces he could not control.

What would happen if a liberal colonial power suddenly ceded power to a
small clique of bloody-minded natives backed by the Soviet Union? "The
result must be inefficiency, anarchy, and chaos," Alan warned a group of
industrialists in Geneva in early 1950.[89] Colonial "foundations" laid in a

hurry would not last, as Alan's favorite Kipling poem had sung. The gap of "centuries" that separated the West from the rest could not be wished away, even as pressures to "quicken" the pace to self-government grew. "Many years ago Britain undertook the gigantic task," of preparing peoples for self-government, Alan told the group. "In many parts of the world the task has not yet been completed and it is inconceivable that we should abandon it half-done."[90]

Why the sense of panic? Several things were colliding in Alan's mind when he made this warning. There were barbarous insurgencies in Kenya and Malaya, labor riots throughout the British West Indies, and a sudden radicalization of political parties in British Africa. The Soviet Union and its anti-colonial allies were applying the lash to European colonial powers at the UN. The British public, still recovering from the war, had adopted "a defeatist attitude" in the face of the critics and was "anxious to shrug off the remaining colonies as quickly as possible and at any cost."[91] "The question that keeps cropping up," Alan pointed out, "is 'When?'" His answer: no time soon. "We would be making a grave blunder if we tried to hurry the pace of constitutional advance."[92]

The question of setting UN time targets for decolonization was raised by India in 1946 and then by the Soviet colonial regime in Czechoslovakia in 1949. Both attempts failed, mainly because the General Assembly in those years was largely composed of Western powers. It did not take much of a crystal ball to foresee that fixed dates would foil preparations for self-government because nationalists would have no incentive to work with colonial powers. "The mechanical timetable becomes a self-wrecking mechanism," the *Times* argued.[93]

The question was revived in 1950 when the Soviet Union insisted that the new Italian trusteeship over Somalia (or Somaliland) be put onto a ten-year schedule to independence, a unique situation because Moscow was one of the victors in the war against Italy. Under the plan, the British and French would hand over their bits of Somalia to the Italians, who would then launch the new country. The French refused, holding true to their conviction that ethnic-based states were a bad idea. The British, however, agreed, against their better judgment. A new nation of 2.5 million illiterate pastoralists surrounded by hostile forces would become independent on December 2nd, 1960, come what may.

As the clock began ticking on Somalia, discussions at the UN took on an anxious tone: "It is part of [UN] responsibilities to see to it that independence for Somaliland does not simply mean bankruptcy and chaos," Alan warned in one meeting.[94] The UN advisory commission was bitterly divided by personal recriminations between Carpio of the Philippines and the Colombian delegate. Carpio, Alan noted in one internal memo, was accused by commission members of conspiring with Somalian rebels, whom he frequently took on tour in the territory with an official car flying the UN flag. The Colombian delegate, meanwhile, was accused of being "generally drunk" and "completely in the pocket of the Italians."[95] He feared that Somalian rebels might slip into New York to slit his throat and slept "with a revolver under his pillow." Alan, then serving as Trusteeship Council president, was asked to suppress the juicy allegations against both men so as not to cause a "public scandal." He refused, adding to the sense of unease. Indeed, he worked behind the scenes with a lady friend, a British countess living in New York, to ensure the allegations reached the press, hoping that both men would resign. "Please write to me at home if your schemes for inducing resignations meet with the success such Machiavellian planning deserves," the self-styled "old-fashioned girl" wrote to Alan.[96]

Predictably, Somalia was a disaster. In 1956, elections were held in the Italian section, where 650,000 votes were cast out of a total eligible electorate of 300,000. As the fixed date approached, political chaos erupted. Italy and Britain cast off the place five months early on July 1st, 1960. Within months, Somalia was plagued by border wars, famine, and a new Soviet air base. As one advocate of the Somalia model wrote ruefully: "It would be ironic, and tragically so, if Somalia were to . . . lend credibility to the argument against the entire United Nations approach."[97]

In 1951, those lessons were yet to come. India resubmitted what it called a "historic" resolution for time targets. It was cosponsored by Haiti, whose victims of anti-colonialism had flooded Alan's colonial Bahamas. Another cosponsor was Yemen, a failed medieval regime eager to seize Britain's prosperous Aden colony and surrounding protectorate. No one doubted the potential impact of the resolution. The representative from Indonesia noted that the "psychological effect" would be "far reaching."[98] Even though the resolution would technically apply only to trust territories, it would imply that most colonies should already be independent.

Alan took the stand at the Fourth Committee in Paris in January 1952 to face down the India resolution. It was, he said, a triumph of hope over reason. It was impossible to know in advance when a colony would be ready for independence. "There are not enough astrologers assigned to the UN for this task." Britain was sincere in its aims, as shown by the many independent (and democratic) countries that were products of the British Empire. "If anyone doubts this, they need only look around this committee table, or at a map of the world," Alan remarked coldly.[99] Political development could not be determined by "mathematical formulae." This was Britain's empirical tradition—practical facts, not abstract principles. In any case, what if the people of a colony did not *want* a timetable? Would it be undemocratic to force one upon them? Who exactly spoke for colonial peoples: coffee-house radicals in

London and Soviet stooges at the UN, or the elected native representatives of colonial legislatures? Political development, Alan insisted, with echoes of Edmund Burke, should happen "by evolution, not by resolution."[100]

The Iraqi representative sought to divide the colonial powers, calling Alan his "friend and colleague" and praising British efforts to move colonies to independence while assailing France's attempts at integration. Alan called the moment "embarrassing."[101] An attempted Scandinavian compromise to set targets only for intermediate steps to independence satisfied neither side. The original resolution went to a vote and was passed in the Fourth Committee. The General Assembly made matters worse by voting for both intermediate and final time targets.

The Trusteeship Council simply ignored the resolution as far as trust territories were concerned. "From the purely British standpoint, little if any harm was done; and indeed a new respect was shown for the wide personal knowledge of Sir Alan Burns," the *Times* enthused.[102] One saving grace was that Alan's arguments hit home in Washington. It abstained on both the 1952 votes and those of the next two years.[103] The sudden burst of American prudence was reflected in an editorial in the *New York Times* entitled "The Bogey of Colonialism." "National sovereignty of itself solves no problems, and usually creates new ones temporarily which are worse than the old," it noted, pointing to the rapid collapse of political and economic conditions in independent Libya and Indonesia.[104] The Saudi Arabian delegation at the UN flew into a rage over the editorial, accusing the State Department of being the author. As the London *Times* observed: "One has the uneasy feeling that the crisis is yet to come."

NOTES

1. Edward Stettinius, *Roosevelt and the Russians: The Yalta Conference* (1949), p. 246.

2. Inis Claude, *Swords into Plowshares: The Problems and Progress of International Organization* (1959), p. 343.

3. H. Duncan Hall, *Mandates, Dependencies, and Trusteeship* (1948), p. 291.

4. Arthur Creech Jones, *Labour's Colonial Policy* (1947).

5. FBCE-G, p. 17.

6. Robert Pearce, *The Turning Point in Africa: British Colonial Policy 1938–48* (1982), p. 113.

7. FO/371/81010/25150/IR, "Creech Jones to ACB," February 3, 1950.

8. CO/967/ 115, "Creech Jones to ACB," April 10, 1947.

9. CO/967/115, "ACB to Creech Jones," April 1, 1947.

10. "Service in the colonies," *Times Literary Supplement*, August 26, 1949.

11. "Weather," *The Times*, August 10, 1951.

12. "Review of 'In Defence of Colonies,'" *Africa Today* (1957).

13. Jeffrey Herbst, *States and Power in Africa: Comparative Lessons in Authority and Control* (2000), p. 257.

14. CBAA, p. 176; CCT-G, p.1.

15. UN-G, p. 12.

16. IDOC, p. 105.

17. FBCE-G, p. 16.

18. CCC, pp. 317–24.

19. John Kenton, "United Togoland urged by African," *New York Times*, December 9, 1947.

20. "Ewe Union opposed by French, British," *New York Times*, December 10, 1947.

21. "Agreement on treatment of Ewes reached in U.N. Trusteeship body," *New York Times*, December 11, 1947.

22. UN/T/PET.2/40, October 30, 1947.

23. Marius Fortie, *Black and Beautiful: A Life in Safari Land* (1938), pp. 9, 45, 58.

24. Mallory Browne, "Trusteeship fight splits council," *New York Times*, June 25, 1948.

25. IDOC, pp. 119, 116, 105.

26. Walter Crocker, *Can the United Nations Succeed?* (1951), p. 7.

27. IDOC, p. 130.

28. "Right kind of help to Africans urged," *New York Times*, December 16, 1947.

29. H. V. L. S., "Review of 'Colour Prejudice,'" *African Affairs* (1949), p. 161.

30. CP, p. 29.

31. CBAA, p. 11.

32. CPCW-G, p. 8.

33. IDOC, p. 5; CP, p. 45.

34. CP, p. 143.

35. CCC, p. 310.

36. CRP-G, p. 7.

37. CP, pp. 151, 136.

38. H. V. L. S., op. cit., p. 162.

39. Denis Pierre de Pedrals, *La Vie Sexuelle en Afrique Noire* (1950).

40. CO/554/161/4, "ACB to Lloyd," September 8, 1948; CO/554/161/4, "Lloyd to ACB," September 11, 1948.

41. CO/554/161/4, "File notes on Burns Committee," December 17, 1948.

42. "ACB to Blackburne, Gold Coast," personal letter, September 26, 1949, private collection.

43. CO/554/161/4, "File notes on Burns Committee," April 4, 1950.

44. Alan Burns, Robert Gardiner, Colonial Office, and Central Office of Information, *Other People, Other Ways: Some Suggestions to Africans and Europeans Visiting One Another's Countries* (1951), p. 4.

45. Marie-André du Sacré-Cœur, *La Femme Noire en Afrique Occidentale* (1939).

46. UN/T/PET.4/2, December 4, 1947.

47. UN-G, p. 8.

48. UN/T/3S/SR.7, June 23, 1948; "Wives total 110, not 600, Fon says," *New York Times*, January 28, 1949.

49. John Hohenberg, "Why have 110 wives? The bedeviled Fon of Bikom puts a mental hex on four U.N. diplomats probing into the evils of polygamy," *Esquire*, December 1950.

50. IDOC, p. 119.

51. UN-G, p. 8.

52. "The Fon of Bikom," *Adelaide Advertiser*, October 6, 1950.

53. Mervyn Jeffreys, "Some Notes on the Fon of Bikom," *African Affairs* (1951), pp. 247–48.

54. IDOC, p. 74.

55. CCC, pp. 319, 323.

56. Amelia Fry, "Rebecca Hourwich Reyher: Search and Struggle for Equality and Independence, Third Research Trip: The Fon and His Hundred Wives," University of California at Berkeley, Regional Oral History Office, Oral History (1973).

57. Rebecca Hourwich Reyher, *The Fon and His Hundred Wives* (1952), pp. 21, 312.

58. Karen Knop, *Diversity and Self-Determination in International Law* (2002), p. 340.

59. IDOC, pp. 151, 172.

60. OPT, p. 7.

61. UN/T/SR.389, March 3, 1952.

62. UN/T/SR.410, March 31, 1952.

63. UN/T/PV.454, July 23, 1952.

64. CCT-G, p. 7.

65. John Blacker, "The Demography of Mau Mau: Fertility and Mortality in Kenya in the 1950s: A Demographer's Viewpoint," *African Affairs* (2007).

66. IDOC, p. 61, 34.

67. "ACB to Lady Burns," personal letter, June 6, 1950, private collection.

68. "ACB to Lady Burns," personal letter, June 15, 1950, private collection.

69. FO/371/88582/UP/24169, "ACB to Colonial Office," May 11, 1950.

70. "ACB to Lady Burns," personal letter, May 7, 1950, private collection.

71. "ACB to Lady Burns," personal letter, July 12, 1950, private collection.

72. "ACB to Lady Burns," personal letter, May 7, 1950, private collection.

73. "ACB to Lady Burns," personal letter, June 28, 1950, private collection.

74. "UK's Trusteeship Council protest," *Scotsman*, February 4, 1950; "Britain denies breach of trust charge," *Scotsman*, March 7, 1950; "Trouble over the Cameroons," *Manchester Guardian*, March 8, 1950.

75. "ACB to Galsworthy (Foreign Office)," personal letter, February 17, 1950, private collection.

76. UN/A/C.4/SR.50-85, September 21–November 22, 1948.

77. FO/371/95679/UP/24152, "ACB to Foreign Office," November 17, 1951.

78. "ACB to Lady Burns," personal letter, July 9, 1950, private collection.

79. FO/371/88582/UP/2416/11, "ACB to Galsworthy," July 27, 1950.

80. FO/371/88582/UP/2416/9, "ACB to Colonial Office," May 11, 1950.

81. "ACB to Lady Burns," personal letter, July 4, 1950, private collection.

82. "ACB to Lady Burns," personal letter, June 15, 1950, private collection.

83. "ACB to Lady Burns," personal letter, May 7, 1950, private collection.

84. FO/371/95679/UP/24152, "ACB memo," November 17, 1951.

85. UN/A/C.4/SR.168, November 6, 1950.

86. "ACB to Lady Burns," personal letter, June 6, 1950, private collection.

87. FO/371/88582/UP/2416/11, "ACB to Galsworthy," July 27, 1950.

88. "Air mail rates for British journals: reduction urged," *The Times*, October 10, 1950.

89. FBCE-G, pp. 13, 16.

90. IDOC, pp. 302–3.

91. IDOC, p. 293; CBAA, p. 158.

92. RCD-G, p. 14.

93. "Trusteeship," *The Times*, January 11, 1952.

94. UN/T/PV.465, June 22, 1953.

95. FO/371/95679/UP/24152, "ACB to Foreign Office," November 17, 1951.

96. "Rachel Caroline Maxtone Graham to ACB," personal letter, April 10 (no year), private collection.

97. Gilbert Ware, "Somalia: From Trust Territory to Nation, 1950–1960," *Phylon* (1965), pp. 178, 184.

98. UN/A/C.4/SR.240, January 9, 1952.

99. UN/A/C.4/SR.239, January 8, 1952.

100. UN/A/C.4/SR.297, December 8, 1952.

101. CO/936/60/2, "UK Delegation at UN in Paris to Foreign Office," December 23, 1951.

102. "UN and the Colonies: Onslaughts in the Fourth Committee," *Times Review of the British Colonies* (1952).

103. UN/A/C.4/SR.241, January 9, 1952; UN/A/Res558(VI), January 18, 1952.

104. "The bogey of colonialism," *New York Times*, November 10, 1952; "British UN aide lauds trust role," *New York Times*, November 20, 1952.

Chapter 11

The Wildest Schemes

From his arrival in 1947, Alan found himself listening to lectures on the evils of colonialism from representatives of the Soviet Union. The Soviets always waited to speak last "to be sure of the best propaganda effect," he observed.[1] Their criticisms were "a monotonous propaganda tirade" that repeated the same formulaic points no matter what place was under discussion.[2] Alan drew laughter at the Trusteeship Council when he suggested that the Soviet delegation should have its standard criticisms printed on a form with an empty box to fill in the name of the place being discussed.[3] When the Soviet delegate complained about the lack of democracy in Tanganyika, Alan scoffed: "I can assure the Soviet Union representative that more than one political party exists in the territory and that any individual wishing to start another party will not be liquidated."[4]

The Foreign Office wanted to ignore most Soviet resolutions. Any attempt to debate them, a diplomat noted, would suggest that "we are a bunch of nineteenth century reactionaries who must be prodded into action by the Trusteeship Council stimulated by the USSR."[5] Alan was less restrained. "The representative of the Soviet Union talks a great deal about democracy and the alleged anti-democratic practices" of the British colonial administration, he said at one point. Britain was "prepared to rest with confidence on the reputation of its own type of democracy as against the type of democracy in which the representative of the Soviet Union believes."[6] In a debate on arrest and imprisonment, he asked if the council could discuss Soviet practices, to which the Soviets responded "under no circumstances."[7]

All the indignity of lectures from the Soviet Union would eventually get a full venting in Alan's 1957 book *In Defence of Colonies*. "The victims of Soviet expansion and absorption are certainly less 'free' than the inhabitants of British colonies," he would write.[8] While anti-colonial delegates from other countries might be foolish, at least they meant well. Moscow, by contrast, saw anti-colonialism as part of a program of world domination. The Soviet aim was "that the record of their interventions [at the UN] . . . find their ways into the hands of active politicians in trust and colonial territories and that, read out of their context, they . . . create the impression that only the Soviet Union is devoted to the real interests of these inhabitants."[9] This made it "all the more necessary" for the colonial powers "to be indefatigable in going on record against Soviet proposals." His efforts won him plaudits in the Colonial Office: "The most effective way you have responded" has "caused great delight throughout the office," one liaison wrote.[10] "Burns has been quite pugnacious," the British ambassador to the UN added.[11] After the Conservatives returned to office under Churchill in 1951, Alan was given every encouragement to rebut the Soviets on colonial issues.

The communist threat was real, which is why most Third World delegations steered clear of Moscow and Beijing, Alan noted.[12] "If the British Empire were to dissolve or if the too hasty grant of self-government led to anarchy in a colony," he warned in a speech, "there would be a political vacuum into which communism would most certainly enter."[13] The insurgency in Malaya that had taken the life of his friend Henry Gurney was, in his words, "not a case of Malayan patriots fighting for the independence of their country" but instead "a deliberate attempt by Chinese communists to destroy the economy of Malaya."[14]

Two other places had recently experienced communist disruption. In Burma, what one former chief secretary of the colony in 1953 called "a disorderly stampede for independence" had thrust the country into "anarchy and chaos."[15] Backed by Moscow's communists in India, Burma's Red Flag insurgency had "been able to exploit the conditioned reflexes of a people who had been primed for a violent revolution against the British," added a scholar, and thus "when the British tactfully withdrew in 1948 they left a country all dressed up for a colonial struggle with nowhere to go."[16] The military would soon step in for a lengthy tenure, and Burma, once the rice basket of Asia, would become a failed state. "People are beginning to look back wistfully to the law and order which prevailed under the British Government," another former colonial official in Burma wrote in 1949.[17]

The same pattern emerged in British Guiana: "We have recently seen the effects of Russian teaching and the danger of handing over the destinies of an immature people to indoctrinated communists," Alan warned in a speech.[18] Colonial authorities suspended self-government there in 1953, and Churchill sent a detachment of troops to restore order. After winning legislative elections, the communist-inspired People's Progressive Party, led by an ethnically Indian dentist named Cheddi Jagan, had brought the colony to a standstill. Jagan and his American wife were "zealots in the cause of communism," Alan added.[19] Jagan titled his autobiography *The West on Trial.*

British Guiana was doubly upsetting to Alan because of Jagan's links to brother Emile. Jagan visited Britain's Communist Party headquarters in 1951 and 1953. Visiting the CPGB at this time was no trifle. Emile and other members had turned it into the central institution imposing Moscow's will on left-of-center political and social movements in Western Europe.[20] Even the eminent Marxist historian Edward Thompson complained that Emile and others were "acting as High Priests interpreting and justifying the Holy Writ as emanating from Stalin."[21] Emile conveyed the latest directives from Moscow on colonial issues, according to meetings bugged by MI5.[22] For Jagan to seek the support of the CPGB at this time was to put himself, and British Guiana, directly in the service of Moscow.

Jagan brought back to British Guiana a shipment of Emile's 1946 pamphlet *The Story of Capitalism*, which argued that economic activity should be in the hands of the state. Jagan praised the killing of white farmers in Kenya and demanded that a "people's police" be formed in British Guiana to counter the colonial police. The moment Jagan became government leader in 1953, he called a mass strike and tried to push new laws through the legislature banning all trade unions except the communist one. His government walked out of the legislature when the speaker did not oblige.[23] Even Britain's Labour Party condemned his behavior. Emile coined the term "right-wing Labour" to describe Labour's perfidy.[24] People began to flee the colony, and the economy nosedived. Independence for what became the "cooperative republic" of Guyana in 1966 would offer an object lesson in what Alan called "the tyranny of self-government."[25] The post-colonial leaders replaced the British monarchy as the symbol of national unity with an eighteenth-century rebel named Cuffy the House Slave. When not in Moscow or Havana, Jagan kept the country on the boil, accusing the socialist government of being "pro-imperialist" and "neo-fascist."[26] Alan was not about to sit idly by and watch the cancer spread.

At the heart of colonial disputes at the UN were two questions. First, what exactly was a "non-self-governing territory"? Since virtually every country was a result of conquest, over land or over sea, most UN members should in theory be providing information on their "colonial" holdings. The "salt-water fallacy" held that only expansion over seas was "colonialism," while expansion over land was "nation-building." Moscow's colonial rule over the peoples of Central Asia, Siberia, and now Eastern Europe, to say nothing of the expansion over diverse peoples by Latin American countries, India, the United States, China, Pakistan, Indonesia, Egypt, Iraq, and others should on this view be the subjects of Fourth Committee inquiries. "It is indeed

difficult for the British to understand," Alan wrote, "why countries which
have expanded across oceans . . . should be classed as brutal imperialists,
while on the other hand nations which have expanded across continents . . .
are subjected to no such stigma."[27]

This question led to another. Even if the arbitrary "salt-water" criteria
were used to distinguish colonialism from noncolonialism, it still left open
the question of how to judge "progress to self-government." Presumably,
progress should be judged against conditions in similar places. Yet here
again, European powers ran into a seemingly arbitrary distinction: what was
expected in European colonies was much better than what was expected in
independent states. European nations were not allowed to draw attention to
conditions elsewhere and cry, "You too!" (*tu quoque*). This blackout was
formalized in a General Assembly resolution of 1950 that required independent countries to consent to being used as comparisons with colonies.[28]
In one instance, the El Salvador delegation to the UN demanded an official
apology from Alan after a British tabloid ran a story comparing conditions
in El Salvador with those in British Honduras. "The *Sunday Express* is not a
government publication," Alan reported.[29]

Together, the salt-water fallacy and the injunction against *tu quoque* meant
that colonial debates at the United Nations were artificially constrained. The
French and Belgians were critical of the salt-water fallacy, but for different
reasons. The French (and Portuguese) saw their overseas empire as a part
their country. If the French were required to inform the UN about conditions in Algeria or Indo-China, then they should also transmit information
on Normandy and Provence.[30] The Belgians, by contrast, saw even their own
country as only a temporary agreement among groups (Flemish, Walloon
French, and German) who might one day decide to govern themselves sepa-
rately. The so-called "Belgian Thesis" was that *every* UN member should be
transmitting information on *every* group under its rule.[31] "Far from wishing to
restrict these principles, we wish on the contrary that they should be respected
in their fullest meaning," Ryckmans explained, suggesting that at least thirty
of the newest UN members should be considered colonial powers.[32] Alan
concurred. Most Indonesians, he noted, saw independence as "a substitution
of Javanese for Dutch rule," while throughout Latin America, "the people
are still governed by men of Spanish descent and the indigenous Indian has
little control over his own destiny."[33] What made a people "self-governing,"
Alan told the Fourth Committee, was whether they had control over their
fates. This "cardinal and essential feature" implied that a people might choose
something other than outright independence, including outright annexation
by the colonial state or continued colonial rule.[34]

The Belgian Thesis also challenged the ban on *tu quoque* since it implied
that every country was a colony ripe for comparison. Perhaps UN efforts

should be directed toward improving the status of disadvantaged groups in the Soviet Union or India rather than in the Congo, Ryckmans ventured. "It is difficult to understand why the attitude adopted towards the under-developed indigenous populations differs according to the state under whose sovereignty they happen to be. . . . Do some of those populations have more right than others to the attention of the United Nations?"[35] With their subversive thesis, the Belgians could claim to be more anti-colonial than the anti-colonialists: "To restrict the enjoyment of international guarantees to a few indigenous peoples would be an injustice to all the others" and "would constitute a deplorable set-back to the pursuit of the humanitarian ideal to which this Organization is dedicated," another Belgian delegate explained.[36]

While rejecting the Belgian Thesis, the British, Alan noted, accepted its basic humanitarian principle. Most anti-colonial countries, he observed, dared "not accept the challenge in the Belgian Thesis" that would shine a spotlight on subject peoples within their own borders.[37] Among the growing ranks of "professional anti-colonialists . . . little sympathy" was "shown for those who wish to be free from non-white masters."[38] This should not prevent European powers from showing such sympathy, he advised, beginning perhaps with subject peoples in virulently anti-colonial India, Egypt, and the Soviet Union: "Their need for such protection is as great as ever." Frequent resolutions demanding democracy in European colonies were put forward by nations that had never held a national election, he noted.[39] In calling out misrule in independent Yemen, Egypt, the Philippines, or India, he noted, the European powers could offer a model of what constructive criticism looked like: "I would not suggest that in those countries, the position is so simple that it can be cleared up in a short time."[40]

Alan's frequent deployment of *tu quoque* comparisons, one scholar noted, "pointed to very real shortcomings in the UN apparatus for protecting dependent peoples living in territories not under colonial rule."[41] Perhaps the European colonial powers with their long experience and advanced economies *should* be held to higher standards. It was "certainly a tribute to the British reputation for upright administration that our critics expect from us a much higher standard than they themselves can reach," Alan noted. But the critics at the UN sometimes spoke as if their own conquests and conditions were pristine. Resorting to *tu quoque* argument, he admitted, "is never satisfactory but it is sometimes necessary if a proper sense of proportion is to be gained."[42] "It is notorious that the most severe criticism comes from the representatives of countries where the administration is most corrupt, the treatment of minorities or of the working classes the most discriminatory, and the constitution so unstable that it is shaken by frequent revolutions. It is, of course, convenient in such cases to divert attention from their own shortcomings by fervid protestations of devotion to democracy, coupled with denunciations of colonial misrule."[43]

Peering deeply into the anti-colonial soul, what worried Alan was that entire nations were being raised on hypocrisy. Anti-colonial delegates would admit to him privately that they recognized colonial achievements and that their domestic records were much worse. But in public, they were duty-bound to denounce colonialism and urge the coming of "freedom." Over time, angry protest against the West would substitute for good governance as the basis of domestic legitimacy, to the enduring detriment of the people of former colonies.

India's de facto minister for decolonization, Apa Pant, was a good example of the anti-colonial politicians who "may be (as most of them are) personally friendly and reasonable in their approach to colonial questions, [but] are generally bound by anti-colonial convention (or by their instructions) to an extent which does not allow them to deal with such questions publicly in an objective manner," Alan recalled.[44] A whole world was being forged at the UN in which objective inquiry was impossible. Protest against the West rather than cooperation for better lives was becoming the dominant mode of global governance. This psychological tick in the founding mythologies of the Third World nations would confound international affairs for decades to come.

By 1951, colonial debates at the United Nations had shifted to the Fourth Committee. Alan continued to strike a "note of sweet reasonableness," a colleague remarked.[45] But it was inevitable that a breach would occur. "I do not believe that sweet reasonableness has the slightest effect on United Nations opinion," Alan rued.[46] He scolded the Fourth Committee for veering into "acrimony, bitterness, and recrimination" with its "arid and meaningless verbal quibbles." Rather than concentrating "on the practical and the material," the members preferred "intoxicating but abortive and acrimonious discussions."[47]

Alan found solace in dry humor. One session was held up when the Iraqi delegate insisted that the term "teacher training" was archaic and should be replaced in all UN documents with the swanky new term "teacher preparation." Training, the Iraqi theorist declared, was for horses. "I spent many years being trained as a civil servant," Alan insisted, "and I most emphatically deny that I am a horse."[48] On another occasion, when the delegate from Syria asked Alan what laws protected farmers in British colonies from "exploitation," he replied, "The laws of supply and demand."[49]

The first breach came in November 1951 after several delegates offered unsolicited advice to France on a political crisis in French Morocco. Iraq proposed a resolution that would make political discussions formally part of the Fourth Committee's mandate—in effect revising the UN Charter through a floor motion.[50] Alan stepped in to insist the resolution be submitted in writing given its "far-reaching implications." France walked out of the meeting, a first for a colonial power. The issue was held over until the following Monday. Alan telegraphed London to advise the British ambassador to the UN to be present when the committee resumed in order to show they meant "business."[51] The resolution needed to be defeated so that they were "not gradually pushed into acceptance of some degree of United Nations supervision" over the British Empire. The ambassador's appearance had its intended effect, frightening the anti-colonial bloc with the prospect of the major colonial power's abandoning the Fourth Committee. Alan won "a détente for the moment," a Foreign Office colleague wrote to him, but there was no promise that "our enemies will not return to the attack."[52] Alan was promised extra staff to remain "at full strength . . . while we are in the thick of this battle."[53]

The following summer, Alan was asked by Churchill's new secretary for colonies to continue as Fourth Committee representative. He wrote back expressing disillusion: "Quite frankly, I would rather not accept it. I am finding it more and more difficult, as United Kingdom representative, to accept the role of a defendant in a trial conducted by ignorant and prejudiced judges of 'the colonial system.' I happen to be rather proud of the colonial service and of the work this country has done in the colonies, and I resent the general anti-colonial atmosphere of the United Nations."[54] But he would not say no. His heart was too much in it. His only request was an extra allowance to allow Katie to accompany him more often.

As he prepared to resume the "thick of battle" in the summer of 1952, Alan wrote a long memo to the foreign and colonial secretaries outlining a new strategy.[55] There was a danger that "our colonial policy will be perverted and virtually dictated by a majority of the irresponsible in the United Nations." Thus "the time has come for us to take a stand." This stand "should take the form of a positive counter-attack and leave no doubt in the minds of our critics that they can push us so far but no further." All the various attempts to bend and invent rules at the UN—allowing discussions of political issues in colonies, allowing natives to sit as independent delegates from trust territories—should be thwarted. The defeat of the Iraqi resolution had shown that "a strong line taken by us would have an excellent effect." Otherwise, British colonial officials would find their policies being driven by "undue and increasing regard to the ill-considered opinions" of UN members. "We should not allow our work to be undone in this way." The memo ended with a stark defense of the British Empire: "We should sum up by a forceful affirmation that we are as, if not more, zealous and interested in promoting the welfare of the peoples for whom we have responsibility than our irresponsible critics who cannot even decently order their own domestic affairs."

The Burns Memo of Summer 1952 does not appear in any public records, but its resonances were immediately apparent. In late 1952, the Fourth Committee passed a Soviet-Egyptian resolution demanding that the British reverse a resettlement scheme in Tanganyika undertaken to boost food production. Most of the new farmers were white, which is what attracted the censure. Alan denounced the thirty-two countries who voted for it (as opposed to only seventeen Western powers against) for engaging in a "blatant example of racial prejudice" with their insinuations that the government had acted to favor whites (rather than to raise food production). The whole UN system for trusts and colonies, he warned, would "collapse" if such resolutions continued.[56]

In retrospect, the Tanganyika resolution showed that the system had already collapsed. The Mau Mau bloc, in Alan's words, was "less concerned with the welfare of the indigenous inhabitants than with the spread of ideological propaganda." This had caused colonial powers to refrain from sharing evidence at the UN since it "would be seized on as a damning admission of national guilt, and the criticism would be twisted and exaggerated almost beyond recognition by unscrupulous opponents." The resulting "absurd situation" was such: "Those best qualified to offer constructive suggestions and advice are almost silent while those who know too little talk too much."[57] Alan's growing silence at the UN reflected a dangerous divide (see figure 11.1).

Figure 11.1 Trusteeship Council Meeting at Lake Success, 1952. *Source*: Private Collection of Alan Dixon.

Again, Alan wrote a long memo to the colonial and foreign secretaries to summarize the state of the fight.[58] Like his summer memo, this one did not mince words. "While the results may be more satisfactory than last year, I think the atmosphere is much worse," he began:

> On the whole, the [Fourth] Committee has been more irresponsible than ever and I foresee that it will be worse at the next session unless we take action. . . . There are continual attacks on the colonial powers . . . and there is a complacent assumption that only the Mau Maus have the interests of the natives at heart. All these things are hard to bear, particularly when we know what goes on in the countries represented by the Mau Maus. . . . What is important is the effect on Africans and others in our dependent territories. I believe the behavior of the Mau Maus in the Fourth Committee is based on a deliberate attempt to weaken the position of the colonial powers and to encourage "subject" peoples to revolt. . . . The speeches made by the Mau Maus are intended to lower the prestige of the colonial powers among their native "subjects," and I am afraid that they are going to have the desired effect.

In the course of just a few months, Alan's advice had shifted from active rebuttal to utter rejection of the UN system. "Our good work has been ignored, our good faith has been impugned, and we have been made to feel that we are regarded by the Fourth Committee as criminals, on trial for our crimes, and not as colleagues with the same ideals, working towards the same ends." By continuing to sit on the committee, colonial powers were in effect participating in their own destruction: "We are doing positive harm by our presence in the Fourth Committee, which seems to be an admission that we are prisoners at the bar, and that the best we can hope for is a light censure for our crimes." A firm line was needed with a threat to abandon the UN on colonial issues altogether. "I am convinced that we will come to this position very soon and early action may save us trouble in overseas territories."

The breach finally happened over a special committee that had been created by a Cuban-Iraqi initiative of 1946 to "examine" the information reports sent to the Fourth Committee. This "Committee on Information" was not contained in the UN Charter and was seen as illegal by colonial powers. It was an attempt at "empire-building" by anti-colonial states, the Colonial Office warned.[59] Belgium's Ryckmans foresaw the results: "A committee means discussion, and discussion means criticism."[60]

Sure enough, the information committee veered sharply into anti-colonial criticism from day one.[61] Because of this, the colonial powers repeatedly thwarted attempts to make it permanent. In 1952, the Fourth Committee, swollen with new anti-colonial countries, sent the resolution to the General Assembly again. Alan, representing the colonial bloc, issued an ultimatum:

reject the motion, or we walk. The threat worked: thirty countries abstained, while only eleven voted in favor and eighteen (including the United States) against. Only the Soviets and "their trained seals," as Alan called them, voted in favor. The *Times* bubbled that "for once, a warning of the Assembly's limitations did not pass unheeded."[62]

Alan was toasted back home for the success. "It is a very remarkable achievement to have achieved such a *volte face* on the part of our adversaries," the Colonial Office wrote to Alan. It had vindicated the point in Alan's memos: "When we decide to stand firm, the opposition are powerless to shift us." The only regret was that the threat had not been carried out: "It would have been interesting, to put it at the least, to see what would have happened" if colonial powers had abandoned colonial discussions at the UN.[63] Alan was less sanguine. The thirty countries that abstained did so "with no good grace."[64] The delegate from India had stated, "Whether we agree or not," the participation of the colonial powers was "necessary if the committee is to yield maximum results."[65] It was no fun to put the West on trial with no Westerners in the dock.

The final collapse came in August 1953. Enduring endless censure of their administration in Ruanda-Urundi and the Congo, the Belgians declared that the information committee was "absolutely useless" and formally withdrew. The five-page Belgian indictment of the committee stands as a testament to the failed experiment that was UN-led decolonization.[66] The damage, nevertheless, was done. The "fumbling fingers" of the UN would usher in more than a half century of horror for the Congo, Rwanda, and Burundi, as well as other places.

By late 1953, the UN had lost interest in preparations for self-government in favor of an obsessive concern with ending colonialism at all costs. Hundreds of millions of lives lay in the balance as ideology replaced empiricism. Alan had won tactical battles, but he was losing the war. "It is the attitude of this [Fourth] Committee, more than anything else," he warned in a speech in Geneva, "which will lead to the break-up of the United Nations."[67]

Alan's alarm about the direction of events at the United Nations led him to take his case public even though he continued to serve in a diplomatic capacity. The venue he chose for his *crie de coeur*—entitled "The Movement Towards Self-Government in British Colonial Territories"—was *Optima*, a recently launched magazine of South Africa's Anglo-American Mining Corporation. The June 1954 article summarized the salient points of what by now we might call "the Burns Thesis" on colonialism: that compared to what might have happened in most colonial areas, the coming of colonialism was mostly good for subject peoples; that it enjoyed broad legitimacy as a result; that racial and national feeling, far more than economic or political need, was driving the movement for self-government; and that the growing anti-colonial clamor at the United Nations was both hypocritical, coming from nations that were themselves "colonial" or which could not govern themselves, and dangerous, given the likely consequences of sudden decolonization. There were "considerable differences of opinion" among subject peoples about how quickly to decolonize. Britain's views on the matter were "worthy of some regard" because its "record for liberal humanity, in spite of its black spots, is better than that of most countries." The article was variously described as "hard-hitting" and "realistic."

Alan's defense of the British Empire was directed at many audiences. There were the Soviets and their "trained seals," including brother Emile in London, who seized "every opportunity to fan into a flame any smoldering embers of economic or racial troubles" in the colonies.[68] There were the newly independent states like India that took up the anti-colonial mantle with a "holier-than thou" attitude toward European powers, pretending they "were competent to be the nagging conscience of the world" despite their flawed domestic records.[69] There were the ambitious native politicians who had foresworn cooperation with colonial authorities in favor of appearances in New York, each of whom wished "to see his [UN] speeches reproduced in the press of his own country to show what a fine fellow he is."[70] There was the average person in Britain, increasingly dismayed by reports of unrest in the empire who felt it better to "go comfortably to bed at night, with confidence that we are not likely to get our throats cut while we sleep, and that, in any case, the wearisome struggle in distant and primitive lands is no concern of ours."[71]

Above all, there was the United States where "traditional hostility to British colonialism so often blinds the American to the facts of life."[72] In the years since the Atlantic Charter, Britain had convinced Washington to refrain from pushing for sudden decolonization. A State Department official warned publicly in 1953 that premature independence for many colonies and trust territories would be "dangerous, retrogressive, and destructive."[73] Outside the State Department, however, anti-colonial sentiment was growing. In mid-1954, President Eisenhower asked London to moderate its blanket opposition to anti-colonial resolutions at the UN.[74]

The changing U.S. attitudes were personified in the new U.S. representative on the Trusteeship Council, Mason Sears. A patrician New Englander, the Harvard-educated Sears had been a member of the Massachusetts house and senate before his appointment. He saw himself as sweeping away the tired old empires of Europe and bringing a new dawn of Yankee freedom to everywhere he visited—"to make as many friends for the United States as possible without being offensive to our Allies in Europe," as he put it in his confirmation hearing.[75] He entitled his memoirs *Years of High Purpose*, in contrast to the humble title of Alan's memoirs. "Pictures of him standing or moving against some tropical background were frequently published," noted the American ambassador to the UN.

Widely travelled in Asia, Sears was a newcomer to Africa and made his first visit to the continent in 1954. After a week in the Gold Coast, he declared it ready for independence. There were, he averred, no grounds for concern that "political instability [would] be the characteristic of the new state of Ghana."[76]

It was that attitude that unnerved Alan when Sears was chosen as one of four members of a visiting mission to Tanganyika in 1954 (see figure 11.2). The giant trust territory was a refuge of good governance in East Africa. The de facto leader of the independence movement was a lovable intellectual, Julius Nyerere, whose soaring rhetoric about community democracy and *ujamaa* (familyhood) development struck a chord with Western progressives. Sears fell for the diminutive "Teacher of the Jungle" who in turn flattered Sears for standing up to the imperialists. "Sears was regarded by the colonial authorities of Britain as a dangerous and irresponsible American, dabbling in matters which he did not understand and doing considerable damage in the process," Nyerere wrote of his American mentor.[77]

Sears expressed puzzlement about Alan. On the one hand, Alan was the author of many progressive measures as governor of the Gold Coast and

Figure 11.2   At a School in Somaliland after the Tanganyika Mission, 1954. *Source:* Private Collection of Alan Dixon.

frequently spoke about moves to self-government. Yet he was cautious and defended the colonial record vigorously. "Sir Alan was also plainly anti-American, in part due to his irritation with the anti-colonial mood of the American public," Sears wrote. The senator from Boston could not understand how someone could be both "progressive" and "pro-colonial."

The mission was in Tanganyika for five weeks in July and August 1954. Alan joined for the critical six days in Dar es Salaam when political issues were discussed. Having sworn to Katie that he would never again join such a mission, Alan went because he viewed Sears as an imminent threat to the British Empire.

As with the Pacific mission, the delegates understood that the point was to go on safari in order to legitimate their differing views once they returned to New York. The real action began with the drafting of the mission report. For Sears, the report should represent a major break with the "no time targets" position that the State Department had taken. "He is invariably annoyed when he feels that obstacles are being placed in his way by the State Department or other source," noted one magazine profile.[78]

The Tanganyika mission was, in retrospect, a final attempt to bridge what had become a vast divide on the issue of colonialism. The mission delegates from India and El Salvador inserted into the draft report that the territory would be ready for independence "much earlier" than the twenty to twenty-five years set for neighboring Ruanda-Urundi.[79] Sears ignored his instructions and supported the position. Only a great public row with the British, he believed, would direct attention to the question of independence. "Unless there was a major dissent with the mission, the statements about conditions in Tanganyika which I wanted emphasized would lose their impact," he wrote.

The New Zealand chair of the mission tried to find a consensus position in a meeting with Sears. "During this conference, I was delighted to have him ask me, 'What do you think Sir Alan Burns will think about the report?,'" Sears recalled. "This gave me the perfect opportunity to explain . . . that I represented the United States and not the British government." The Kiwi chair dissented from the draft report, calling the time target "a fraud."[80]

When the draft appeared in January 1955, it hit like a storm. The Colonial Office sent an emissary to Washington asking for clarification on whether U.S. policy had changed. A colonial official brought in from Tanganyika told the Trusteeship Council that most Africans opposed timetables because it was "certain" that independence in less than twenty years would result in "chaos." Alan dismissed the target as "purely arbitrary." The *Times* called his dissent "scathing."[81] More significantly, Alan declared that Britain would "in no circumstances accept or implement any recommendations which in its view are inimical to the real interests of the inhabitants of Tanganyika."[82] Britain had finally broken ranks with the UN.

The American Secretary of State, John Foster Dulles, wrote an internal memo calling the situation "quite embarrassing" and making clear that Sears had *not* represented the U.S. position. This was not simply Cold War strategy, Dulles explained, but the best policy for the lives of ordinary Tanganyikans: "It is precisely because we attach importance to the sound development of self-government that our policy emphasizes economic, social, and educational advancement." Sears had affixed the United States' name to a draft report that was "unnecessarily controversial and tendentious."[83] Sears was ordered to inform the UN that the U.S. position remained that time targets would not be helpful "in any way."[84] Sears felt humiliated: "It made our government look like a conspirator on the side of imperialism instead of a champion of independence," he wrote. A new committee composed of Australia, Belgium, China, and Haiti wrote a final mission report that deleted all references to time targets.

Alan's declaration that the United Kingdom no longer felt itself bound to comply with UN instructions was an admission that the global governance of decolonization had failed. The same year, he declared that Britain was ruling its colonies "in accordance with the [UN] Charter, and it will continue to do so" even though it "might not be satisfying some of the members" of the UN.[85] This was Britain's returning to the "sacred trust" that had motivated the spread of the British Empire. It was the same message he had issued less diplomatically in his *Optima* article: "We have a duty to the people of the dependent territories and to the world at large that it would be cowardly to shirk, and we could not later escape the responsibility and the blame for the disasters that would follow if we abandoned our trust."

It would take another year for the immensity of this shift to become apparent. Along with the Belgian withdrawal from the information committee, Alan's dissent over Tanganyika was a watershed moment when the UN's collaborative approach to decolonization shattered. "In respect of her colonial territories, the United Kingdom has an immense responsibility, but this responsibility is to the people of those territories and not to the self-appointed critics of 'colonialism,'" he would explain later.[86] From this point forward, decolonization became a game of threat and power rather than law and legitimacy. The road to breakdown in the colonies was prepared.

Although Mason Sears was forced to retreat on time targets, his views were advancing in Washington. A congressional resolution of 1955 sided with Sears, demanding that Washington vote in favor of *all* anti-colonial resolutions at the UN. This tipped the UN decisively to the anti-colonial. For ambitious politicians in the colonies, it was like the sounding of a starter's pistol.

Jungle teacher Julius Nyerere came to New York in March 1955 to testify on the mission report. He was no firebrand and seemed unnerved by the rapidity of the change. His country needed twenty more years of colonialism, he averred. Sears too seemed rattled by talk of "independence now" at the UN and urged Nyerere to "steer" his people away from this question.[87] Nyerere replied that the population was not for steering. "My big problem now is how to control what is likely to be a mass movement."[88]

Events elsewhere in East Africa were moving fast. Britain had been forced by Egypt to abandon their joint control of Sudan in 1953, leading to a disputed election in 1954 and a rebellion in the south in 1955 that ended in the execution of three hundred rebels. Sudanese refugees were now streaming into colonial Uganda, which was the bridge into colonial Tanganyika.[89] A spillover of the chaos from Sudan into Tanganyika would be disastrous. Nyerere returned home to find his movement in a restive mood. He symbolically quit the legislature in protest against British foot-dragging, lest he become a target. Sears convinced the State Department to support a resolution in the Trusteeship Council encouraging time targets for independence in Tanganyika "where appropriate" lest the United States become a target as well. He knew the resolution would draw another *démarche* from the British and wrote to his superiors, appending a copy of Alan's criticisms: "If the British by chance should come to see you in order to protest against the United States position in the Council, I hope you will privately agree with me that it is a little unbecoming for a nation which is doing so much for self-government all over the world to take objection because the United States joined other nations in asking them merely to consider a course of action."[90]

In retrospect, the Tanganyika issue exposed the inherent problems with the global governance of colonialism. By offering an alternative venue for native politicians, the UN system had sabotaged the orderly transition to independence in European colonies. No longer bound to adhere to the dynamics of power within colonial institutions, native politicians end-ran the process by appealing for help to the UN. A malign precedent was set in which disgruntled groups would appeal to outside forces when they did not get their way. Tanganyika's independence would come like a firecracker in 1961. Within three years, Nyerere's military would mutiny, and he would be briefly chased from power before being reinstalled by a British military intervention. *Ujaama* socialism and one-party authoritarianism would then send the country into a three-decade downward spiral.

Evidence of the decolonization debacle emerged at Duala, the coastal town where Alan had had his baptism of fire in World War I. On May 22nd, 1955, a rebel group that had failed to win any support in the French Cameroons trust territory began an insurgency there that would continue through the independence era, costing between sixty and a hundred thousand civilian lives.[91] The so-called Bamileke War was launched by a movement under Ruben Um

Nyobe, whose counterpart in British Cameroons was an avowed Marxist and a frequent visitor to Beijing and Moscow.[92] Thwarted by French colonial officials and denied a hearing at the Trusteeship Council, Nyobe won a warm welcome at the Fourth Committee and in the General Assembly. He made three appearances at the General Assembly in the early 1950s and passed on documents stolen from the French authorities to the UN Secretary General, who made them public, acting like a sort of decolonizing WikiLeaks. Nyobe's tenor was wholly different from Nyerere's. He was violently anti-colonial and made no attempt to mollify the colonial power.

When the Duala insurgency began, the future of the two Cameroons was the subject of delicate talks in the Trusteeship Council. The armed attacks "seriously retarded the political progress of the territory," Alan noted in one session. "It showed with great clarity how easily the peaceful tenor of those relatively under-developed parts of Africa could be seriously disturbed." Local administrators in both the British and the French sectors, he added, needed to hear from the UN that it "was conscious of their sense of disappointment," implying that the UN shared some of the blame because of its encouragement of Nyobe.[93]

As in Somaliland, the result of these "fumbling fingers" was to undermine colonial authority just when it was needed most. If European colonial powers were seen as having lost control of events to the UN, Alan said in one speech, it would be used as "a lever with which to apply direct pressure" to colonial rulers, undermining the incentive for local politicians to work cooperatively with colonial authorities.[94] The street protestors, not the elected native politicians and party leaders—whom the French and Belgians called the *évolués* or "advanced leaders"—would seize power. They would act as if the colonial authorities were no longer relevant and that the real decision-makers were in New York, Washington, and Moscow.[95]

The UN could hardly claim it was supporting preparations for self-government, Alan declaimed. Its handling of colonial questions was " a constant source of irritation and hostility between otherwise friendly nations, and, more important, does positive harm to dependent peoples."[96] In the Cameroons, as in Somaliland, the result was that the colonial powers lost control and had to hand over in a rush with predictable consequences. Formal independence ceremonies for Cameroon in 1960 had to be canceled because of armed conflict. "The effect of the UN's actions," wrote a New York human rights lawyer who had initially supported the Duala insurgents, "has been to leave the Cameroons in chaos, with no official international guidance."[97] The country would never recover, becoming one of the world's poorest and most despotic countries. Colonial foundations easily succumbed to the pounding sea.

The Cameroons and Tanganyika debates revealed the fissure that had now opened up between the anti-colonial majority at the UN and what was informally called the "tripartite" colonial powers of Britain, France, and Belgium. The three countries had been consulting informally on colonial issues at the UN since 1953. At a meeting in July 1955,[98] they concluded that the UN's handling of colonialism had failed. Anti-colonial countries like India and Syria, "assisted by the unreliability of Mr. Sears," a memo of the meeting noted, had abandoned attempts at compromise on colonial issues in favor of using the bully-pulpit of the UN to bring about mass decolonization. Colonial powers should reject outright any attempt to compromise "vital principles" about their sovereign right to determine the future of colonies and trust territories.

The slide was now rapid. Sears avenged his earlier humiliation and convinced the State Department to back targets for decolonization everywhere. Events were moving so rapidly that the trust territories risked falling behind the formal colonies. In the British and French Togoland trusts, agitation was rising, because the neighboring Gold Coast was now slated for independence as Ghana in 1957. This created the ironic demand by Togolese to be colonized by the British so that, as part of the Gold Coast, they could become independent. The Americans pressed for plebiscites in both sectors of Togoland. The British sector voted for amalgamation with Ghana, in effect approving the British decision to administer it as part of the colony, which had drawn wide censure in the UN. Nkrumah wrote a personal letter to Alan thanking him for his "successful lobbying in favour of the union."[99] Unbeknownst to Nkrumah, Alan had forced Mason Sears, "with some difficulty," to delete from a UN statement a commendation of Nkrumah's handling of the issue, believing he had been a positive disruption.[100] The French sector voted for outright independence. The French were enraged and threatened to withdraw from NATO. Alan, who as Gold Coast governor had supported the demands of the French Togolese, now swung around to the consensus view in London that the top priority was to avoid a break with the French.[101] Eventually, Paris was sweet-talked into accepting the result.

Whatever the technicalities, immediate decolonization everywhere had become de facto UN policy by 1956. The Cameroons and Tanganyika denouements signaled to native politicians everywhere that colonial powers had lost control. The Soviet Union in 1956 tabled a resolution in the General Assembly calling for two to three years to political independence for all trust territories, even as it was sending tanks into Hungary. In retrospect, this was not far off as an estimate for the entire decolonization process. By 1960, the UN would declare that colonialism was a threat to world peace and should be ended forthwith.

Alan's disillusion was complete. His thoughts now turned to public life outside of the UN, free of the constraints of a proconsul. He had declined an
interview with the BBC to discuss the work of the UN on the grounds that
if he spoke honestly, he would be fired.[102] A piece of doggerel found in his
papers reflects his dismay:

In the United Nations, day by day,
Anti-colonial members have their say,
And seek by flowery speech and waving hands,
To prove their interest in backward lands.

They speak at boring length on well-worn themes,
And vote in favour of the wildest schemes,
But backward peoples still in darkness walk
Unaided by this cataract of talk.

Meanwhile with patience, far from this turmoil,
The agents of "imperialism" toil
To help the backward peoples on their way
To independence and a brighter day,
Knowing full well that time is better spent
In quiet work than noisy argument.[103]

London asked Alan to continue for another two years. By this time, he was
burning to be free of the constraints of diplomacy. He had completed a new
book—which would be *In Defense of Colonies* of 1957—with the understanding that it would not be published until he was retired.[104] Extending his
tenure would delay its appearance. Alan decided to take up his own bully-
pulpit rather than continue to face reckless abuse at the UN. Nine years at the
UN, he explained, "has completely disillusioned me."[105] Remaining would
only contribute to the "positive harms" the organization was doing to colonial
areas. He wanted out. The secretary for colonies was thankful for a decade
of Burns: "It would not have been possible for anyone to have defended our
interests in the Council . . . more ably and skillfully than you have so bril-
liantly done."[106]

Alan had failed to turn the tide of global anti-colonialism. He had, however, chastened many countries with his arguments and laid the basis for a
later defense of the British Empire. As a junior secretary for colonies would
note: "His work [at the UN], I think, was of outstanding importance. Whereas
before our colonial policy was generally thought of as pretty unattractive or
bad in various ways, by the time he finished at the United Nations I think
everybody realized that our policy and what it stands for, colonialism, was
good. There is a great debt of gratitude owing to him for that."[107]

The official explanation of Alan's retirement was that Britain had decided to make their colonial delegation at the UN a permanent fixture in New York. For family reasons, Alan was not amenable to an extended posting overseas. This was partly true. Katie was becoming ill and unable to travel as much. The girls were planning their nuptials. Sister Essie had been struck by a car in London and needed constant care. Mainly, Alan was ready to speak and act from the outside.

Alan's retirement coincided with the Suez crisis. In July 1956, Egypt nationalized the Suez Canal, and the United States pressured the British and French to give it up. Alan was particularly critical of the Egyptian regime, whose radio stations "broadcast the most violent attacks against the Western world," including calling for Mau Mau–style uprisings throughout Africa.[108] Alan arrived home in Britain in August, a week before an international conference in London to resolve the dispute. His formal retirement came in September, a month before the ill-fated British-French attempt to reassert control over the canal.

Alan and his generation came home to indifference and hostility. Most retired civil servants were happy to take their pensions and reminisce about colonial days. Alan was too much the imperialist for that. Everyone in the Colonial Office was looking forward to reading *In Defense of Colonies*, the secretary for colonies wrote to him, and to Alan's public advocacy for colonial peoples: "I have a feeling that your retirement from public life is not going to be the beginning of a lazy time for you."[109]

NOTES

1. UN/T/SR.374, July 17, 1951.
2. UN/T/SR.365, July 3, 1951; UN/T/SR.356, June 20, 1951.
3. FO/371/95751/UP/2426/51, July 2, 1951.
4. UN/T/SR.681, March 9, 1956.
5. FO/371/95749/UP/2426/12, "Wilson to Mathieson," May 11, 1951.
6. UN/T/PV.442, July 10, 1952.
7. FO/371/95750/UP/2426/32, June 23, 1951.
8. IDOC, pp. 16, 141.
9. "ACB memorandum to Foreign Office and Colonial Office," Summer 1952, private collection.
10. "Poynton (Colonial Office) to ACB," personal letter, July 16, 1948, private collection.
11. "Jebb (UK ambassador to UN) to Foreign Office," confidential minute, July 24, 1951, private collection.
12. "ACB memorandum to Foreign Office and Colonial Office," Summer 1952, private collection.
13. FBCE, p. 16; OPT, p. 7.

14. CCT-G, p. 9.

15. Frank Donnison, *Public Administration in Burma: A Study of Development During the British Connexion* (1953), p. 71, 106.

16. Edward Law Yone and David Mandelbaum, "The New Nation of Burma," *Far Eastern Survey* (1950), p. 190.

17. John Furnivall, "Twilight in Burma: Independence and After," *Pacific Affairs* (1949), p. 171.

18. OPT, p. 7.

19. HBWI, p. 717.

20. Julie Waters, "Marxists, Manifestos, and 'Musical Uproar': Alan Bush, the 1948 Prague Congress, and the British Composers' Guild," *Journal of Musicological Research* (2011).

21. Geoff Andrews, *The Shadow Man: At the Heart of the Cambridge Spy Circle* (2015), p. 191.

22. KV/21762/297, April 2, 1951.

23. Ronald Sires, "British Guiana: The Suspension of the Constitution," *Western Political Quarterly* (1954).

24. Spencer Mawby, "The Limits of Anticolonialism: The British Labour Movement and the End of Empire in Guiana," *History* (2016); Emile Burns, *Right Wing Labour: Its Theory and Practice* (1961).

25. CBAB, p. 180a.

26. Harold Lutchman, "The Co-Operative Republic of Guyana," *Caribbean Studies* (1970), p. 109.

27. IDOC, pp. 18–19.

28. UN/A/PV.320 and UN/A/Res.447.V, December 12, 1950.

29. UN/T/PV.425, June 20, 1952.

30. UN/A/915, June 14, 1949.

31. Fernand van Langenhove, *The Question of Aborigines before the United Nations: The Belgian Thesis* (1954); Belgian Information Center, New York, *The Sacred Mission of Civilization: To Which Peoples Should the Benefits Be Extended?* (1953); Jessica Lynne Pearson, "Defending Empire at the United Nations: The Politics of International Colonial Oversight in the Era of Decolonisation," *Journal of Imperial and Commonwealth History* (2017).

32. UN/A/C.4/SR.253, October 23, 1952.

33. IDOC, pp. 177, 157.

34. UN/A/AC.58/1, July 16, 1952.

35. UN/A/C.4/SR.253, October 23, 1952.

36. UN/A/PV.402, December 10, 1952.

37. IDOC, p. 113.

38. CBAA, p. 5.

39. IDOC, pp. 114, 104.

40. UN/A/C.4/SR.232, December 20, 1951; CO/936/60/2, "UK delegation to Foreign Office," December 23, 1951.

41. Pearson, op. cit., p. 526.

42. IDOC, pp. 294, 6–7.

43. OPT, p. 7.
44. IDOC, p. 6.
45. "J. M. Martin (Colonial Office) to ACB," personal letter, November 21, 1951, private collection.
46. "ACB memorandum to Foreign Office and Colonial Office," Summer 1952, private collection.
47. UN/A/C.4/SR.206, November 19, 1951.
48. "Not a horse," *Daily Telegraph*, January 25, 1950.
49. UN/T/SR.570, February 3, 1955.
50. "Moroccan issue in UN," *The Times*, November 24, 1951; UN/A/C.4/SR.210, November 23, 1951.
51. "ACB memorandum to Foreign Office and Colonial Office," Summer 1952, private collection.
52. "J. M. Martin (Colonial Office) to ACB," personal letter, November 21, 1951, private collection.
53. "ACB to Selwyn Lloyd," personal letter, November 30, 1951, private collection.
54. "ACB to Secretary for Colonies," personal letter, August 18, 1952, private collection.
55. "ACB memorandum to Foreign Office and Colonial Office," Summer 1952, private collection.
56. "Welfare of the Meru tribe," *The Times*, December 4, 1952.
57. IDOC, pp. 115, 117.
58. "ACB to John M. Martin (Colonial Office)," personal letter, December 18, 1952, private collection.
59. CO/936/60/2, "Cabinet steering committee on international organizations: Brief for the UK delegate to the sixth session of the General Assembly," November 1, 1951.
60. Robert Godding, "Les Deviations de l'ONU," *La Revue Coloniale Belge* (1950), p. 8.
61. IDOC, p. 300.
62. "British warning to assembly," *The Times*, December 11, 1952.
63. CO/936/166/IRD/166/03, "John M. Martin (Colonial Office) to ACB," December 15, 1952.
64. "ACB to John M. Martin (Colonial Office)," personal letter, December 18, 1952, private collection.
65. UN/A/PV.402, December 10, 1952.
66. UN/A/AC.35/L.142, August 18, 1953.
67. UN-G, pp. 9, 12, 14.
68. OPT, p. 7.
69. CBAA, p. 21; IDOC, p. 151.
70. UN-G, p. 8.
71. CCT-G, p. 1.
72. OPT, p. 7.
73. "Danger of 'new colonialism,'" *The Times*, November 2, 1953.

74. United States, Department of State, Office of the Historian, "US–UK Colonial Policy Talks, July 26, 1954," *Foreign Relations of The United States, 1952–1954, United Nations Affairs, Volume III* (1979).

75. United States Senate, Committee on Foreign Relations, "Nomination of Mason Sears to be U.S. Representative on the Trusteeship Council of the United Nations," June 8, 1953, HRG-1953-FOR-0095.

76. Mason Sears, "What Success Means," *Africa Today* (1957), p. 23.

77. Mason Sears, *Years of High Purpose: From Trusteeship to Nationhood* (1980).

78. "Profile: Mason Sears," *Africa Today* (1955), p. 12.

79. UN/T/1169, April 4, 1955, paragraph 430.

80. UN/T/SR.594, March 8, 1955.

81. "British Policy in Tanganyika," *The Times*, February 25, 1955; UN/T/SR.584, February 24, 1955.

82. UN/T/SR.596, March 10, 1955; "Time targets," *UN Review*, April 15, 1955, p. 55.

83. United States, Department of State, Office of the Historian, "Letter From the Secretary of State [Dulles] to the Representative at the United Nations [Lodge], Washington, February 9, 1955," *Foreign Relations of the United States, 1955–1957, Africa, Volume XVIII* (1989).

84. UN/T/SR.594, March 8, 1955.

85. UN/T/SR.574, February 9, 1955.

86. IDOC, p. 300.

87. Sears, *Years of High Purpose*, p. 82; UN/T/SR.592, March 7, 1955.

88. UN/T/SR.592, March 7, 1955.

89. Eva Meyerowitz, "The Southern Sudan Today," *African Affairs* (1963).

90. United States, Department of State, Office of the Historian, "Letter From the Representative at the Trusteeship Council (Sears) to the Assistant Secretary of State for International Organization Affairs (Wilcox), New York, April 3, 1956," *Foreign Relations of the United States, 1955–1957, Africa, Volume XVIII* (1989).

91. FO/371/176876, "Goodfellow, British Embassy, Yaounde, to Mellon, West and Central Africa Department," July 22, 1964.

92. Margaret Roberts, "Political Prospects for the Cameroun," *The World Today* (1960).

93. UN/T/SR.692, March 22, 1956.

94. UN/T/SR.697, April 2, 1956.

95. Meredith Terretta, "'We Had Been Fooled into Thinking that the UN Watches over the Entire World': Human Rights, UN Trust Territories, and Africa's Decolonization," *Human Rights Quarterly* (2012).

96. IDOC, pp. 8, 99.

97. Elizabeth Landis, "Cameroons in Chaos," *Africa Today* (1960).

98. FO/35/6966, "Anglo-French-Belgian Talks, Brussels," July 1, 1955.

99. "Nkrumah to ACB," personal letter, August 6, 1956, private collection.

100. FCO/141/5025, "UK Delegation to UN to FCO telegram on Togoland issue," June 29, 1954.

101. John Kent, *The Internationalization of Colonialism: Britain, France, and Black Africa 1939–1956* (1992), pp. 222, 230.

102. "Roger Cary to OTM, Langham, re: Sir Alan Burns," BBC Archives, April 21, 1.

103. ACB, unpublished poem, ca. 1955, private collection.

104. "ACB to Sir Thomas Lloyd," personal letter, July 10, 1956, private collection.

105. IDOC, pp. 8, 99.

106. "Alan Lennox-Boyd to ACB," personal letter, December 11, 1956, private collection.

107. David Drummond, 8th Earl of Perth, "Opening remarks: Recent Developments in Fiji," *Journal of the Royal Society of Arts* (1960), p. 758.

108. IDOC, pp. 300, 172–73.

109. "Alan Lennox-Boyd to ACB," personal letter, December 11, 1956, private collection.

Chapter 12

Probably Bloodshed

At midnight on March 5th, 1957, Alan stood incognito on the Old Polo Grounds in Accra. He had been invited to the independence celebrations for Ghana by Prime Minister Kwame Nkrumah. That day, Nkrumah had unveiled a monument along the road to Alan's former castle redoubt where rioters in 1948 had been shot dead by police. The people had "regained" their freedom, an inscription on the monument read. Now, the final session of the colonial legislature was taking place across from the Old Polo Grounds. Alan chose to remain in the crowds outside. At the final session, Nkrumah wore worker's overalls and a cap emblazoned with "P.G." for "prison graduate," the status symbol within the ruling party for those who did time under the British. As midnight struck, Nkrumah's supporters carried him in his chair out the door with such disorder that they nearly bashed his head on the lintel of the doorway. The crowd dispersed, and within an hour the streets were deserted.

Alan walked slowly back to his government lodging to prepare for the formalities of the following day. He felt keenly the disquiet of the crowds. Everything he heard was in contrast to the bubbling optimism of the dignitaries. It had taken all the efforts of Lady Quist's husband, the speaker of the legislature, to prevent Nkrumah from ditching British parliamentary tradition under the new constitution. Ghana, he told Nkrumah, should practice "humility" if it were to be a model of successful decolonization.[1] Nkrumah had appointed himself minister of defense and minister of external affairs, and he had stuffed his cabinet with other prison graduates, whom Alan called "the wild men." The flag of Ghana carried the black star of Marcus Garvey's movement, now reduced to little more than a second-hand Israeli freighter. Nkrumah called himself a "revolutionary" and declared that capitalism was "too complicated" for his new nation.[2] Most of Nkrumah's guests came from the pantheon of anti-colonial fanatics: Cheddi Jagan, the deposed communist leader of British Guiana; John Koinange, a son of Chief Koinange, the architect of the Mau Mau insurgency in Kenya; and Alan's brother Emile, as yet unmoved by the official denunciation of Stalin's crimes in the Soviet Union. Alan used his ten days in Ghana to meet a broad cross-section of Africans. The sudden deterioration in conditions—power outages, police reports not filed, trains breaking down—worried his interlocutors. Nkrumah's cabinet members seemed to positively delight in every act of sabotage. The Ghanaian elites he met "spoke quite bluntly of Nkrumah's inability to restrain his wild men," Alan wrote in a memo to the Colonial Office. Secession was brewing in Togoland and Ashanti, because Nkrumah had rejected a federal constitution. The Ashanti king, whom Alan met twice, was "a very worried man . . . a very frightened man." CPP thugs threatened to deport him unless he jumped to attention for the so-called Redeemer of Africa. "Unless Nkrumah shows more statesmanship than he has yet shown," Alan concluded in his memo, "something certainly will happen, probably bloodshed."[3]

Lady Quist accompanied Alan everywhere he went. It was not clear whether she was guiding him or clinging to him. The assorted anti-colonials whom Nkrumah had invited seemed surprised that Alan moved so freely and to such warmth. Two delegates from Mao's China were taken aback, Alan recalled, "when I received a warm welcome from a number of my African friends. I suppose that they expected (and perhaps hoped) that I, as a former governor, would be greeted with a volley of rotten eggs."[4]

Nkrumah had nationalized the cocoa industry and steered profits into crony projects. He had sidelined all opposition, including Joseph Danquah, who begged an American journalist to expose the rot. "You have the choice of telling the truth or assuming some of the responsibility for the creation of the first black totalitarian dictator in history," Danquah blustered.[5] The journalist demurred, noting that anyone in the United States who was critical of African independence was immediately labeled "an enemy of people of color." Whatever problems arose after independence would be conveniently blamed on colonialism. The "blameless Ethiopian" would live on eternally. The U.S. State Department's point-man on colonial affairs, a historian of Africa, warned of the chaos to come: "What is now needed," he wrote in *Foreign Affairs* in 1957, "is not faster political advance but a still greater effort to build economic and educational foundations for the social cohesion necessary to make freedom meaningful."[6]

Alan had devoted his life to building the foundations of human flourishing in the British Empire. Then he had spent a decade watching the UN system tear them down. His final task was to limit the damage. He was without suit jacket when he left Accra. Lady Quist stood at his side, a moment captured by an alert press photographer but otherwise unremarked upon. He was going back to practical work, sleeves rolled up, tie blowing in the hot wind.

It was fortunate that *In Defense of Colonies* did not arrive in the bookshops until after Alan returned from Accra. His blunt and unapologetic defense of colonialism was well known in diplomatic circles. Now it landed in the public with a thud. The book attracted wide attention and transformed Alan into a lightning rod for the increasingly rancorous debate on colonialism.

One group of reviewers praised his straightforward case for the British Empire as a much-needed tonic. "If the author sometimes shows excessive zeal in his praise of the British record, his object is laudable, and it is as a valuable, constructive, and much needed piece of propaganda that the book must be viewed," the *Times* wrote.[7] A British scholar noted that Alan "does not mince words. . . . [I]t can only be hoped that some non-British readers will take notice."[8] An American scholar agreed with Alan's assessment that the British Empire had "rescued millions from utter degradation, cannibalism, human sacrifice, slavery, and the slave trade" and that such progress "could not have been made without tutelage and the wise guidance provided by British administrators and statesmen."[9] A Canadian official called the book "an earnest effort to account for the less rational kinds of anti-colonialism" and concluded that Alan "very persuasively . . . shows the incongruity of anti-colonial charges."[10]

Alan had made no attempt to draw up a balance sheet of the British Empire. Instead, he began from first principles, namely that there could not possibly have been a better outcome than having been colonized by the most advanced and liberal country on Earth. "Is this a one-sided book?" asked an American law professor. "Perhaps, but after all it is written in defence of colonies. Let those who remain skeptical read it carefully and answer the arguments if they can."[11]

A second group did just that. Alan's aims in defending British policy were laudable, the *Economist* allowed, but his ten years at the UN "seems to have made him too touchily sensitive to present a reasoned case. . . . His frustration after ten years is understandable but the same kind of sparring has weakened his case for the defence."[12] An Oxford scholar noted how Alan "strikes out lustily, often overzealously, at any criticism of the British colonial record" but called his prescription for slower transitions to independence "sadly unrealistic."[13] A German scholar doubted whether Alan's book would change any minds: "Whether sharp accusations are the right means of gaining a more objective attitude is questionable because the very nationally proud peoples will surely parry them with reference to the injustice of the early colonial times."[14] A Canadian scholar and Nyerere-admirer who would later head Tanzania's first university charged Alan with producing an "angry and at times immoderate reply" to critics of British colonialism. "A strong and persuasive case along these lines can be made. Sir Alan, however, has not made it."[15]

The third camp got closer to the heart of the matter. If the revolt against colonialism was in some degree emotional and psychological, as Alan had assayed in *Colour Prejudice*, then perhaps his own retort to anti-colonialism was as well. Putting Alan on the couch, an American scholar wrote that the book "provides a highly illuminating insight into the mechanism of thought of a dying species of British colonial administrators who still like to talk about 'The Empire' and still believe in 'the great civilizing mission.'"[16] The U.S. State Department's colonial expert took the same psychological approach, perhaps because he had spent time with Alan at the UN:

> Sir Alan had to listen too often to a venomous berating of the major ideas and ideals of his life. . . . A man of intelligence and integrity, Sir Alan would no doubt acknowledge that his attack is one-sided. Perhaps the key to the understanding of the book lies in the fact that Sir Alan, now in private life, is airing the feelings he would like to have expressed in the Trusteeship Council and General Assembly had he not been shackled by UN rules of procedure and by his own sense of propriety as a British representative. . . . In Defence of Colonies should not be judged as a scholarly analysis of UN disputes over the colonial issue but as a partly autobiographical narrative by one of the partisans in the controversy.[17]

The UN years had left Alan bitter. This was no way to end a happy career. Aged seventy in 1957, he would throw his final energies into hands-on work. Like Churchill, he might regain a shot of colonial vigor as wintertide rolled in.

Much of Alan's work after leaving the UN was an echo of his younger days. Almost as an afterthought, he had in 1954 published an 800-page *History of the British West Indies*, which would, like *History of Nigeria*, remain a standard reference well into the 1970s. With his wide experience of the Caribbean, Alan was then asked by London to hustle the scattered colonies of the region into a single federation. Despite his official optimism, he seemed to know the project was doomed because of petty jealousies.[18] "I travelled hopefully. But I have returned a disappointed man, rather depressed by what I have seen and heard," he wrote after one visit to the West Indies to urge the federation.[19] At Port Antonio in Jamaica, he noted, the workers loading bananas used to laugh and sing. Now they were surly and objected to being photographed by tourists: "Jamaica seems to have changed—and not for the better!" In the end, the only things to survive from the ill-fated federation when it collapsed in 1962 were a university and the West Indies cricket team.

Alan was perhaps too much *of* the West Indies. His *History* was gently mocked by the future Nobel Laureate V. S. Naipaul as too uncritical of the

West Indies people. "How can the history of this West Indian futility be written? What tone shall the historian adopt?" Naipaul asked in his savagely realistic 1962 book about returning to Trinidad, *The Middle Passage*. "Shall he be as academic as Sir Alan Burns, protesting from time to time at some brutality, and setting West Indian brutality in the context of European brutality?"[20] In Naipaul's fictional accounts of decolonization in the region—*The Mimic Men* (1967) and *Guerrillas* (1975)—locals express bewilderment at why Britain is giving up so easily. "It was as though, in a tug-of-war contest, the other side had suddenly let go," the narrator of *The Mimic Men* notes. "We wondered at the ease of our success. We wondered why no one had called our bluff."[21]

Alan, like Naipaul, had been rescued from the West Indies by the "universal civilization" of the West, as Naipaul called it. Alan drafted plans for a book on this topic to be titled *The British Contribution to Modern Civilization*. His regular publisher, Allen & Unwin, rejected the proposal, since it had published an almost identical book in 1941 to little acclaim.[22] Imperial fatigue had set in, and Britons were in no mood to read about their historical virtues, only their vices.

Alan's thoughts were turning back to the foundations of his career in other ways. In a BBC broadcast of 1958, he paid homage to Lugard, his mentor and the greatest of imperialists (see figure 12.1). Describing Lugard's restless

Figure 12.1   BBC Broadcast on Lugard, 1958. *Source*: Private Collection of Alan Dixon.

youth on garrison duty in Gibraltar, Alan seemed to be describing himself. Lugard's enthusiasm for freeing slaves from Arab stockades was "a mission of mercy with a large slice of danger" and "just the sort of adventure that [he] was looking for."[23] Alan was still looking for adventure himself.

At first, the only adventures that came Alan's way seemed to involve teas and lunch talks. His bookish endeavors landed him in the chair of the Royal Empire Society's library in London, where he hosted the young Queen Elizabeth II when it reopened from war damage. "Massive and impassive, he presided over the Library Committee with brisk efficiency," a colleague at the Society recalled.[24] The Colonial Office realized that those talents could be put to better use.

Alan's finale came in 1959. It would form a grand coda to his colonial life. Fittingly, it would be a close re-enactment of Her Majesty's West Indies Royal Commission that had arrived at Basseterre in 1897 to the wide-eyed admiration of the young Alan Burns. The purpose was the same: to offer hope to a remote island colony wracked by sugarcane-cutter riots and racial strife. The assignment: Fiji.

The islands of Fiji had been beset by internal conflict and external threats in the mid-nineteenth century. Rival Tongans had been expanding through brutal conquests, and the paramount Fijian chief requested British annexation twice in 1859 and 1868. Britain finally agreed to take over in 1874 through a deal signed by thirteen chiefs of the islands. "If matters remain as they are," the paramount chief warned, "Fiji will become like a piece of drift-wood on the sea, and be picked up by the first passer-by."[25] The terms of the British takeover made it clear that the purpose was to transform Fiji from scattered tribal fiefdoms into a constitutional state.[26] Sovereignty was vested in the British crown as a representative of all native Fijians, now imagined as a single people. When the first British governor retired, the chiefs gave him two small islands in perpetuity, "that it may be known that it was he who established the working of good and suitable government in our land, which has brought us prosperity, rest, and peace."[27]

The prosperity of colonial Fiji soon attracted migrant labor from India to work on the growing sugar plantations. The Indians were confined to the coastal and urban areas since most land was set aside for native Fijians under the terms of the British annexation. Alan loved to tell the story of the naughty Indian shopkeeper whose mischief had caused the international dateline to be kinked around Fiji. "He maintained that the meridian passed through the middle of his shop, so that when it was Sunday at one end of the shop it was Saturday or Monday at the other end. In this way he was able to evade the law regarding Sunday trading, and to keep open for business seven days a week."[28]

Jollity aside, Indian success and large families caused growing tensions. By 1958, Indians were 50 percent of the population, compared to 42 percent Fijian and 8 percent European and Chinese. The governor wrote to London asking for a commission to report on the colony's "land and population" problems, a euphemism for racial tensions. The first choice to lead the commission, a former Fiji governor, was shy of the task. The job was offered to Alan as the second choice because of his role in heading the UN commission to the Pacific trust territories in 1950. That mission, which he hated to the core, became his entrée back into colonial life.

The Colonial Office was frank to Alan about the task. The mandate of the commission was fudged by the legislature, "overt reference to political problems suppressed." This "political element, studiously unexpressed by the legislature, is, of course, fear of the growing Indian section of the population and its potential political and economic predominance," a mandarin explained.[29] The problem of "the rapidly multiplying Indians swamping the native Fijians" had prompted the commission, whose implicit role was to state these realities "in a way which no one in Fiji is prepared to do in public."[30] The commission was "being brought in to say the necessary harsh truths," namely that continued Indian ascendance would threaten Fijian status.

At the time, the colonial legislature was barely democratic, and seats were allocated by group rather than by population. Fijians held most seats—an untenable situation, because the Indians were inspired by India's own democratic rule. We are "putting off our responsibilities for a political solution on someone else," the mandarin noted.[31] Alan suggested that if he took the job, he might write a separate "confidential" report on these political issues.[32] The Colonial Office would have none of it: "What is really wanted is for the commission to state *publicly* the political implications of its study."[33] Alan agreed. Tough tasks and home truths were his specialty. The commission was announced in September 1958.

Alan was told he could spend up to six months in Fiji for this "commission to end all commissions."[34] It would be the most intensive project of his career. Throughout the winter of 1958–1959, he was, in his own words, "slowly reading myself into the Fijian picture."[35] A key work, *The Fijian People,* appeared in early 1959 by an Australian geographer named Oskar Spate who offered an unsparing criticism of the shielding of the Fijians from modern life. The policies of communal land for Fijians and Fijian native governments, Spate wrote, had created "a dangerously unrealistic psychology of pride and self-pity" among the Fijians. The native governments had become "a state within a state."[36] He recommended a shift to individual farming with individual land ownership, preserving only some village areas as commons. Otherwise, Fiji would gradually become two countries: a rural Fijian society

ruled by a "rigid authoritarian collectivism" and "looked upon askance by the free world" and a wealthy, democratic, and open Indian one in the cities.[37]
    Spate's bleak assessment was shared by the British governor. "The Fijians have been sheltered from external influences for too long," the governor wrote to Alan. "If they are to hold their own in the decades that lie ahead, they must be exposed to the uncomfortable facts of life."[38] A Fijian chief came to London to warn Alan that the natives feared an abolition of their privileges.[39] Cries were rising for Indians to be "sent home," the chief warned. A former governor defended the old system, explaining that Fijians feared the fate of native Hawaiians, swamped by outsiders and "hired by the Americans to shout *aloha* through a megaphone at arriving and departing steamers."[40]
    Alan realized he was stepping into a minefield. He asked Colonial Office legal advisors to clarify the exact terms of the 1874 cession and the various laws, winks, and handshakes that had piled on top since then. His conclusion: Britain had a moral obligation to honor the promise that crown lands would remain set aside for native Fijians. He objected strenuously to a suggestion by another former governor that the government should simply buy out the lands, a proposal that the Colonial Office called "half-baked."[41] The ex-governor had suggested in the *Times* a "lordly bonus" of twenty-five to fifty million pounds (two to four *billion* dollars in contemporary money) to buy out the land claims, otherwise "the seeds of bloodshed will be sown." Alan called the article "monstrous." In addition to exciting Fijian fears, the article would encourage the Indian community to press for full conversion of lands through the generosity of the British taxpayer. Alan had by this time seen enough of the dispossession of natives of their lands in Africa to not want to repeat the mistake in Fiji. "Governors, like Generals, should be muzzled on retirement," he grumbled.[42]

    The choreography for the arrival of the Burns Commission in Suva on July 3rd, 1959, was carefully planned to emphasize the long-standing assurances of Fijian preeminence and the protection of native lands (see figure 12.2). The first meeting was with the Council of Chiefs, where Alan promised that the commission would "make no recommendation which does not take into consideration these assurances." The chiefs in turn repeated their demand that Fijian interests "which have always been acknowledged to be paramount must continue to remain so."[43] Alan received the *tabua*, a sperm whale's tooth pierced at each end with a cord, which expressed both respect to Alan and a hope that he would assist the donors.[44]
    With those preliminaries, Alan and his two fellow commissioners set out on a torrid ten-week tour. As in 1950, Alan's hectic pace drove the accompanying staff to rebellion and annoyed the spouses in tow, who wanted the adventure stretched out to the maximum six months. Katie remained in Suva

Figure 12.2   Receiving Whale Tooth, Fiji, 1959. *Source*: Private Collection of Alan Dixon.

most of the time, where torrential rains marred the "dry season." Alan had boasted during the Pacific mission of 1950 that his health was rude enough for the rigors. Now he was slowing. A fall in a boat left him bed-ridden for a day and nursing back pain for most of the rounds.[45]

Every group voiced complaints. The Indian community was alarmed at the prospect of permanent relegation to second-class citizenship, and Delhi started to grumble about the issue as well. The community leaders demanded "one man, one vote" in all elections and accelerated conversion of native reserves into leasable crown land. "The problem," Alan observed in private, "is that over time 'the crown' is likely to become 'the Indians.'"[46]

What worried Alan most was how little life had changed for the Fijians since 1874. "The Fijians are a charming people. But they are finding it difficult to compete with those of other races under modern conditions," he told a gathering in London after his return. "In most countries, customs change with the years, allowing people to adapt themselves to changing conditions. This is, unfortunately, not the case in Fiji, where the customs have been maintained, or perhaps I should say petrified."[47]

Colonial officials saw the two groups on a collision course.[48] It would be the "height of folly" for the commission to blandly accept the Fijian view that they should remain special forever given the "terrifying" speed with which independence movements had spread elsewhere demanding "one man, one vote," the local colonial secretary testified. Above all, London needed to avoid a repeat of the chaos erupting in the Belgian Congo, where intergroup rivalries had led to a hasty grant of independence by Brussels, with all the inevitable suffering. "Government has still the chance to grasp and hold the initiative in this respect and that it must do."

Alan and Katie returned to London in October. There, Alan had a frank meeting with the secretary for colonies to offer his "political" assessment. Minutes of the meeting make grim reading. The problems had grown acute under the previous two governors, Alan charged, the first of whom "did not know the problems" and the second of whom "did not care." The colony had "got completely out of hand."[49] There was a lack of drive from the bottom and a lack of leadership at the top. British officials had become "more Fijian than the Fijians,"[50] treating the natives like some precious artifact to be observed and lovingly cared for under a glass case. While the moral obligation to protect Fijian lands remained, the commission should recommend other changes needed to advance Fijian interests by bringing them into the modern world. He would later write: "The Fijians will certainly not learn to compete successfully with anyone if they are screened from all contact with the cruel world."[51] Alan's views of the dangerous dance between gone-native colonial officials and Fijian traditionalists were widely shared in London, a mandarin noted. "Although he puts them in a more extreme fashion."[52] Carte blanche, he was told. And so the writing began. Two rooms were set aside in the Colonial Office for Alan and his colleagues to write their report. Alan promised an honest report clothed in "tactful language."[53]

The starting point for Alan was the moral obligation to abide by the protection of most of Fiji's land as native reserves. There was in any case plenty of land already in private hands on the coast or available for lease from the government, especially if the colony was weaned off sugar production. The island of Jamaica had a population six times that of the main island of Fiji despite being likewise mostly confined to coastal areas, he noted later. "So when we hear that there is a shortage of land in Fiji what is really meant is that there is a shortage of the rich, level land on which sugar-cane could be grown."[54]

The commission report walked gingerly around the land issue, recommending stiff taxes on undeveloped private land and measures to make the leasing of crown land easier. At the same time, the commission recommended all sorts of educational and regulatory reforms that would allow native Fijians to join the modern economy. Customary constraints such as mandatory communal labor and the sharing of individual wealth with the community had weakened incentives to join the labor force, turning Fijians into paupers. As Alan would note: "There is no reason why they should be kept in a sort of zoo separated from the facts of this horrid world."[55]

The real bombshell was the commission's recommendation to abolish the native Fijian governments which, Alan noted, paraphrasing geographer Spate, had "in fact, become almost a separate government, parallel to the central colonial government and to some extent independent of it."[56] Integrated multiracial local governments would be formed instead. The report did not touch on whether this might be extended to the national level.

The final contentious issue was population control, and it split the commission. Given the colony's rapidly growing population, noises had been made about birth control policies since the mid-1950s. The government did not want to be seen as targeting the Indian population, however, and thus remained passive. By 1959, the government had changed to a more active approach, opening clinics and broadcasting family planning messages in both Hindi and Fijian. In their testimony at the arrival ceremony, the Fijian chiefs complained of a "conspicuous lack of any organized endeavor by the Indian leaders and people generally to encourage among themselves methods of birth control or family planning."[57]

Alan's faithful Catholicism prevented him from endorsing birth control, although not family planning in general. The result was that the Burns Commission recommendation for more family planning clinics and free contraceptives for married couples was rejected by Burns himself. Alan agreed that better child-rearing support was needed to help native Fijians, whose children died more often than Indian children. His opposition to birth control was also practical. Coercive birth control would lead to all sorts of unintended consequences, he believed, including female infanticide, Indian radicalization, a reinforcement of the false idea of land scarcity, labor shortages, and an ageing society.

Alan's dissent against population control policies would later became a common refrain among anti-colonial scholars. They used a sharply reductionist and conspiratorial tone to suggest that *any* colonial policies designed to have *any* impact on population were *wholly* motivated by racism and eugenics. As one reviewer asked about such dogmatic interpretations: "Was there no argument about population growth that was not racist and imperial?"[58] Indeed, there was, and Alan's "colonial" dissent took aim at such arguments. His dissent was informed by a careful understanding of realities on the ground and of the multiplicity of causes and consequences at stake. In later decades, Alan's dissent would be vindicated: Indian population growth slowed naturally, while Fijian population growth accelerated. Over time, most of the birth control policies were abandoned.[59] The "colonial" argument against population policies, it turned out, was far more germane than the heated-up anti-colonial arguments of later critics.

The 124-recommendation report was issued in March 1960.[60] The cost of implementing the recommendations was estimated to be about 650 million dollars in contemporary terms, a fifth of which would come as grants from the United Kingdom. Alan called the recommendations "the only hope for the survival of the Fijian people in a competitive world."[61] The *Times* called it "a ruthless dissection" of the colony's woes.[62] Geographer Spate applauded the report: "The Fijian Way of Life as an abstract aesthetic ideal, or the Fijians as a truly live people—that is the choice, clearly posed by the Burns Report."[63] The governor of Fiji wrote to Alan with thanks. It was just the sort of "plain speaking" that was needed, and he hoped to implement the entire report within months. The reaction of Fijians was "better than I feared," the governor reported, although they were "indignant" about the abolition of their local government.[64] Alan was surprised by the positive response from the European officials in Fiji "of whom I have but a poor opinion (as they probably have of me)."[65]

The timing was, alas, unfortunate. Rioting erupted in Suva in late 1959 against a white-owned oil company, with an equal number of Fijian and Indian workers taking part. The riots seemed to vindicate the colonial secretary's warnings that African-style "liberation" movements would not be long in coming to the islands. A military curfew was imposed, and the territorial army mobilized for the first time since the war—some were surprised that the island paradise even had one.[66] In March 1960, as the report was issued, Indian sugar workers went on strike, throwing the economy into turmoil.

Despite their initial acceptance of most of the recommendations, the Fijians slowly began to think of the entire report as a threat to their paramountcy. "The thought that Fijians might lose their identity and land has drawn divergent types together who were formerly in opposition," the governor reported. The recommendations, he advised London, "were regarded by the Fijians as likely to promote Indian interests at the expense of their own." Trying to implement them in the wake of the riots might provoke "outbreaks of violence against Indians or Europeans, or both." Since Fijians accounted for 80 percent of the security forces, it might lead to breakdown.[67]

Debate on Alan's report raged for over a year. It put Fijians in "a touchy mood,"[68] the Colonial Office told Alan, and had "set in motion a defensive mechanism, making the Fijians retreat into their shell."[69] A leading Fijian politician demanded that if the British would not protect the status quo, then, "the running of this colony must be handed over to the Fijians." Finally, in his Cession Day speech in October 1961, the governor backed down, promising to take no action on the report without Fijian consent. The Burns Commission Report was dead, "a sorry waste of time and money" according to the *Pacific Islands Monthly*, "due as much, perhaps, to Fijian native intransigence as to official failures."[70]

As with the *ju-ju* murder case, some historians have argued that the Burns Commission made anti-colonial sentiment worse by hardening attitudes in the Fijian community against reforms.[71] Yet it is hardly plausible that if Alan had politely sidestepped the entire issue there would have been more progress toward equality and reform. A later work on the road to independence in Fiji was entitled *A Time Bomb Lies Buried*.[72] Alan had tried to clear it.

Having rejected modest reforms, Fijians set themselves onto a path of conflict. The insistence on communal privilege and Fijian paramountcy led to a continuation of ethnic voting at the national level up to independence in 1970. By then, the Indian community had become so afraid of ethnic pogroms by the Fijians that they accepted their second-class status. A frightened Delhi, chastened by communal violence at home, took an uncharacteristically cautious attitude, having previously denounced communal voting as British colonial oppression.[73] Far from trying to perpetuate racial divisions, then, Alan and his commissioners did everything in their power to end them. Those divisions were perpetuated by the groups themselves. By "accommodating indigenous privilege," as one scholar called it, the Fijian government and Colonial Office had acceded to an abandonment of the colonial mission just when it was needed most. Fiji was about to embark on independence with an unresolved conflict between its two major ethnic groups. The Burns Commission Report would be remembered as the path not taken.

Alan made sure that his reinterpretation of Fiji's problems did not die as an obscure legislative paper. After some heated back-and-forth with the government in Fiji about his frank discussions of cannibalism, administrative slack, and Fijian privileges, the report was turned into a book in 1963.[74] It came richly illustrated with sharp photographs, dainty pencil drawings, lush watercolors, and end papers carrying a textile pattern of Fijian *tapa* (bark-cloth). "The Fijians and their islands are patently so congenial to the writer that one can but regret that he was never able to include them before retirement in his gubernatorial career," one reviewer of the book noted.[75] Another was more sober: "For some time yet the British administration will have to hold the balance between Fijian conservatism and Indian ambition, while the scales are rocked by suspicion and incomprehension on both sides. . . . This book, at least, will increase the awareness of these dangers."[76]

Of all the British colonies that expected a long time to independence, Nigeria loomed greatest. Yet the acceleration of events since the time targets debate at the UN had been incredible. The independence of Nigeria in 1960, Alan admitted, was "something I did not anticipate in my lifetime."[77]

As in Ghana, local events had caused shivers. A deal had been worked out among the three main groups to form a federal government. That left most of the country's 250-odd ethnic groups under the "alien rule" of a major tribe. Up on the River Benue, riots had broken out among the bridge-building Tiv, who feared domination by the Muslim northern government to which they were attached. Over 4,500 were arrested in the week leading to independence, and scores were killed by police.

Alan and Katie were in Lagos for the celebrations, where the greatest words of caution came from Nigerians themselves. "All too soon," the new prime minister said as he took the constitutional instruments into his hands. There was an echo of Kipling in his assurance that "Nigeria now stands well built upon firm foundations." The *Times* applauded Nigeria's cautious leadership for avoiding "grandiose cliché-mongering about the African personality or the unmitigated evils of colonialism."[78] But were words enough?

The prime minister called attention to "the startling events which have occurred in this continent" and implored his fellow Nigerians "to show that our claims to responsible self-government are well-founded." The early catalog of post-colonial horrors was startling: Congo in free fall; hundreds of Tutsis killed in a Hutu rampage in Rwanda known as the "wind of destruction" that hastened a Belgian exit from that trust territory; a military coup in recently decolonized Sudan; growing ranks of political prisoners in Nkrumah's Ghana. Farther abroad was much of the same: a coup in East Pakistan precipitating a brutal civil war; the abolition of democracy and the expulsion of Chinese and Dutch in Indonesia; dozens killed in riots in Bombay; the list went on.

London had loosed the blocks of decolonization, and the airplanes were whirring down the runway—Tanzania, Kenya, Uganda, Sierra Leone, Nyasaland, and Rhodesia—not to mention colonies in Asia. The same was happening in French, Belgian, and Portuguese colonies. London now offered full cooperation with the UN's Fourth Committee to update it on political progress toward independence throughout the British Empire. No more talk of empiricism. The Burns line, one historian noted, was "no longer the true expression of the British official attitude."[79]

Alan and Katie paid their respects to the new Nigerian nation. Then it was time to go home for the last time. Time for grandchildren, who were coming fast—four already. Time for siblings: Essie was gravely ill, and Katie's health seemed fragile, as did Bertie's. How much more could a man give of his life? A mission of mercy with a large slice of danger. It had been just what he wanted, except for the lack of time. "All that we have to regret is that we left our work unfinished and that to some extent we deserted our friends," Alan would write. "The British colonial service asked only for time, time to lay the foundations securely, and time was denied us."[80]

NOTES

1. "Ghana speaker to resign," *The Times*, November 15, 1957.

2. Kwame Nkrumah, *Ghana: The Autobiography of Kwame Nkrumah* (1957), p. xvi.

3. Sir Alan Burns, "Confidential memo to Colonial Office on Ghana," March 16, 1957, private collection.

4. CBAA, p. 148.

5. Robert St. John, "Too Early for Judgement: Ghana, One Year After," *Africa Today* (1958), pp. 5–8.

6. Vernon McKay, "Too Slow or Too Fast? Political Change in African Trust Territories," *Foreign Affairs* (1957), p. 308.

7. "Colonial powers," *The Times*, February 7, 1957.

8. Charles Carrington, "Review of 'In Defence of Colonies,'" *International Affairs* (1957).

9. Paul Knaplund, "Review of 'In Defence of Colonies,'" *American Historical Review* (1958).

10. Eric Beecroft, "Review of 'In Defence of Colonies,'" *Annals of the American Academy of Political and Social Science* (1957).

11. O. Hood Phillips, "Review of 'In Defence of Colonies,'" *Modern Law Review* (1959).

12. "Hitting back," *The Economist*, March 23, 1957.

13. Francis Carnell, "Review of 'In Defence of Colonies,'" *Pacific Affairs* (1959).

14. Wahrhold Drascher, "Review of 'In Defence of Colonies,'" *Historische Zeitschrift* (1958).

15. R. Cranford Pratt, "Review of 'In Defence of Colonies,'" *International Journal* (1957).

16. Dale Harrison, "Review of 'In Defence of Colonies,'" *Africa Today* (1957).

17. Vernon McKay, "Anti-Colonialism Attacked," *Africa Special Report* (1957).

18. Sir Alan Burns, "Towards a Caribbean Federation," *Foreign Affairs* (1955); Great Britain Colonial Office and Hilary Blood, *The Plan for a British Caribbean Federation* (1955).

19. Sir Alan Burns, "Weakness of British West Indian administration," *Crown Colonist*, March 1949.

20. V. S. Naipaul, *The Middle Passage* (1962), p. 29.

21. V. S. Naipaul, *The Mimic Men* (1967), p. 200.

22. Donald Cowie, *The British Contribution: Some Ideas and Inventions That Have Helped Humanity* (1941).

23. Sir Alan Burns, "Lord Lugard," *BBC Home Service, Schools Program*, June 25, 1958.

24. Donald Simpson, "Sir Alan Burns," *Library Notes* (Royal Commonwealth Society), October 1980.

25. Sir Alan Burns, *Fiji* (1963), p. 98.

26. Colin Newbury, "History, Hermeneutics and Fijian Ethnic 'Paramountcy': Reflections on the Deed of Cession of 1874," *Journal of Pacific History* (2011).

27. Burns, *Fiji*, pp. 122–23.

28. Sir Alan Burns, "Recent Developments in Fiji," *Journal of the Royal Society of Arts* (1960), p. 759.

29. CO/103/6435, "MacPherson to ACB," August 18, 1958.

30. CO/103/6435, "Fiji Commission file notes by Kitcatt," February 21, 1957.

31. CO/103/6435, "Fiji Commission file notes by Rogers," March 13, 1957.

32. CO/103/6435, "ACB to Colonial Office," August 22, 1958.

33. CO/103/6435, "Fiji Commission file notes," August 27, 1958.

34. CO/103/6435, "Grantham to MacPherson," May 1, 1958.

35. CO/103/6435, "ACB to Hall," October 25, 1958.

36. Robert Norton, "Averting 'Irresponsible Nationalism,'" *Journal of Pacific History* (2013).

37. Oskar Spate, *The Fijian People: Economic Problems and Prospects* (1959), p. 9.

38. CO/103/6437, "Governor Maddocks to Secretary for Colonies," April 2, 1959.

39. CO/103/6437, "ACB to Hall," April 4, 1959.

40. Harry Luke, "Discussion," *Journal of the Royal Society of Arts* (1960), p. 759.

41. Ronald Garvey, "Guiding Fiji past the rocks," *The Times*, August 6, 1959.

42. CO/103/6438, "ACB to Hall," September 14, 1959.

43. CO/103/6438, "Memo by Council of Chiefs Chambers to Burns Commission," July 3, 1959.

44. Steven Hooper, "'Supreme Among Our Valuables': Whale Teeth Tabua, Chiefship and Power in Eastern Fiji," *Journal of the Polynesian Society* (2013).

45. CO/103/6438, "ACB to Hall," September 14, 1959.

46. CO/103/6774, "Maddocks to Secretary for Colonies," February 28, 1961.

47. Burns, "Recent Developments," p. 759.

48. CO/103/6438, "Colonial secretary of Fiji (MacDonald) to Burns Commission," May 8, 1959.

49. CO/103/6438, "ACB to Hall," September 14, 1959.

50. CO/103/6439, "Fiji Commission file notes," November 17, 1959.

51. Burns, *Fiji*, p. 229.

52. CO/103/6438, "Brief for the Secretary for Colonies meeting with Burns Commission," November 15, 1959; CO/103/6439, "Notes on meeting with Sir Alan Burns," November 17, 1959.

53. CO/103/6438, "ACB to Hall," September 14, 1959.

54. Burns, "Recent Developments," p. 759.

55. Ibid., p. 758.

56. Ibid., p. 759.

57. CO/103/6438, "Memo by Council of Chiefs Chambers to Burns Commission," July 3, 1959.

58. Thomas Robertson, "Review of Karl Ittmann, 'A Problem of Great Importance: Population, Race, and Power in the British Empire, 1918–1973,'" *Journal of Social History* (2016), p. 446.

59. Timoci Bavadra and Jozef Kierski, "Fertility and Family Planning in Fiji," *Studies in Family Planning* (1980), p. 22; Judith Roizen, Fajat Gyaneshwar, and Zoe Roizen, *Where Is the Planning in Family Planning: Fiji After Three Decades of Family Planning Programmes* (1992).

60. "Fiji: Population and Resources," *Journal of the Fiji Legislative Council* (1960).

61. Sir Alan Burns, "Solving Fiji's problems," *The Times*, August 19, 1960.

62. "Fiji's stiff fight," *The Times*, March 15, 1960.

63. Oskar Spate, "The Burns Commission Report," *Pacific Commentary* (1960).

64. "Maddocks to ACB," personal letter, March 14, 1960, private collection.

65. "ACB to Morris (Colonial Office)," personal letter, January 20, 1962, private collection.

66. James Heartfield, "'The Dark Races Against the Light'? Official Reaction to the 1959 Fiji Riots," *Journal of Pacific History* (2002).

67. Robert Norton, "Accommodating Indigenous Privilege: Britain's Dilemma in Decolonising Fiji," *Journal of Pacific History* (2002).

68. "Carstairs (Colonial Office) to ACB," personal letter, August 1, 1961, private collection.

69. "Morris (Colonial Office) to ACB," personal letter, December 29, 1961, private collection.

70. "The Burns Commission in Fiji," *Pacific Islands Monthly*, April 1963, p. 21.

71. Brij Lal, *A Time Bomb Lies Buried: Fiji's Road to Independence, 1960–1970* (2008), p. 29.

72. Ibid.

73. Robert Norton, "India's Part in the Politics of Fiji's Decolonization: From 'Outworn Slogans' to 'Pragmatism and Realism,'" *Journal of Pacific History* (2017).

74. "ACB to Colonial Office re: Fiji book," personal letters, July 29, 1961, July 30, 1961, December 30, 1961, January 20, 1962, and February 23, 1962, private collection; "Colonial Office to ACB re: Fiji book," personal letters, August 1, 1961, and December 29, 1961, private collection.

75. Philip Snow, "Review of 'Fiji,'" *Journal of the Polynesian Society* (1964), p. 99.

76. Colin Newbury, "Review of 'Fiji,'" *Geographical Journal* (1963), pp. 539–40.

77. Allen.

78. "Nigeria celebrates the great day," *The Times*, October 3, 1960.

79. Giuliano Ferrari-Bravo, "The Development of International Trusteeship at the United Nations with Particular Reference to British Reactions: 1944–1960," University of Cambridge, Department of History, Doctoral Dissertation (1980), p. 364.

80. CBAA, p. 197.

Chapter 13

Who Heeds How They Perished?

Alan's siren about the "wild men" taking over Ghana was vindicated after that somber independence day in 1957. The death of Lady Quist's husband in 1959, before Nkrumah turned truly despotic, was probably for the best; later defenders of British constitutionalism in Ghana began to disappear into the jungle. The Nkrumah terror affected many close friends of Alan. Nkrumah purged the government economist Robert Kweku Atta Gardiner, Alan's coauthor on *Other People, Other Ways*, as part of the "decolonization" of the bureaucracy. He also forced assistant police commissioner H. A. Nuamah, who had cracked the *ju-ju* murder case, into retirement without a pension, accused of complicity with one of the growing number of assassination attempts. It took the intervention of Julius Nyerere, whom Nuamah had advised on Africanization of the police services in Tanganyika, to have the pension restored and Nuamah spared from prison.

Joseph Danquah of course was not so fortunate. His death in prison, which Alan read about while transiting with Katie in New York on their way to St. Kitts in 1965, was only the latest evidence of the strangulation of democracy and progress by Nkrumah. By this time, the Black Star and Deliverer had declared Ghana a one-party state and was spending most of his time cajoling smaller African nations to unify under his rule. "President Nkrumah has just about read himself and his government out of the comity of civilized nations," asserted the *New York Times* in an editorial on the death of Danquah.[1]

Facing mounting criticism after Danquah's death, Nkrumah called on "all patriotic Ghanaians to act as security officers and bring alarmist rumor mongers and saboteurs to justice."[2] All journalists, he declared, should adopt a "revolutionary morality" to expose enemies of his regime. Fortunately, by the time Alan contacted Lady Quist with concerns for her safety, she was already on her way to the UK with her two daughters. She would remain there for several years.

Alan also fretted about Emile's daughter Marca, who, along with Labour Party backbenchers in Britain, had dug in like a terrier to support Nkrumah as his reign of terror worsened. Alan could not persuade her to leave because Nkrumah had offered assurances to Emile that all was well. Not until 1966, when the Ghana military overthrew Nkrumah while he was in Beijing, did Marca leave. She bought a farm in the Lake District, where she wrote a book extolling Nkrumah's socialist policies for agriculture and headed a branch of the Anglo-Cuba Solidarity Committee.[3] Nkrumah was given exile in Guinea, where the spiral of chaos since French colonial days had been even faster. He expected to be returned to power and kept up a torrid correspondence with Emile about his plans. When he died of cancer in Romania in 1972, he asked that his body be embalmed in a public temple like Lenin's (and later Mao's). Instead, it was flown home and buried in his home village.

The collapse of Ghana was one of the saddest chapters in the annals of decolonization for Alan. A *New York Times* headline of 1966 captured it all: "Ghana, Now in Dire Straits, Began as a Showcase."[4] The country had become "farcical" under Nkrumah, Alan lamented, and had, along with the chaos in the Congo, contributed to "a general mood of disillusionment" with Africa as a whole.[5] The brigadier who overthrew Nkrumah complained, "The British handed over to us a decent system of government in which everyone had a say. But the country had been corrupted."[6] For those like Alan or Lady Quist who were present in the late colonial period, the blame lay squarely on those who had ceded power too quickly and on those who seized it.

Nkrumah's overthrow was the beginning of a long, dark night for Ghana. As the night lengthened, the colonial era was increasingly seen as a golden age. A few years after Nkrumah's overthrow, Bertie's grandson, studying at the University of British Columbia, was accosted by a Ghanaian woman student during an anthropology class. "You should be ashamed of being related to a colonial governor," she charged when he told her of his connection to the country. Western professors had begun to instruct their charges that colonialism was evil, and the general mood that prevailed on campus was one of ideological terror. Over the summer holidays, the fired-up Ghanaian woman returned home where she received a tongue-lashing from her elders after relating the incident. Back in Vancouver, she sought out Bertie's grandson: "I'm sorry for what I said. It turns out my people loved your great uncle."

Alan's hands-on career did not come to an abrupt ending with the Fiji commission. The Colonial Office kept bringing him in for odd jobs in the West Indies: last-ditch efforts to save the Caribbean federation, which finally fell apart in 1962; participation in a Bahamas constitutional reform conference in

London in 1963, where he lunched with his old nemesis Etienne Dupuch to unravel a snarl in the talks; a follow-up commission on the failed Caribbean federation in 1964 to sort out what to do with the smallest islands; and an inquiry into official salaries in the Bahamas in 1965, a delicious irony for those who remembered the Alan Burns Act of 1926. He seems to have steered clear of the Monday Club, formed within the Conservative Party in 1961 to defend what was left of the British Empire against the siren calls of independence.[7] The Club lobbied mainly over the protection of what became Zambia, Malawi, and Rhodesia, where the post-colonial horrors were so acute that even this "right-wing" group's warnings were too optimistic in retrospect.

The shrinking pool of liberal internationalists in British foreign policy to which Alan belonged included an Oxford historian who condemned the "cowardice and treachery" of British flight that had allowed a "reversion to barbarism" in most former colonies.[8] It seemed that everywhere Alan went, the reception grew warmer as the sheen of decolonization wore off. On a trip to British Honduras in 1963, he was treated as a hero, and his views on an upcoming constitutional conference in London were eagerly sought (see figure 13.1). No anti-imperialism here—indeed the main opposition party opposed independence altogether. Before Alan's time as governor, the *Times* noted, the colony was an embarrassment. Now it was firmly committed to lengthy British tutelage, "prohibited [only] by international morality to remain colonial."[9]

Those colonies fortunate enough to be spared a virulent anti-colonialism could look forward to years of peace and prosperity even as they transitioned to self-rule. Alan and Katie were in Basseterre in 1967 when the new union of St. Kitts, Nevis, and Anguilla was formed. The six thousand Anguillans, whose forefathers had submitted to the tender ministrations of Alan in 1911, did not like the new arrangement and demanded a reinstatement of British colonial rule. To show they meant business, they put the entire constabulary of fourteen police on a boat back to St. Kitts. One imagines Alan greeting the gendarmes on arrival at the St. Kitts Club with a glass of rum punch and a sympathetic handshake. Two years later, Alan and Katie were back in St. Kitts when the Anguillans voted to form an independent republic, having lost their bid for re-colonization. A Colonial Office mediator was sent for talks. He too was put on a dory and rowed back to St. Kitts. Perhaps again rum punch and a handshake from Alan at the St. Kitts Club when the jilted functionary arrived at Basseterre. In March, one hundred London policemen and British paratroopers landed on Anguilla armed with polite pamphlets to subdue the "revolution." The "rebels" lined the streets singing God Save the Queen. Having conquered the island, the oppressors stripped naked and went for a swim. The so-called "Bay of Piglets"[10] invasion was a moment of light relief in a world reeling from post-colonial trauma. Anguilla became a

Figure 13.1   Official Welcome in British Honduras, 1963. *Source*: Private Collection of
Alan Dixon.

permanent British colony while St. Kitts and Nevis took their own sweet time
before independence, never missing a beat.

Alan, the *Times* would note, "made no secret of his disgust for those—
whoever they might be—who sought to denigrate British 'colonialism'
while conveniently ignoring the fact that many sovereign states tolerated
for their own peoples or imposed upon others conditions far inferior to
those enjoyed by the communities under British rule."[11] The longer he
lived, the more those inconvenient facts—which during his late career had
been only inconvenient predictions—came to life. "Probably bloodshed"
had become "actual bloodshed."

Alan wrote a final book on this dominant theme of many post-colonial
states. Completed around 1973, *Colonialism: Before and After* is a wretched

catalog of post-colonial coups, famines, wars, rigged elections, political prisoners, economic collapse, mass migrations, and anti-colonial bluster. By the
1970s, it was possible to finally arbitrate on the question of time targets and
the rush to independence. Alan respected the practical arguments of those
who had insisted that independence could not be delayed, because local
demands and external pressures were too great. It was a reasonable argument,
and the costs of fighting anti-colonial movements in places like Algeria,
Vietnam, and Aden had shown this danger.

Yet the rushed independence had virtually guaranteed failure in many
places at the cost of hundreds of thousands of lives. Britain and other
European powers had "yielded too quickly to the demands of nationalist
leaders."[12] The list of countries that fell into some form of chaos and poverty
was just too long to name—the Sudan, Uganda, Nigeria, Indonesia, Angola.
Grinding poverty plagued India as socialism replaced the markets of the Raj.
Throughout the former French and Portuguese empires, men who could only
be described as off their trolley—Amílcar Cabral of Guinea-Bissau caused
nearly half the population to flee the country—came to power to the adulation of Western progressives. "Later events make one doubt whether moving
a little slower would have had more disastrous results," he summarized in
the book.[13]

The first problem, as Alan saw it, was indifference and ignorance. The
decades of the 1960s and 1970s witnessed some of the most horrific events
in human history, and yet no one in the West seemed to care as long as there
were no pith-hatted Colonel Blimps on hand. An incredible forty thousand
black Angolans were killed in a month of brutal savagery by the "liberation"
movement of Holden Roberto that began in the northern town of Quitexe
in 1961—children fed through sawmills, women's heads cut off and placed
on top of mounds of coffee beans, men digging their own graves with their
legs cut off.[14] "They massacred everything," Roberto proclaimed proudly.[15]
A further four hundred thousand Angolans in the areas of the "liberation"
movement fled to the Congo. The event passed into oblivion, as with so many
like it, even as research on colonial atrocities, some real, others imagined,
became a cottage industry in the West.

Alan noted that more people had been killed by police firing on riotous
mobs in independent India than in the entire period of the Raj—this before
the worst violence of the 1970s and 1980s. Yet the comparatively small punitive action at Amritsar by Acting Brigadier-General Reginald Dyer of 1919
continued to dominate "atrocity studies" in India. In Pakistan, military rule
and then a "savage and medieval butchery" waged on Bengalis at the cost of
one to three million civilian lives in addition to forty thousand soldiers, as
Alan called it, led to a Bangladeshi secession after Indian intervention.[16] India
by this time had abandoned nonviolence in 1961 with an imperial invasion of

the Portuguese enclave of Goa—in Lisbon's hands since 1510. Native Goans fled to Portugal.

After Togo's Sylvanus Olympio was gunned down in a bloody heap in 1963, he was replaced by a series of military dictatorships that would last for half a century. Under Teacher of the Jungle Julius Nyerere, Tanzania suffered for two decades under the corrupt and coercive idea of *ujaama* socialism, which remained popular only among Western academics. Real per capita income stagnated, food production fell, and inflation raged. Nyerere admitted in 1974 that his policies had failed and withdrew into isolation. The Canadian scholar and chancellor of Nyerere's first university, who had chastised *In Defense of Colonies*, insisted to the end that Nyerere was a man of the people: "Whatever his policy errors, [he] was profoundly committed to their welfare."[17]

Reports from other areas were often worse. The British evacuated the prosperous and humane colony of Aden and its surrounding protectorate in 1967, after which it was taken over by the feudal regime in Yemen and descended into a never-ending tragedy. "It does no good to bend over backwards in avoiding any reference to these things," Alan wrote. Recovery "can only be retarded by a refusal to face the facts or to recognise that everything is not lovely in the garden of independence."[18] The collapse of French rule in Indo-China brought Soviet and Chinese imperialism to the region. It cost 1.5 million lives in the China-backed Cambodian genocide of 1975–1979. In Vietnam, one million soldiers and at least as many civilians died in the failed resistance to the Soviet-backed communist takeover. Another 65,000 were executed by the Vietnamese communists after they seized power, and 250,000 died in communist re-education camps. Nearly two million fled the country altogether, most of them settling in the United States.[19] France, Alan rued, "gave up the attempt to maintain its control over Indo-China" and the result was "a chaotic existence" for the successor countries.[20]

Alan viewed what was happening as deeper than mere conflict. It was an abandonment of the colonial inheritance. "In many states, and even in those where revolution and military dictatorship have not destroyed the ideals of the constitutions agreed to at independence, parliamentary democracy has become little more than a façade as one-party government has been established and opposition rigorously banned and persecuted. Elections, even when they are held, are often rigged."[21] This meant that "independence" had become little more than "the substitution for alien colonial rule, based on respect for the law and the maintenance of order, of local tyranny by a dictator or an elite minority."[22] Tough words. Alan was never one for humbug.

There was a tendency to look outward and backward, to blame the West and colonial legacies, rather than to accept the problems as homegrown and to think of the future. "Until they are prepared to admit their own responsibility for much that has gone wrong, they will not be able to correct the mistakes and to achieve the status which all their friends wish them to attain," Alan cautioned.[23] The Third World would remain third-rate so long as it maintained this anti-colonial mindset. To rage against colonialism was nothing less than to rage against the modern world. Alan drew a comparison with how Britain and Western Europe had needed a Renaissance to recover the classical ideas of their Greek and Roman colonizers. He hoped that a Renaissance would come soon to the post-colonial world, that "this confusion . . . will pass away when the birth pangs of independence and the emotions of the nationhood subside."[24]

Any return to colonialism was unlikely. Independent peoples would not consent, while it was "still more certain that none of the Western European powers would wish to resume the task of colonial administration."[25] Instead, Alan predicted that Western countries—including those that had not been colonizers—would need to find ways to stabilize failing states in other ways. Already by this time, military interventions to restore democratic governments had been required in several places, including Tanganyika in 1964. The independent governments of Kenya and Uganda had requested similar deployments of British troops shortly after. A French military intervention in Gabon the same year prevented a coup, and permanent French garrisons remained in places like Chad.

In some instances like the Congo, Sudan, and Somalia, the UN got involved in military peacekeeping, a great irony for an institution that in Alan's views was partly to blame for the mess. Alan's old American nemesis Mason Sears celebrated the emergent need for UN intervention to clean up these anti-colonial catastrophes as "one of its greatest single strides forward since the Charter was adopted."[26] Alan was less excited about bringing a failed international organization into failed states. He applauded Britain's decision in 1971 to withdraw from the UN's new Mau Mau bloc called the Committee of Twenty-Four, a "useless and dangerous" body that "pontificates on colonial questions."[27]

The more enduring role of the West would be to provide aid and advice to post-colonial states, Alan argued. Much aid in the 1960s had been wasted, Alan complained, either because it was siphoned off into Swiss bank accounts or because there were no conditions attached and no control exercised. Nationalist politicians treated it as guilt money for colonial crimes. "Massive assistance has been provided, for which little credit is given."[28] He cited a 1969 article by the Singapore leader Lee Kuan Yew, whose embrace of the colonial heritage propelled that city-state to prosperity and decency. Lee condemned "the querulous colonies Britain nurtured to independence and into which after independence she poured aid, and in return received churlishness and sometimes abuse."[29] Alan foresaw a growing reluctance by the British public to put up with such abuse: "Up to a point this may be acceptable but in time the charitable (and the bull-dog), like the worm, will turn."[30]

Looming over the entire salvage operation would be the United States. Sooner or later, Alan believed, Washington would need to accept the mantle of world leadership, to be "prepared to sacrifice her anti-colonial emotions by increasing the number of her overseas protectorates."[31] The "informal empire" of the United States that was scorned by later critics was exactly what Alan advocated to lessen human misery. He was a liberal imperialist to the end.

Of all the post-colonial traumas Alan was forced to observe in his retirement, Nigeria's was the most unbearable. Alan had warned London of the disquiet he noticed in Lagos during the independence ceremonies in 1960. It did not take long for the bloodshed to begin, starting with the suspension of democracy, a disputed election, and finally a coup, all of it culminating in the horrific Biafra War of 1967–1970 in which between one and two million people died. The war upset Alan more than any other post-colonial trauma, causing him to wonder whether Lugard's amalgamation of the country had been a mistake. "We thought we were doing the right thing, but perhaps we did the wrong thing."[32] In public though, he put on a brave face. The victorious leader of Nigeria had "been greatly admired" for his "magnanimous attitude" toward the vanquished Igbo rebels, he wrote in the preface to the eighth and final edition of *History of Nigeria* in 1972. "My faith in the future of Nigeria has not been shaken by the tragic events of the last few years."

Anti-colonial critics were quick to blame Nigeria's predicament on colonialism. The rhetorical strategy, which would become generalized in anti-colonial writing, involved identifying some horror, identifying its chronological antecedents in the colonial era, and then attributing the former to the latter. Alan, in the final revision to *History of Nigeria*, did not doubt that critics would always debate whether Britain had the "right" to occupy what became Nigeria. If Britain had not, some other European power would have, and if not them then the strongest of the ethnic groups. Alan's perspective was simply that the British had managed for sixty years to insert themselves as a modernizing buffer in this region, one that improved current lives and future prospects.

An American scholar scornfully summed up the final 1978 print-run of *History of Nigeria* as "benevolent paternalism, British boosterism, and veneration of Lugard."[33] Intended as a put-down, Alan would have taken it as a compliment. If more Nigerians (and others) had supported benevolent paternalism, British boosterism, and a veneration of Lugard, millions might have lived. In one of his last interviews, in 1978, Alan's regrets over the scramble *from* Africa in places like Nigeria and Ghana were palpable. "We were right in what we thought because there has been absolute chaos in some of them, military coups and civil war in Nigeria and other things," he noted. "There was a general feeling that independence was premature and would not be successful. . . . In Ghana and Nigeria those forecasts were not very far out."[34]

With Alan's retirement, the Burns family came together again: Sunday lunch at Bertie's house in the town of Hastings where Bertie, Emile, and Alan would arrive with their spouses and be joined by children and grandchildren. Barbara's husband, a Polish air force officer imprisoned by the Soviets in World War II, loved to retreat with "Sir Alan," as he insisted on calling him, into a back room to play chess. He venerated Alan, not least for Britain's dogged efforts to secure the release of the POWs during the war. His son, Alan, would be the one to carefully preserve Sir Alan's files and folders so that someday a biography might be written.

Katie's final years were spent betting on ponies. As her health deteriorated, she wanted to surprise Alan with a tidy sum. In 1970, she put down 600 pounds (about $20,000 today) on a Triple Crown Winner named Nijinsky, undefeated after 11 consecutive victories. A sure thing. He lost by a head. "Sunday house expense" Alan calmly memoed in his accounts. Katie passed away a month later. Bertie died the same year, and Emile followed in 1972. In rapid order, Alan found himself the last survivor of the Burns dynasty of St. Kitts.

After Katie died, Alan moved into a small apartment on Pall Mall in London. His daily excursions to his cherished Athenaeum Club across the wide avenue with the help of the club porter's intervention in the passing traffic were his joy. His final "colonial" undertaking was to reorganize the club library, which he headed until 1974. He and a colleague counted the volumes (75,000 was the tally) using the long cane handle of a feather duster. He then initiated a reclassification using the Library of Congress system. All the books were physically moved. "So wholesale a migration of volumes from shelves where members had always previously found them not surprisingly caused some annoyance," noted the club history, "for Clubs are conservative, it has been said, as the sea is salt."[35]

Alan found a joyful final lease on life after Katie's death as a founding member of the governing body of St. Edmund's College, to which he donated the whale tooth he had been given in Fiji. "Intelligent but lazy." "Too much time playing cricket and tennis." Alan could not think of St. Edmund's the way that Mr. Chips thought of Brookfield, but the sentiments seemed the same as the years crowded in. He too continued to keep time by the signals of the past, the annual colonial (now commonwealth) report; the meetings on decolonization (what would happen to Hong Kong?); the news on events in the former colonies (the suspension of democracy in India). He too had had a bigger family of sorts, a family of loyal subjects who remembered him as the Sunshine Governor. He too was a remarkable old fellow for his health, one of the lucky ones to escape a horrible disease, except of course, like Mr. Chips, for *anno Domini*.

Even when he was forced to use a walker in the late 1970s, Alan insisted on carrying it around the club most of the time, "typical of his resolution" a colleague noted.[36] He seemed always on call at the new Foreign and Commonwealth Office, a quiet presence with sage advice. Right to the bitter end he was taking interviews from scholars trying to understand the rapid collapse of the British Empire. It had all been a mess, a stampede for the exits, he complained, just when subject peoples needed a little nerve from their protectors.[37]

Sir Alan Burns died on September 29th, 1980, after a short illness. He was ninety-two. A life spent "heaving a new world toward the day," in Kipling's phrase, ended to the subdued tones of Mendelssohn at a Requiem Mass at Westminster Cathedral in London. The lords, viscounts, knights, and ladies who gathered were a "who's who" of colonial stardom—a celebrity funeral in colonial terms. Today, such a gathering would be surrounded by protestors demanding apologies and reparations.

The *Times* obituarist must have known him well: "A strong patriot, and man of vigorous common sense. Downright in his opinions and forceful in expressing them, the enemy of humbug of every kind in private or public life, and an indefatigable worker."[38] Tributes poured in by telephone, telegram, and letter from former friends in the colonies, all gathered in boxes and put away. Alan's life moved into darkness as imperial cringe seized the public.

Alan was "bound rather than crowned" before the colonial achievement. Would he have cared? Probably not. He admired Britain's colonial achievement to the end. "Let us freely admit that our colonial administration has not been perfect, but do not let us for one moment give the impression that we think we have done badly." His words at Oxford in 1947, still ringing on that November day in 1980 when he was laid to rest: "The colonial civil service has little to be ashamed of in its past. . . . I believe we have done very well indeed."[39]

NOTES

1. "Kwame Nkrumah's betrayal," *New York Times*, February 15, 1965.

2. "Dr. Nkrumah warns 'rumour mongers,'" *The Times*, March 8, 1965.

3. Commonwealth Agricultural Bureau, Marca Burns, and Canagasaby Devendra, *Goat Production in the Tropics* (1970).

4. Peter Kihiss, "Ghana, now in dire straits, began as a showcase," *New York Times*, February 25, 1966.

5. CBA, pp. 18, 209.

6. Akwasi Amankwa Afrifa, *The Ghana Coup, 24th February 1966* (1966), p. 27.

7. Daniel McNeil, "'The Rivers of Zimbabwe Will Run Red with Blood': Enoch Powell and the Post-Imperial Nostalgia of the Monday Club," *Journal of Southern African Studies* (2011), p. 735.

8. Hugh Seton-Watson, *Neither War nor Peace: The Struggle for Power in the Post-War World* (1960), pp. 269, 462.

9. "British Honduras," *The Times*, July 23, 1963.

10. Donald Westlake, *Under an English Heaven* (1972).

11. "Sir Alan Burns," *The Times*, October 1, 1980.

12. CBAA, p. 162.

13. Ibid., p. 159.

14. Kenneth Adelman, "Report from Angola," *Foreign Affairs* (1975).

15. "Angola: Alvaro Holden Roberto 1923–2007," *Africa Research Bulletin* (2007).

16. CBAA, p. 178.

17. Cranford Pratt, "Julius Nyerere: Reflections on the Legacy of His Socialism," *Canadian Journal of African Studies* (1999).

18. CBAA, p. 167.

19. Lewis Sorley, *A Better War: The Unexamined Victories and Final Tragedy of America's Last Years in Vietnam* (1999), p. 383.

20. CBAA, p. 176.

21. Ibid., p. 184.

22. Ibid., p. 4.

23. Ibid., p. 18.

24. Ibid., p. 167.

25. Ibid., p. 194.

26. Mason Sears, "The Congo, Africa, and the U.N.," *Africa Today* (1960), p. 15.

27. CBAA, p. 7.

28. Ibid., p. 186.

29. Lee Kuan Yew, "Address at the Royal Commonwealth Society, London, 9 January 1969," *Commonwealth Journal* (1969), p. 8.

30. CBAA, p. 191.

31. Ibid., p. 196.

32. Author's interview with Sarah Pavey, June 14, 2016, Epsom, UK.

33. David Northrup, "Review of 'History of Nigeria,'" *International Journal of African Historical Studies* (1981), p. 344.

34. Allen.

35. Frank Richard Cowell, *The Athenaeum: Club and Social Life in London, 1824–1974* (1975), p. 81.

36. "Sir Alan Burns," *Royal Commonwealth Society Library Notes* (1980).

37. Robert Pearce, "The Colonial Office and Planned Decolonization in Africa," *African Affairs* (1984).

38. "Sir Alan Burns," *The Times*, October 1, 1980.

39. CCC, pp. 317–18.

Chapter 14

The Burns Challenge

Alan was not immune to the belief that, as he put it, "history will one day justify British colonial policy and the work of the men who carried it out."[1] That day seemed a long way off four decades after his death. In left-wing circles, Western colonialism became synonymous with wickedness and suffering, and the men and women who took part in it became objects of protest and vilification. The only memorial to Sir Alan Burns is an unflattering portrait in a hallway at the Athenaeum Club. In a more public space, it would be the object of a "Burns Must Fall" campaign.

Looking down from what one assumes is a writing desk, wearing tie and jacket and a dusty pair of leather shoes, what would Alan have seen in the decades after his death? A clarifying moment in the post-colonial cringe came in 1982 when Argentina, taking its cue from India's violent annexation of Portuguese Goa in 1961, tried to seize the Falkland Islands. Alan had always taken an interest in the various specks of European colonialism that figured so centrally in the wounded national psyche of their neighbors. Argentina's claims to the Falkland Islands, like Guatemala's to British Honduras, and China's to Hong Kong, were logically important because their absolute irrelevance to any economic or geo-strategic needs of those claimant countries showed that the rage against colonialism was emotive, often irrational. Some of these small islands would remain an exception to the general thrust of decolonization, for as Alan explained before his death, "Britain herself would gladly give up the few remaining territories for which she is responsible if she could decently do so, that is, if they were capable and wishful of standing alone. . . . [However] she could not, for example, abandon the Falkland Islands against the wishes of the inhabitants, and she could not shirk her moral obligation to tiny islands with few resources."[2]

Alan jousted with the envoys from Buenos Aires several times over the Falklands while at the UN. He was called upon to assert that Britain had "no doubt" about its sovereignty. But in the 1960s and 1970s, as the "no doubt" of other European powers about their sovereignty over places like Goa and Algeria crumbled in the face of world opinion and military weakness, there was every reason to suppose that Britain too would abandon the Falkland Islanders to the tender graces of one of Latin America's most volatile countries. For that reason, some have pointed to Britain's successful defense of the Falklands as a turning point in the global anti-colonial movement.

Yet events elsewhere suggested that decolonization remained alive and well. The same year as the Falklands war, Prime Minister Margaret Thatcher agreed to hand over Hong Kong to China, in effect jettisoning 80 percent of the remaining British Empire in terms of population. Alan never visited China or Hong Kong, although he was close friends with the Taiwanese delegates who held the UN seat for China until 1971. "The future of Hong Kong is hard to predict," he wrote in *Colonialism: Before and After*. The expiration of the lease signed with the Qing dynasty in 1897 on the mainland sections of the colony would expire in 1997, and "it would be almost impossible to hold Hong Kong if the Chinese government decided to take it over, as they might do at any time."[3] The frequent appearance of British flags and Hong Kong colonial flags during protests against China's attempts to integrate the territory into its regime after 1997 suggested that, as elsewhere, the colonial period began to be seen as a golden era as the post-colonial shadow lengthened.[4]

The continued horrors in post-colonial states did not abate even as many recovered from the spirals after independence. The time bomb in Fiji that Alan had sought to defuse finally went off in 1987. A left-wing coalition government with a strong Indian presence defeated the long-ruling Fijian party, prompting street protests. The military, which the new government threatened to downsize, seized power in what was in effect affirmative action at gunpoint. A new constitution in 1990 was a great leap backward to 1874, reaffirming native Fijian paramountcy. Another coup followed in 2000, and then another in 2006, always to protect that promise. The path-not-taken of the Burns Commission continued to echo through that country's travails.

Alan might have found comfort in Ghana's belated emergence from its long, dark night of authoritarian rule. It began with a return to democracy in 1996, thirty years after Nkrumah's ouster and with an even more grotesque period of repression and misrule since then under Flight-Lieutenant Jerry Rawlings. The legislature elected in 1996 came exactly fifty years after election of the legislature under the Burns Constitution. It marked the first time that democracy had breathed in Ghana since Alan's modest reforms. Alan's colonial democratic "farce," as black nationalists had called it, suddenly measured up quite well against the post-colonial democratic farce.

Nigeria, Alan's true love, was less fortunate. Thirteen years of military government followed the catastrophic Biafra War. A new constitution of 1979 increased the number of federal units to nineteen, including one for the river-diving Tiv in Benue state. But the democratic attempt was overthrown again in 1983, after which Nigeria descended into levels of misrule that Alan's generation would have thought impossible—first under a general whose movement was called the Association for a Better Nigeria—and then from 1994 under another general whose rule from a fortified complex outside of Lagos would give new meaning to the word "crooked." Nigeria was saved from his terror when he died in the arms of two Indian prostitutes in 1998. By 1999, when civilian rule was restored, and despite hundreds of billions in oil revenues since the 1970s, the average income of a Nigerian had risen by only $500 per year since the British handed over. When Chinua Achebe uttered his "heresy" in 2012 about how the British ran the country better than Nigerians, it was a shock only to outsiders who had not paid attention to post-colonial Nigeria.

It is tempting to think of Alan confabbing with his fellow European imperialists from the UN days—especially Pierre Ryckmans of Belgium, but also his colleagues from France, Italy, Portugal, and the Netherlands—as they sit today on the veranda of a heavenly colonial club looking down on the havoc wrought by anti-colonial regimes and wondering if they could have done more. If Alan's interventions, and those of his colleagues, failed to stem that tide, at least they can take comfort in the knowledge that they knew what was at stake. As to the battle of ideas, it will take more time for the evidence to sink in to justify colonial policy and the work of the people who carried it out.

Alan's name was affixed to so many initiatives during his career: the Burns Regime, the Burns Constitution, the Burns Commission. In the end, we are left with something bigger, which we might call the Burns Challenge. At this writing, attempts to recover an objective account of colonialism remain nearly impossible in the West. Some Western leaders even pledge to "decolonize" their own countries, as if the anti-colonial tide will not stop until the Dark Ages that Alan warned against have come to the West as well. Yet countries that were colonial, and colonial for longer, are overwhelmingly richer, more democratic, more liberal, and more peaceful than those that either were not colonies or whose colonial experiences were shorter or less intensive.[5] As Alan noted bluntly during the UN days: "I can assure you that no one exploits the African so effectively as members of his own race, and no one has better protected the African from tyranny than the so-called imperialists who govern the colonies. I am proud that I have been one of them."[6]

NOTES

1. IDOC, p. 41.
2. CBAA, p. 194.
3. Ibid., p. 48.
4. Melissa Chen, "Why Post-Colonial Theory Is Not Helping Hong Kong," *Aero Magazine* (2019).
5. Bruce Gilley, "Contributions of Western Colonialism to Human Flourishing: A Summary of Research," ResearchGate.net (2019).
6. CPCW-G, p. 6.

About the Author

Bruce Gilley is a professor of political science at Portland State University. His 2017 article "The Case for Colonialism" drew international attention after it was withdrawn due to death threats. The London *Times* called him "probably the academic most likely to be no-platformed in Britain." Dr. Gilley holds a PhD in politics from Princeton University and an MPhil in economics from the University of Oxford. He is the author of *The Right to Rule: How States Win and Lose Legitimacy* (2009) and *The Nature of Asian Politics* (2014).

Index